Guru Guru Pon-Chan

2

Satomi Ikezawa

Translated and adapted by Douglas Varenas

Lettering and touchup by Steve Palmer

LONDON

Published in the United Kingdom by Tanoshimi in 2006

1 3 5 7 9 10 8 6 4 2

First published in Japan in 1998 by Kodansha Ltd., Tokyo, copyright © 1998 by Satomi Ikezawa.

Published by arrangement with Kodansha Ltd., Tokyo and with Del Rey,
an imprint of Random House Inc., New York

Tanoshimi
The Random House Group Limited
20 Vauxhall Bridge Road, London, SW1V 2SA

Random House Australia (Pty) Limited
20 Alfred Street, Milsons Point, Sydney
New South Wales 2061, Australia

Random House New Zealand Limited
18 Poland Road, Glenfield
Auckland 10, New Zealand

Random House (Pty) Limited
Isle of Houghton, Corner of Boundary Road & Carse O'Gowrie
Houghton 2198, South Africa

Random House Publishers India Private Limited
301 World Trade Tower, Hotel Intercontinental Grand Complex,
Barakhamba Lane, New Delhi 110 001, India

Random House Group Limited Reg. No. 954009

www.tanoshimi.tv
www.randomhouse.co.uk

A CIP catalogue record for this book is available from the British Library

Papers used by Random House
are natural, recyclable products made from wood grown in sustainable forests.
The manufacturing processes conform to the environmental regulations of the country of origin.

ISBN 9780099504054 (from Jan 2007)
ISBN 0 09 950405 7

Printed and bound in Germany by GGP Media GmbH, Pößneck

Translator and Adaptor – Douglas Varenas
Lettering and Text Design – Steve Palmer

Contents

A Note from the Author

    As her love for Mirai-Kun grows, Ponta's demeanor is becoming more and more woman-like, and she's already changed so much from the beginning of Volume 1. This goes beyond my expectations for Ponta, but I mean that in a good way. By the way, my Pon-Chan and Guts are in the prime of their manhood (they're around 30 years old in human years) but they don't know what it is to love yet. I wonder if they want to love...?

Honorifics

Throughout the Tanoshimi Manga books, you will find Japanese honorifics left intact in the translations. For those not familiar with how the Japanese use honorifics, and more importantly, how they differ from English honorifics, we present this brief overview.

Politeness has always been a critical facet of Japanese culture. Ever since the feudal era, when Japan was a highly stratified society, use of honorifics– which can be defined as polite speech that indicates relationship or status–has played an essential role in the Japanese language. When addressing someone in Japanese, an honorific usually takes the form of a suffix attached to one's name (example: "Asuna-san"), or as a title at the end of one's name or in place of the name itself (example: "Negi-sensei," or simply "Sensei!").

Honorifics can be expressions of respect or endearment. In the context of manga and anime, honorifics give insight into the nature of the relationship between characters. Many translations into English leave out these important honorifics, and therefore distort the "feel" of the original Japanese. Because Japanese honorifics contain nuances that English honorifics lack, it is our policy at Tanoshimi not to translate them. Here, instead, is a guide to some of the honorifics you may encounter in Tanoshimi Manga.

-san: This is the most common honorific, and is equivalent to Mr., Miss, Ms., Mrs., etc. It is the all-purpose honorific and can be used in any situation where politeness is required.

-sama: This is one level higher than "-san." It is used to confer great respect.

-dono: This comes from the word "tono," which means "lord." It is even a higher level than "-sama," and confers utmost respect.

-kun: This suffix is used at the end of boys' names to express familiarity or endearment. It is also sometimes used by men among friends, or when addressing someone younger or of a lower station.

-chan: This is used to express endearment, mostly towards girls. It is also used for little boys, pets, and even among lovers. It gives a sense of childish cuteness.

Bozu: This is an informal way to refer to a boy, similar to the English term "kid".

Sempai: This title suggests that the addressee is one's "senior" in a group or organization. It is most often used in a school setting, where underclassmen refer to their upperclassmen as "sempai." It can also be used in the workplace, such as when a newer employee addresses an employee who has seniority in the company.

Kohai: This is the opposite of "sempai," and is used towards underclassmen in school or newcomers in the workplace. It connotes that the addressee is of lower station.

Sensei: Literally meaning "one who has come before," this title is used for teachers, doctors, or masters of any profession or art.

Anesan: "Anesan" (or "nesan") is a generic term for a girl, usually older, meaning "sister."

Ojou-sama: "Ojou-sama" is a way of referring to the daughter or sister of someone with high political or social status.

-[blank]: Usually forgotten in these lists, but perhaps the most significant difference between Japanese and English. The lack of honorific means that the speaker has permission to address the person in a very intimate way. Usually, only family, spouses, or very close friends have this kind of permission. Known as *yobisute*, it can be gratifying when someone who has earned the intimacy starts to call one by one's name without an honorific. But when that intimacy hasn't been earned, it can also be very insulting.

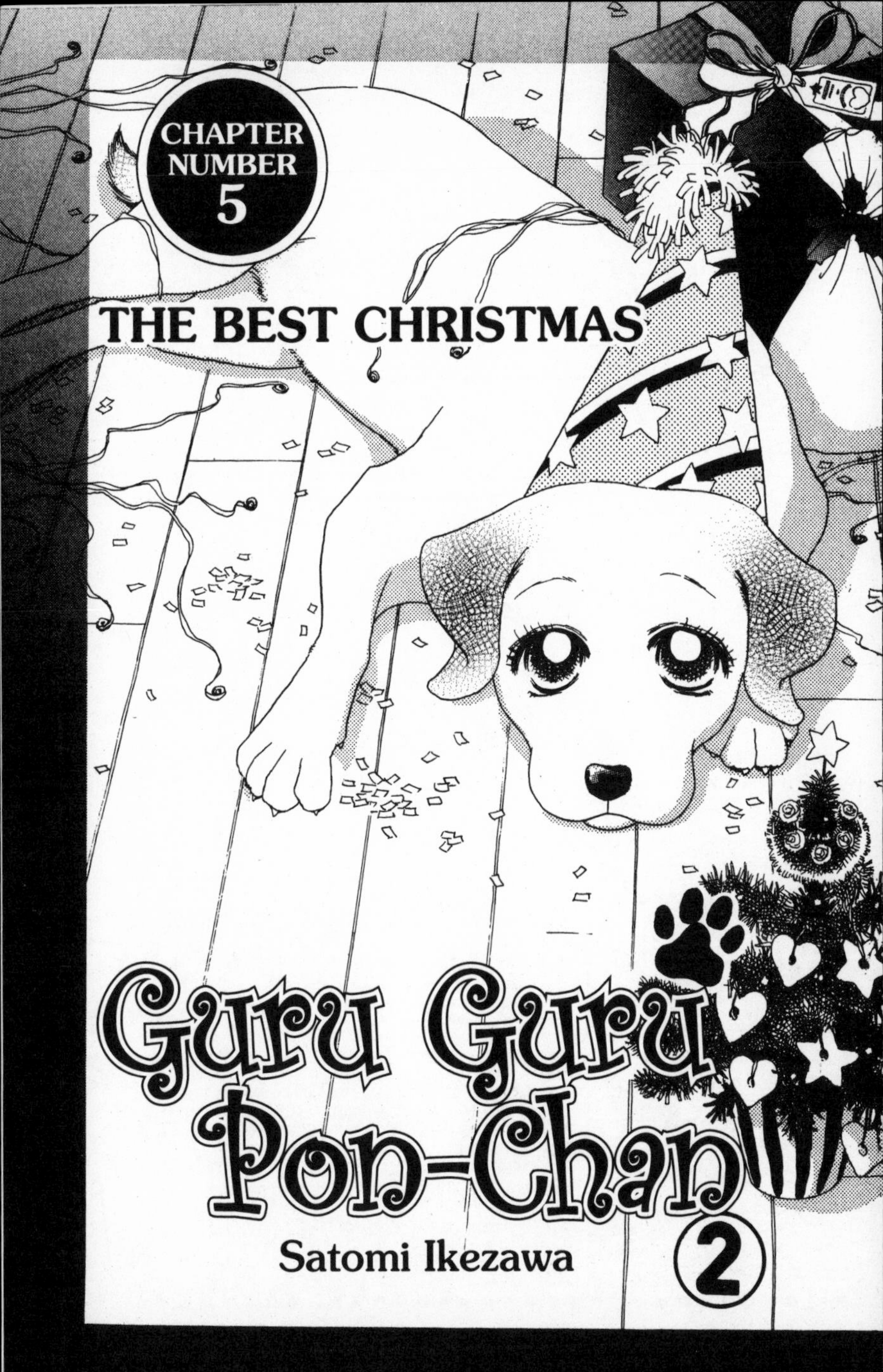
CHAPTER NUMBER 5
THE BEST CHRISTMAS
Guru Guru Pon-Chan
2
Satomi Ikezawa

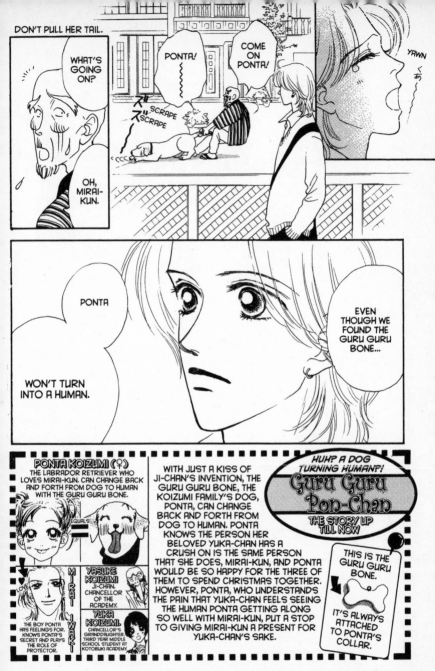

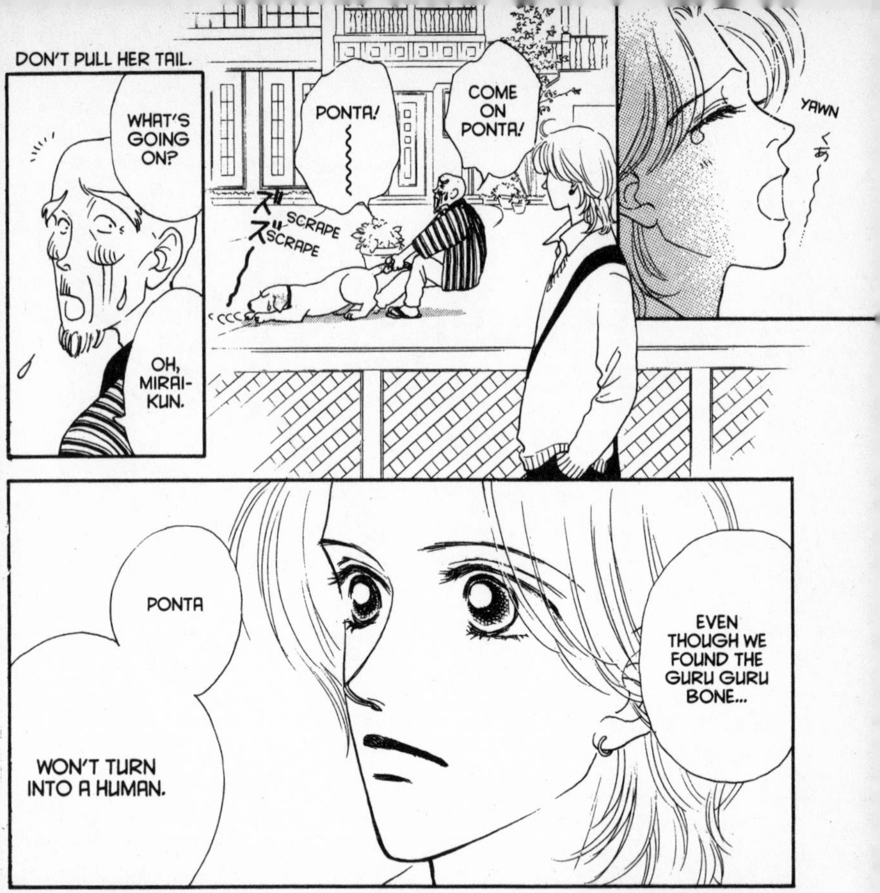
YAWN
COME ON PONTA!
PONTA!
SCRAPE
SCRAPE
WHAT'S GOING ON?
OH, MIRAI-KUN.
DON'T PULL HER TAIL.
EVEN THOUGH WE FOUND THE GURU GURU BONE...
PONTA
WON'T TURN INTO A HUMAN.

HUH? A DOG TURNING HUMAN?!

Guru Guru Pon-Chan

THE STORY UP TILL NOW

PONTA KOIZUMI (♀)
THE LABRADOR RETRIEVER WHO LOVES MIRAI-KUN. CAN CHANGE BACK AND FORTH FROM DOG TO HUMAN WITH THE GURU GURU BONE.

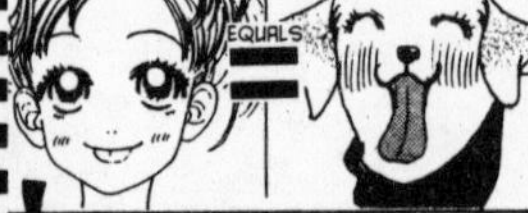
EQUALS

MIRAI IWAKI
THE BOY PONTA HAS FEELINGS FOR. KNOWS PONTA'S SECRET AND PLAYS THE ROLE OF PROTECTOR.

YASUKE KOIZUMI
JI-CHAN. CHANCELLOR OF THE ACADEMY.

YUKA KOIZUMI
CHANCELLOR'S GRANDDAUGHTER. THIRD YEAR MIDDLE SCHOOL STUDENT AT KOTOBUKI ACADEMY.

WITH JUST A KISS OF JI-CHAN'S INVENTION, THE GURU GURU BONE, THE KOIZUMI FAMILY'S DOG, PONTA, CAN CHANGE BACK AND FORTH FROM DOG TO HUMAN. PONTA KNOWS THE PERSON HER BELOVED YUKA-CHAN HAS A CRUSH ON IS THE SAME PERSON THAT SHE DOES, MIRAI-KUN, AND PONTA WOULD BE SO HAPPY FOR THE THREE OF THEM TO SPEND CHRISTMAS TOGETHER. HOWEVER, PONTA, WHO UNDERSTANDS THE PAIN THAT YUKA-CHAN FEELS SEEING THE HUMAN PONTA GETTING ALONG SO WELL WITH MIRAI-KUN, PUT A STOP TO GIVING MIRAI-KUN A PRESENT FOR YUKA-CHAN'S SAKE.

THIS IS THE GURU GURU BONE.

IT'S ALWAYS ATTACHED TO PONTA'S COLLAR.

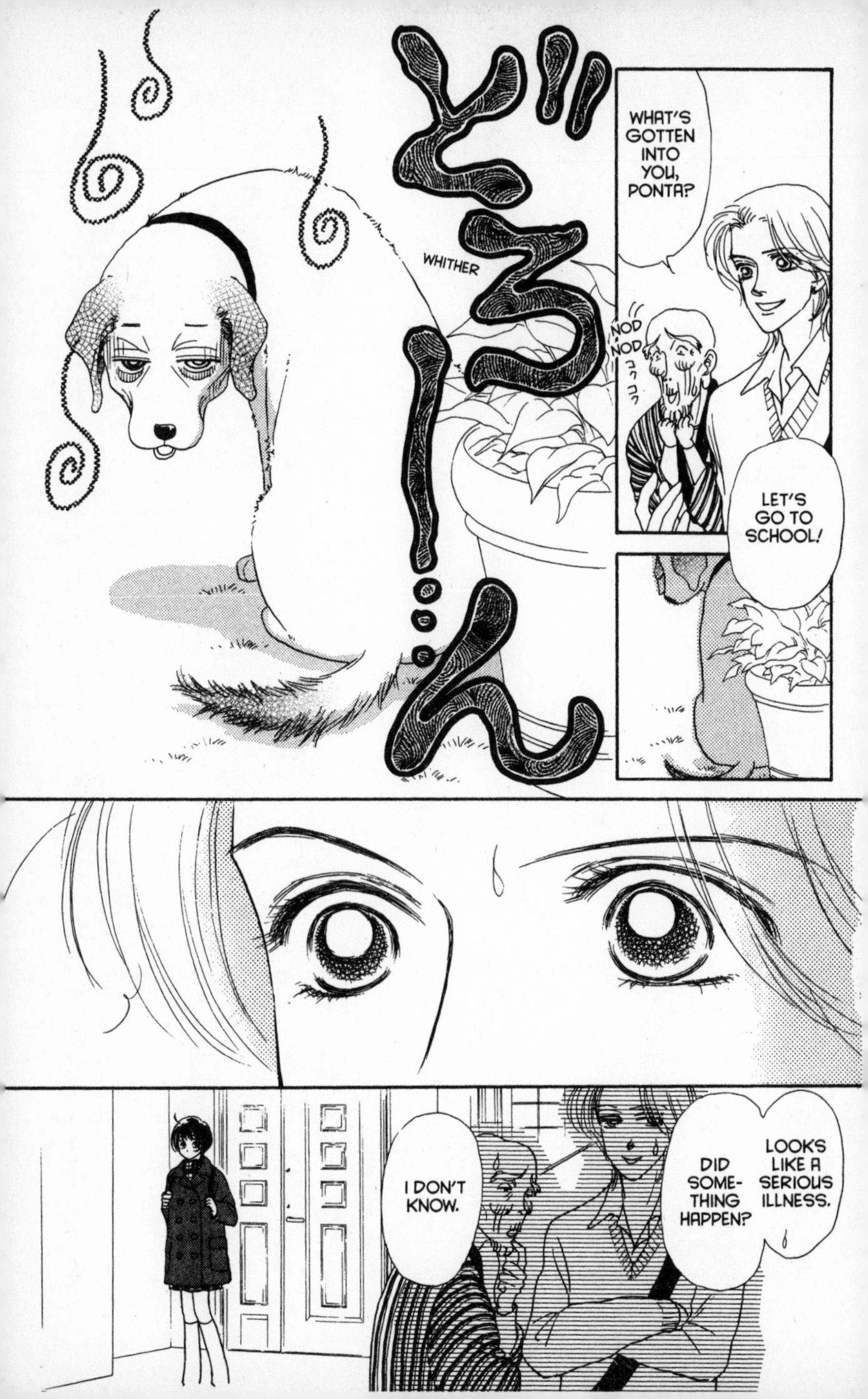
WHAT'S GOTTEN INTO YOU, PONTA?
NOD NOD
LET'S GO TO SCHOOL!
どろー…ん
WHITHER
LOOKS LIKE A SERIOUS ILLNESS.
DID SOME-THING HAPPEN?
I DON'T KNOW.

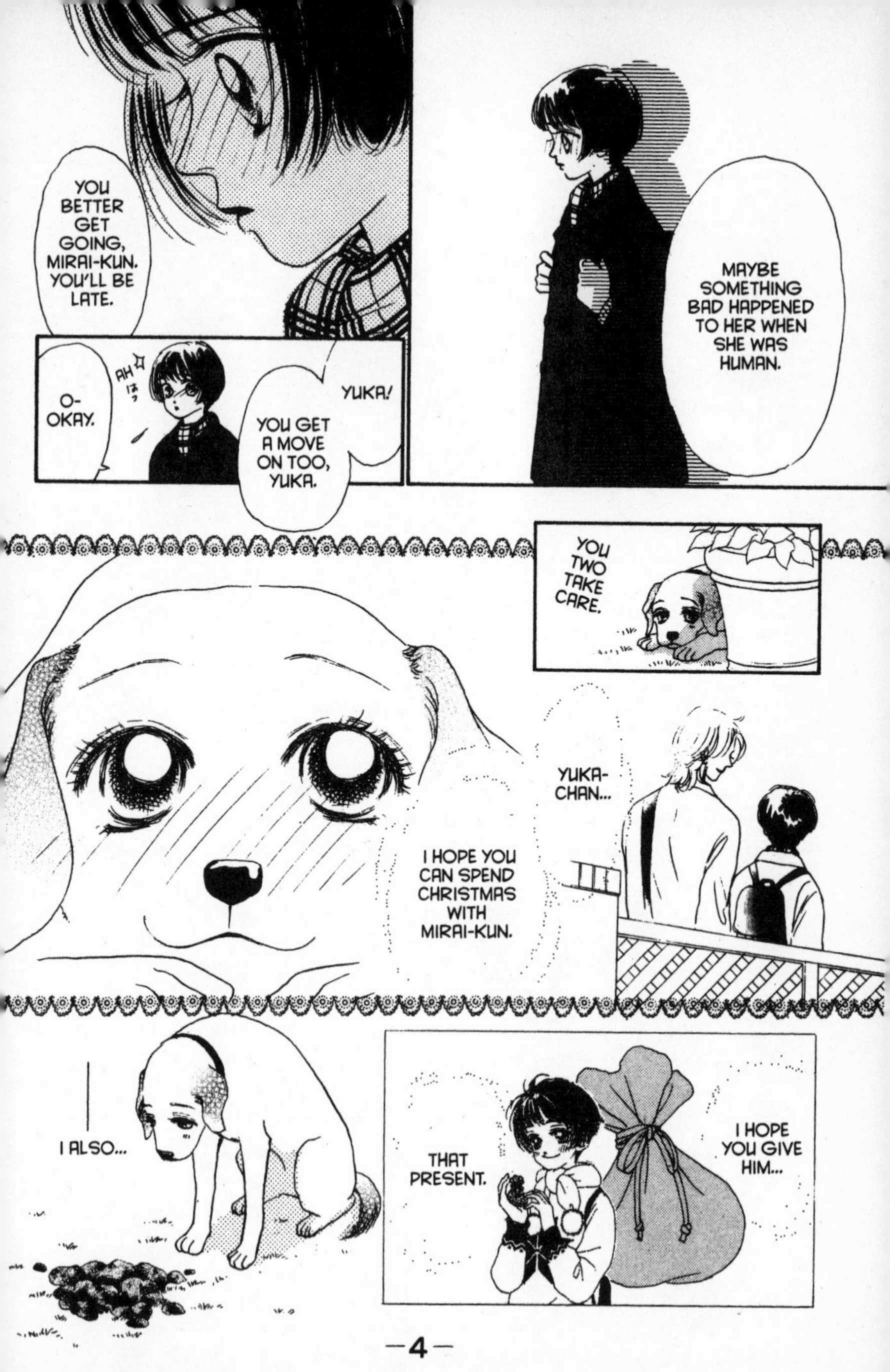
MAYBE SOMETHING BAD HAPPENED TO HER WHEN SHE WAS HUMAN.
YOU BETTER GET GOING, MIRAI-KUN. YOU'LL BE LATE.
YUKA!
YOU GET A MOVE ON TOO, YUKA.
AH はっ
O-OKAY.
YOU TWO TAKE CARE.
YUKA-CHAN...
I HOPE YOU CAN SPEND CHRISTMAS WITH MIRAI-KUN.
I HOPE YOU GIVE HIM...
THAT PRESENT.
I ALSO...

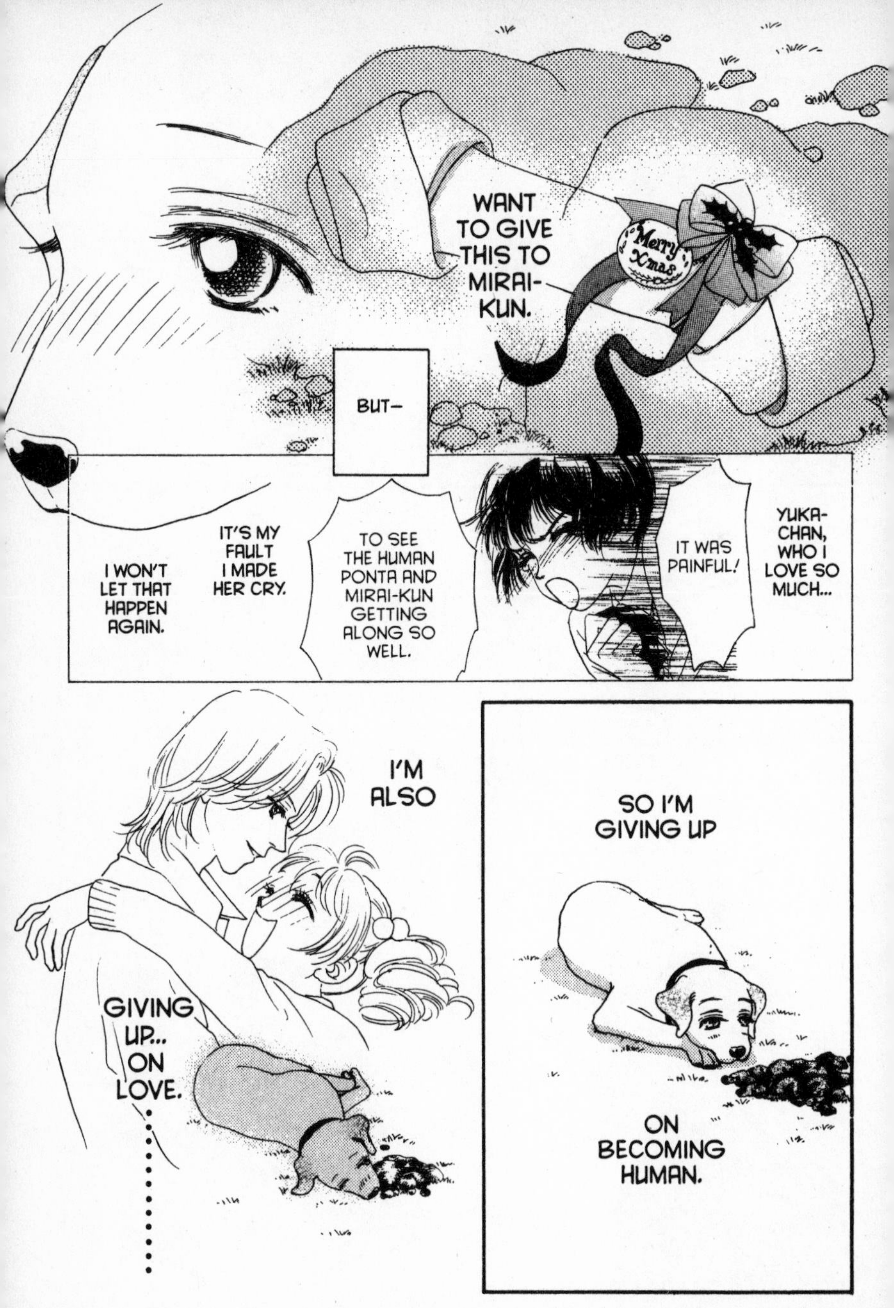

WANT TO GIVE THIS TO MIRAI-KUN.
Merry X'mas
BUT—
YUKA-CHAN, WHO I LOVE SO MUCH...
IT WAS PAINFUL!
TO SEE THE HUMAN PONTA AND MIRAI-KUN GETTING ALONG SO WELL.
IT'S MY FAULT I MADE HER CRY.
I WON'T LET THAT HAPPEN AGAIN.
SO I'M GIVING UP
ON BECOMING HUMAN.
I'M ALSO
GIVING UP... ON LOVE.

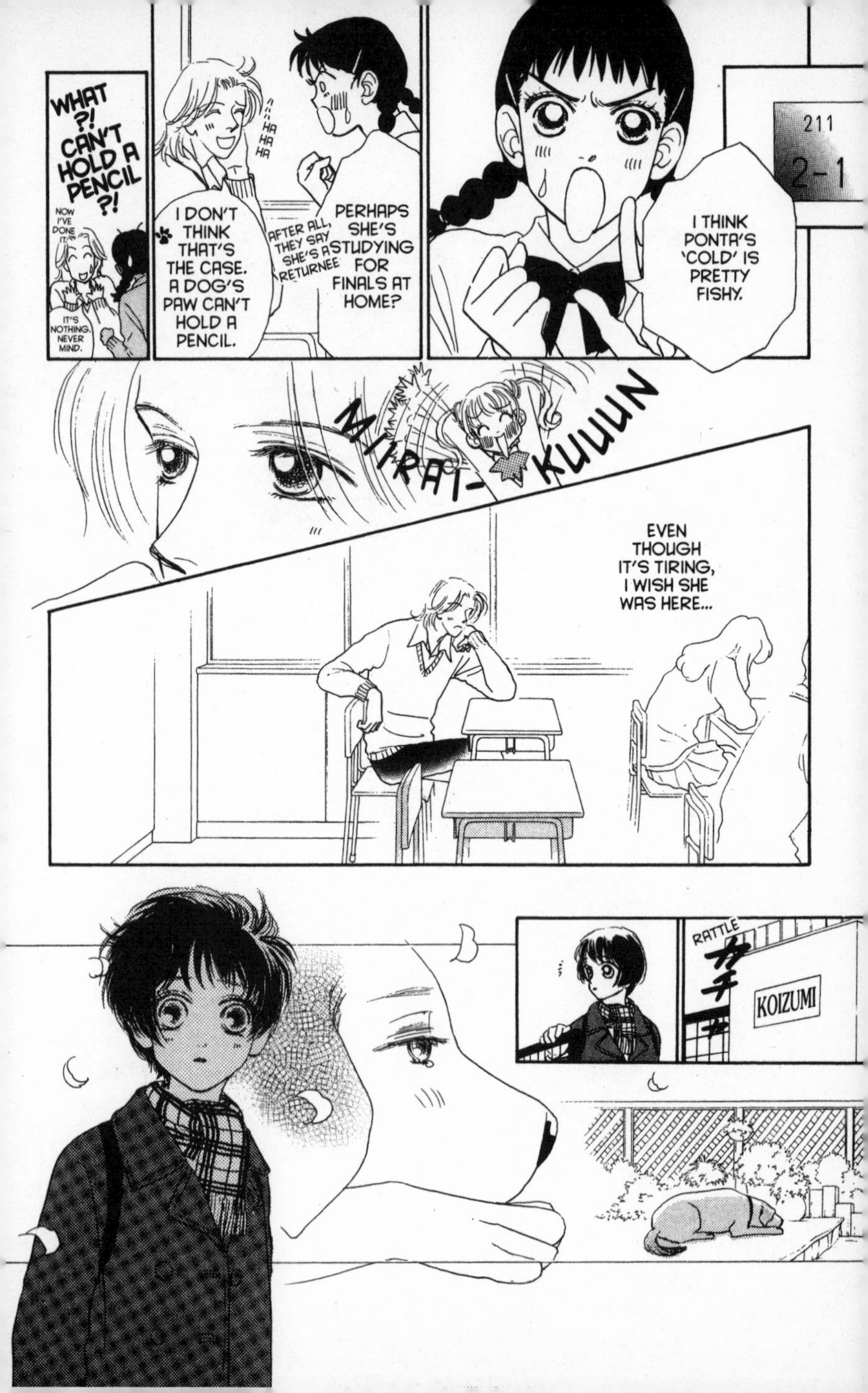
211
2-1
I THINK PONTA'S 'COLD' IS PRETTY FISHY.
PERHAPS SHE'S STUDYING FOR FINALS AT HOME?
AFTER ALL, THEY SAY SHE'S A RETURNEE
HA HA HA
I DON'T THINK THAT'S THE CASE. A DOG'S PAW CAN'T HOLD A PENCIL.
WHAT ?! CAN'T HOLD A PENCIL ?!
NOW I'VE DONE IT.
IT'S NOTHING. NEVER MIND.
MIIRAI-KUUUN
EVEN THOUGH IT'S TIRING, I WISH SHE WAS HERE...
RATTLE
KOIZUMI

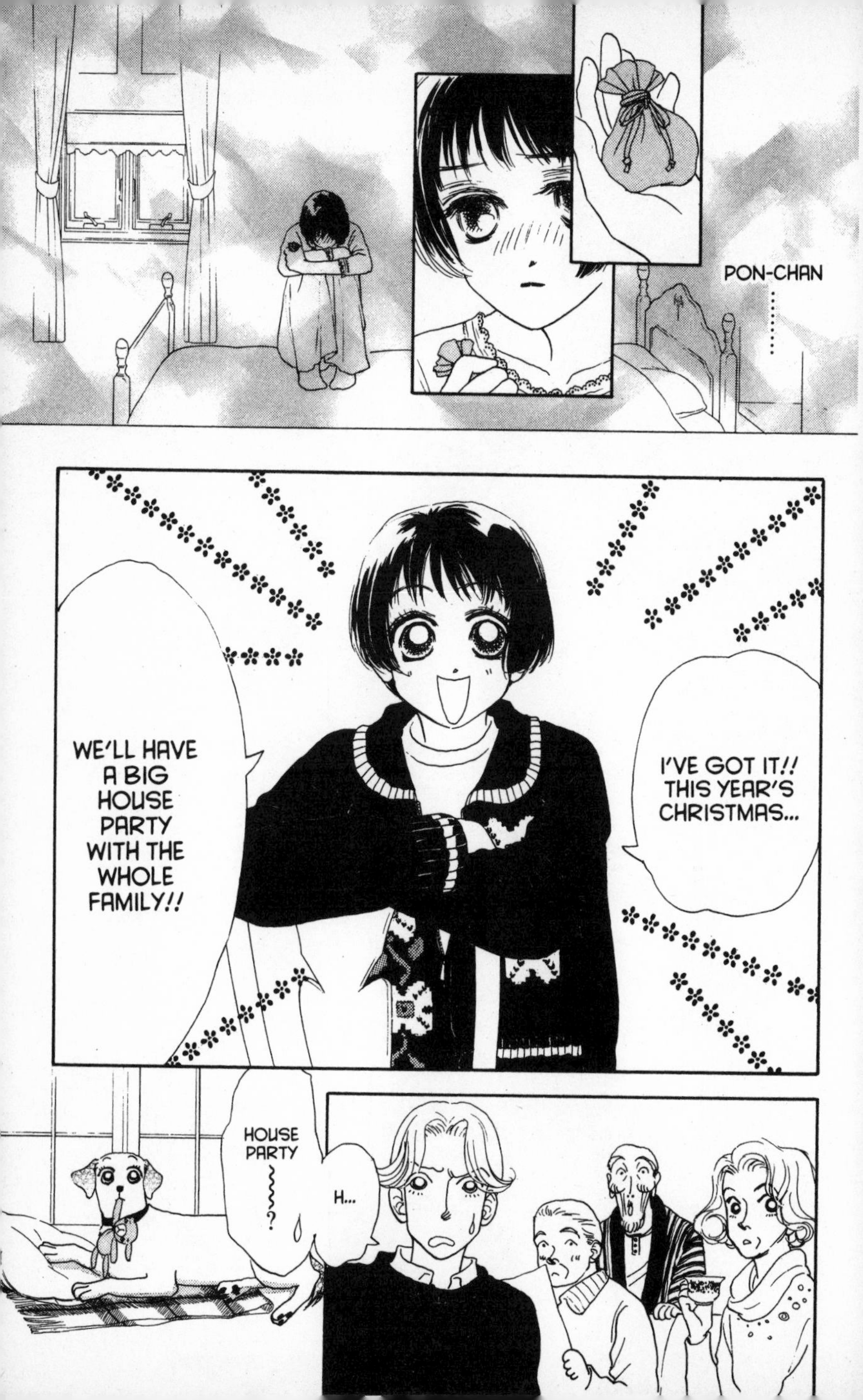
PON-CHAN ......
I'VE GOT IT!! THIS YEAR'S CHRISTMAS...
WE'LL HAVE A BIG HOUSE PARTY WITH THE WHOLE FAMILY!!
H...
HOUSE PARTY ~~~?

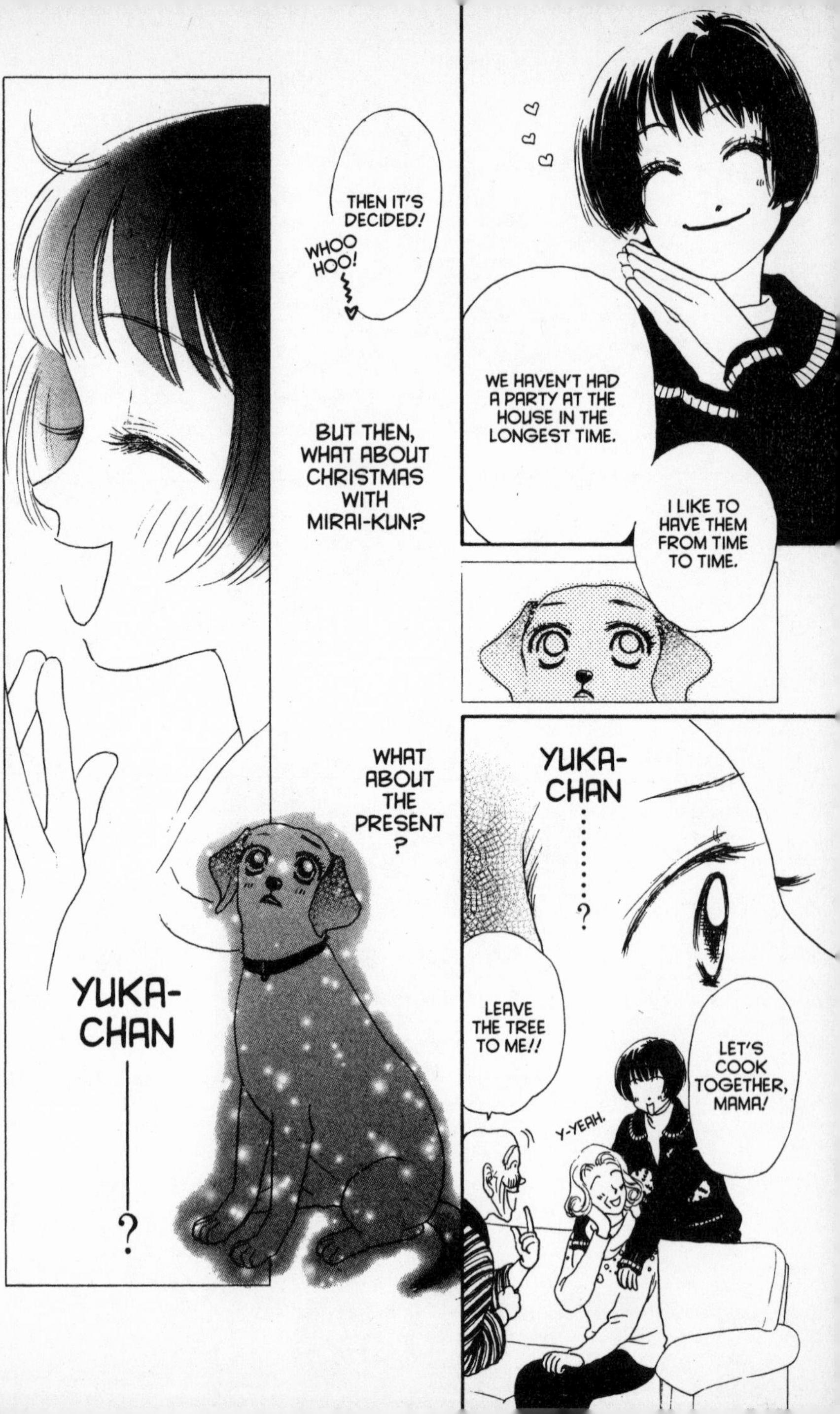
WE HAVEN'T HAD A PARTY AT THE HOUSE IN THE LONGEST TIME.
I LIKE TO HAVE THEM FROM TIME TO TIME.
YUKA-CHAN......?
LET'S COOK TOGETHER, MAMA!
Y-YEAH.
LEAVE THE TREE TO ME!!
THEN IT'S DECIDED!
WHOO HOO!
BUT THEN, WHAT ABOUT CHRISTMAS WITH MIRAI-KUN?
WHAT ABOUT THE PRESENT?
YUKA-CHAN—?

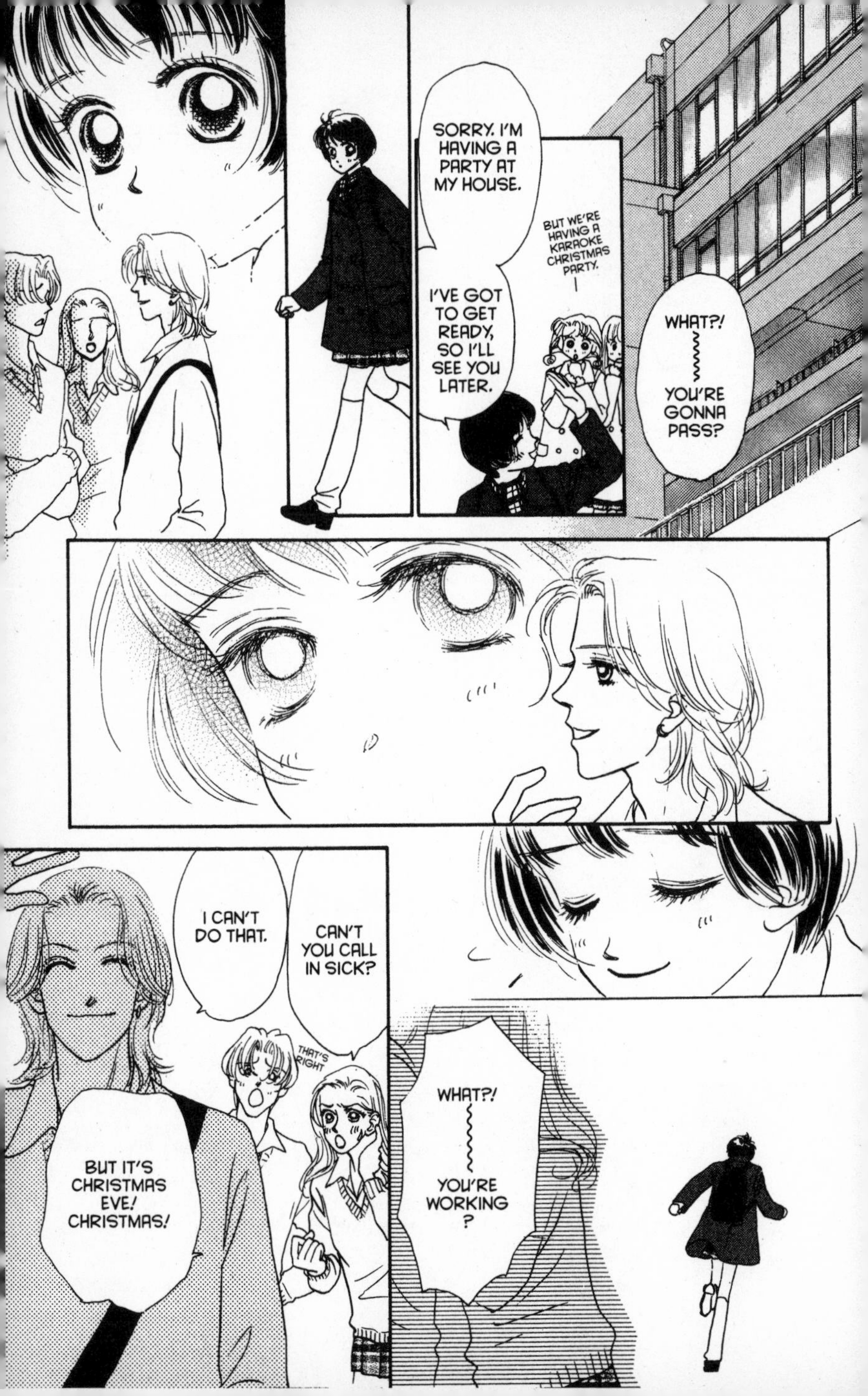
WHAT?! YOU'RE GONNA PASS?
BUT WE'RE HAVING A KARAOKE CHRISTMAS PARTY.
SORRY. I'M HAVING A PARTY AT MY HOUSE.
I'VE GOT TO GET READY, SO I'LL SEE YOU LATER.
WHAT?! YOU'RE WORKING?
CAN'T YOU CALL IN SICK?
I CAN'T DO THAT.
THAT'S RIGHT
BUT IT'S CHRISTMAS EVE! CHRISTMAS!

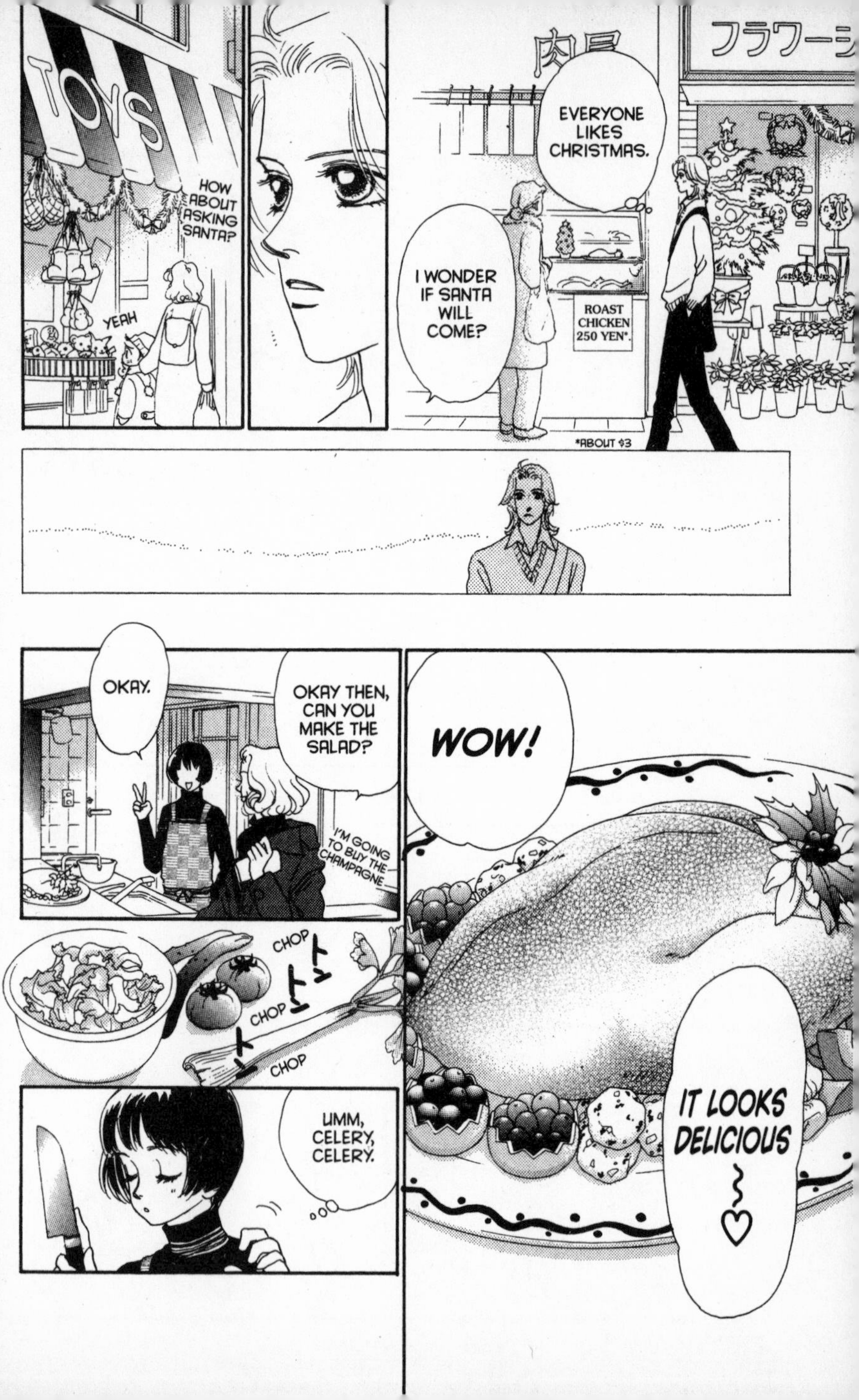
フラワーシ
EVERYONE LIKES CHRISTMAS.
I WONDER IF SANTA WILL COME?
ROAST CHICKEN 250 YEN*.
TOYS
HOW ABOUT ASKING SANTA?
YEAH
*ABOUT $3
WOW!
IT LOOKS DELICIOUS
OKAY THEN, CAN YOU MAKE THE SALAD?
I'M GOING TO BUY THE CHAMPAGNE
OKAY.
CHOP
CHOP
CHOP
UMM, CELERY, CELERY.

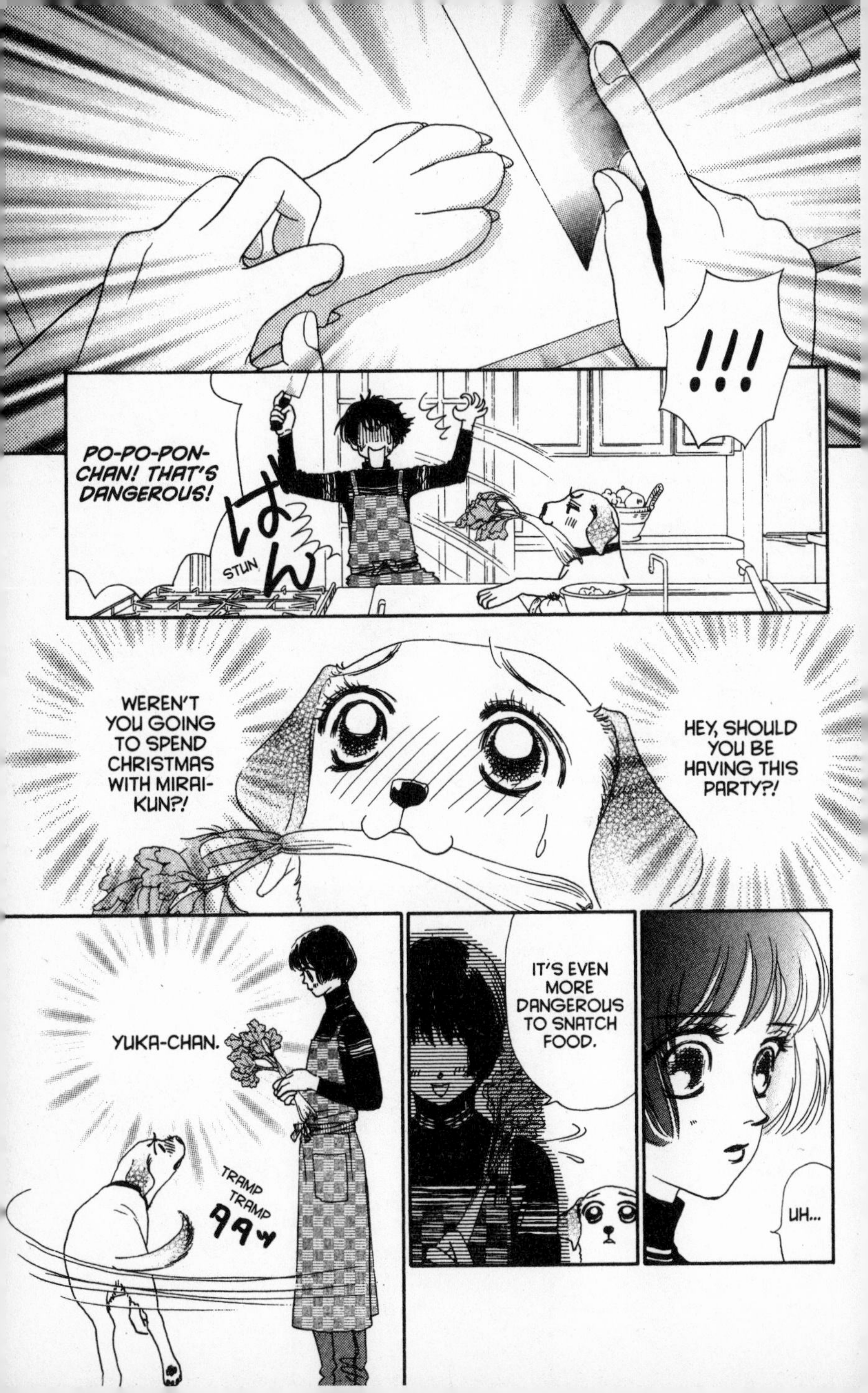
!!!
PO-PO-PON-CHAN! THAT'S DANGEROUS!
はん
STUN
HEY, SHOULD YOU BE HAVING THIS PARTY?!
WEREN'T YOU GOING TO SPEND CHRISTMAS WITH MIRAI-KUN?!
UH...
IT'S EVEN MORE DANGEROUS TO SNATCH FOOD.
YUKA-CHAN.
TRAMP TRAMP
タタッ

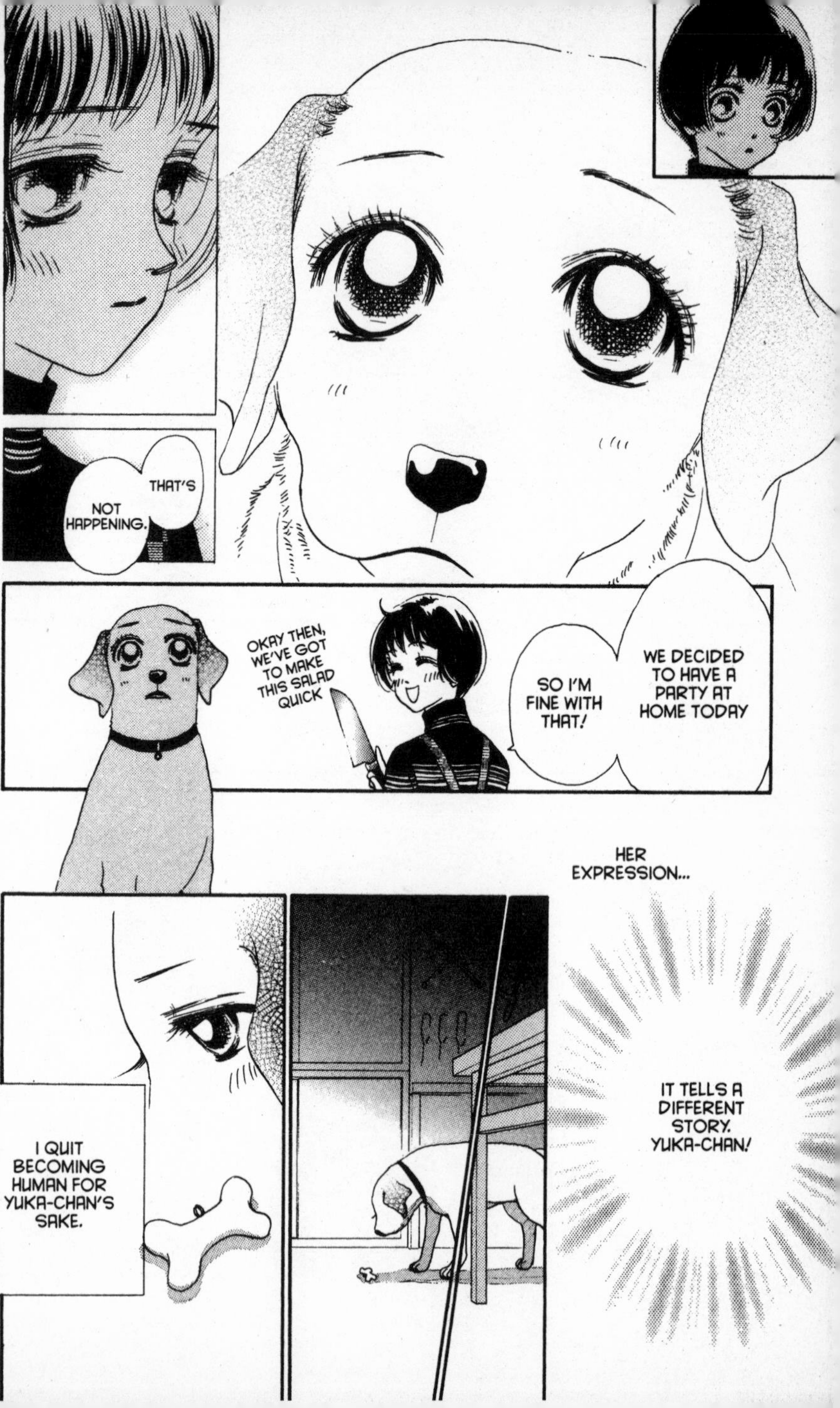
THAT'S NOT HAPPENING.
WE DECIDED TO HAVE A PARTY AT HOME TODAY
SO I'M FINE WITH THAT!
OKAY THEN, WE'VE GOT TO MAKE THIS SALAD QUICK
HER EXPRESSION...
IT TELLS A DIFFERENT STORY. YUKA-CHAN!
I QUIT BECOMING HUMAN FOR YUKA-CHAN'S SAKE.

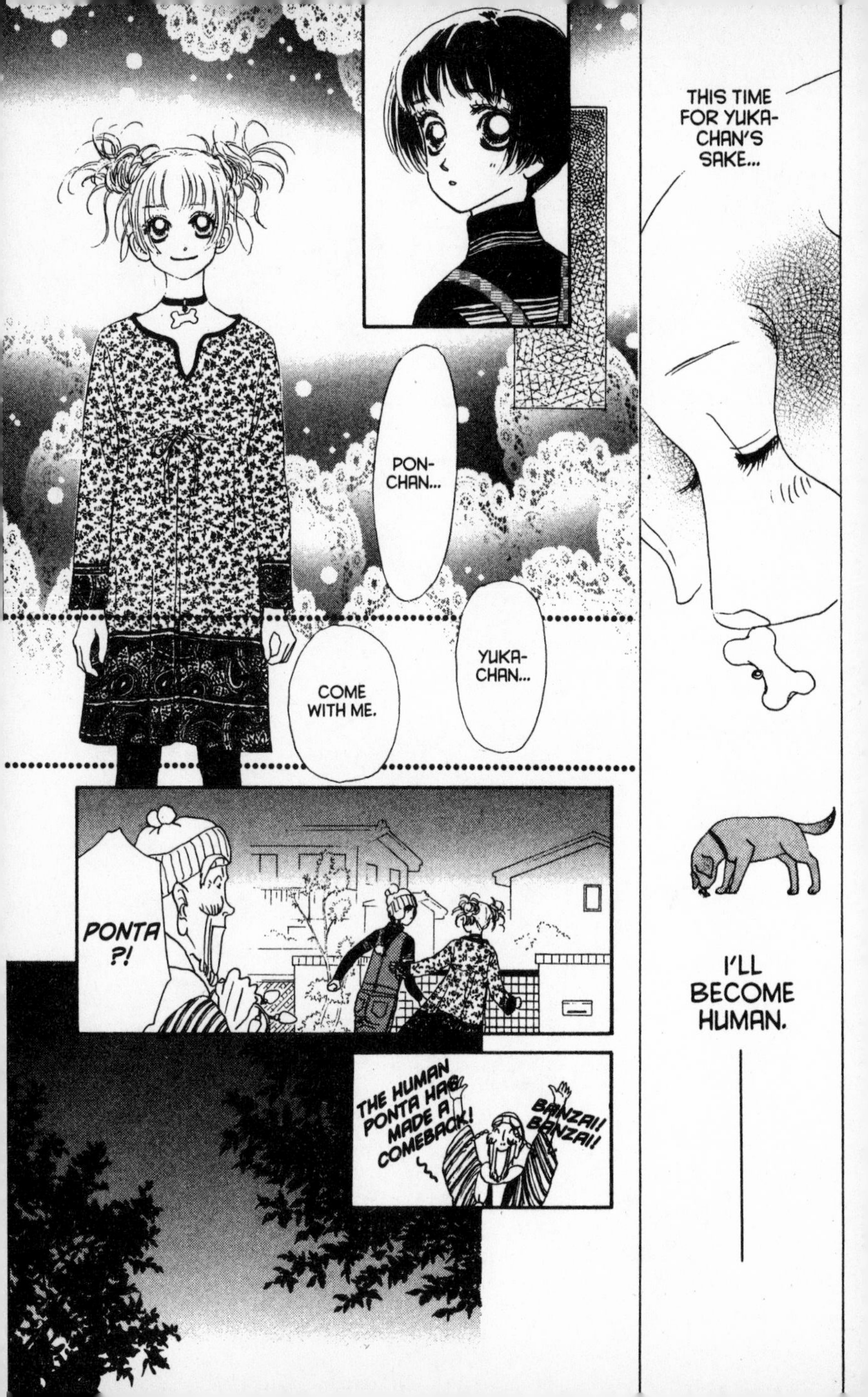
THIS TIME FOR YUKA-CHAN'S SAKE...
I'LL BECOME HUMAN.
PON-CHAN...
YUKA-CHAN...
COME WITH ME.
PONTA ?!
BANZAI! BANZAI!
THE HUMAN PONTA HAS MADE A COMEBACK!

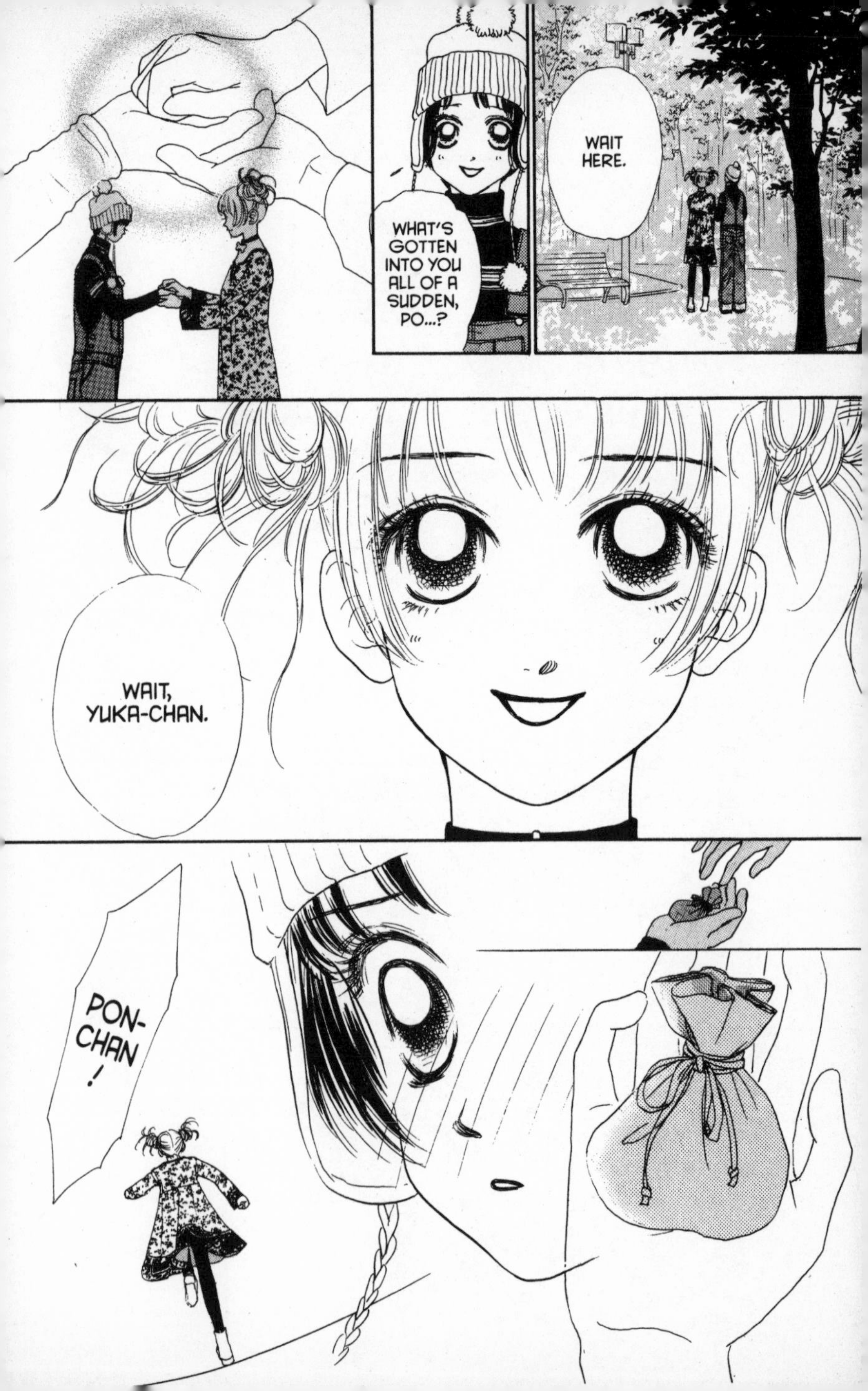
WAIT HERE.
WHAT'S GOTTEN INTO YOU ALL OF A SUDDEN, PO...?
WAIT, YUKA-CHAN.
PON-CHAN!

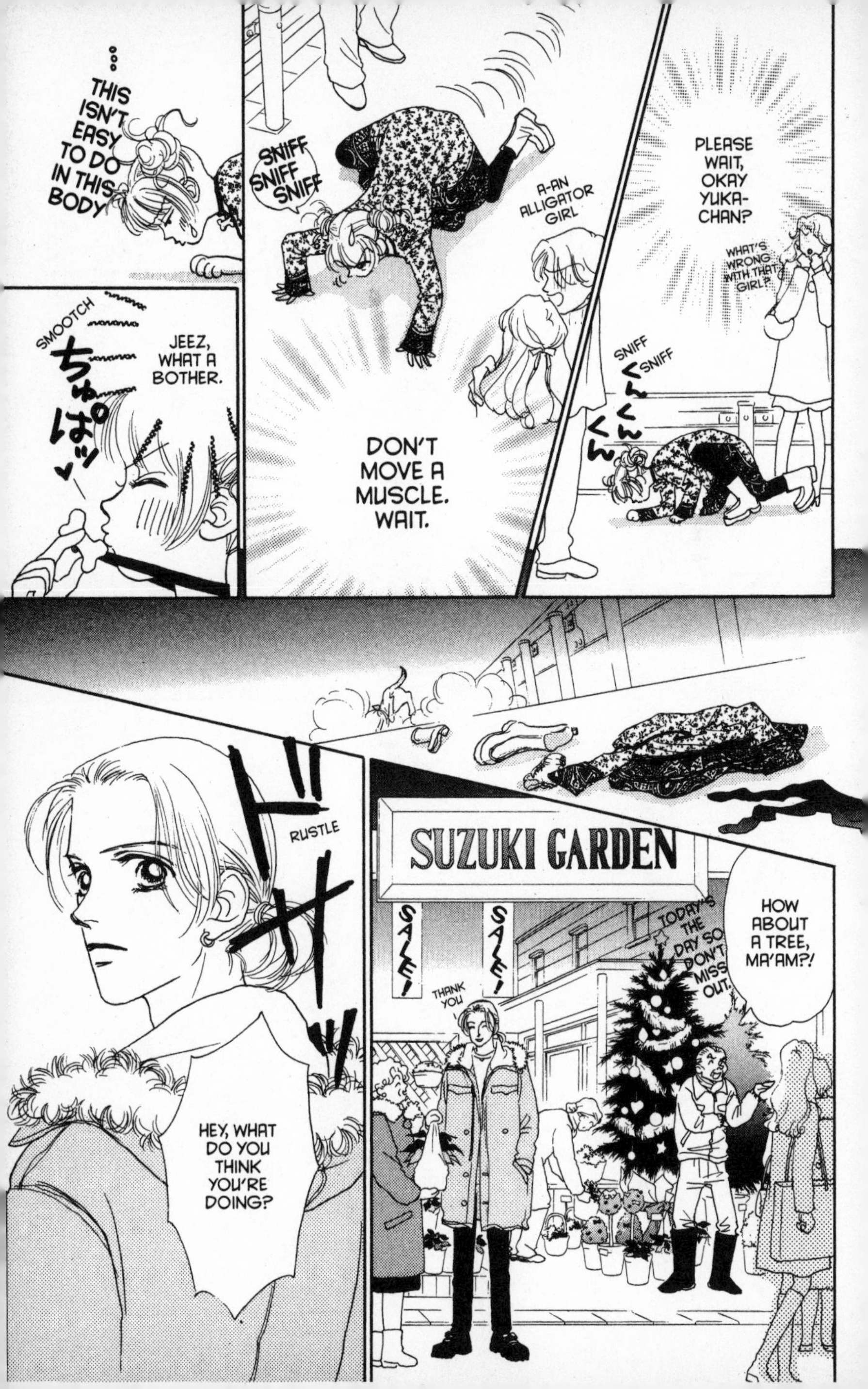

PLEASE WAIT, OKAY YUKA-CHAN?
WHAT'S WRONG WITH THAT GIRL?
SNIFF SNIFF
くんくんくん
A-AN ALLIGATOR GIRL
SNIFF SNIFF SNIFF
DON'T MOVE A MUSCLE. WAIT.
... THIS ISN'T EASY TO DO IN THIS BODY
SMOOTCH
ちゅぱッ
JEEZ, WHAT A BOTHER.
SUZUKI GARDEN
SALE!
SALE!
TODAY'S THE DAY SO DON'T MISS OUT.
HOW ABOUT A TREE, MA'AM?!
THANK YOU
RUSTLE
HEY, WHAT DO YOU THINK YOU'RE DOING?

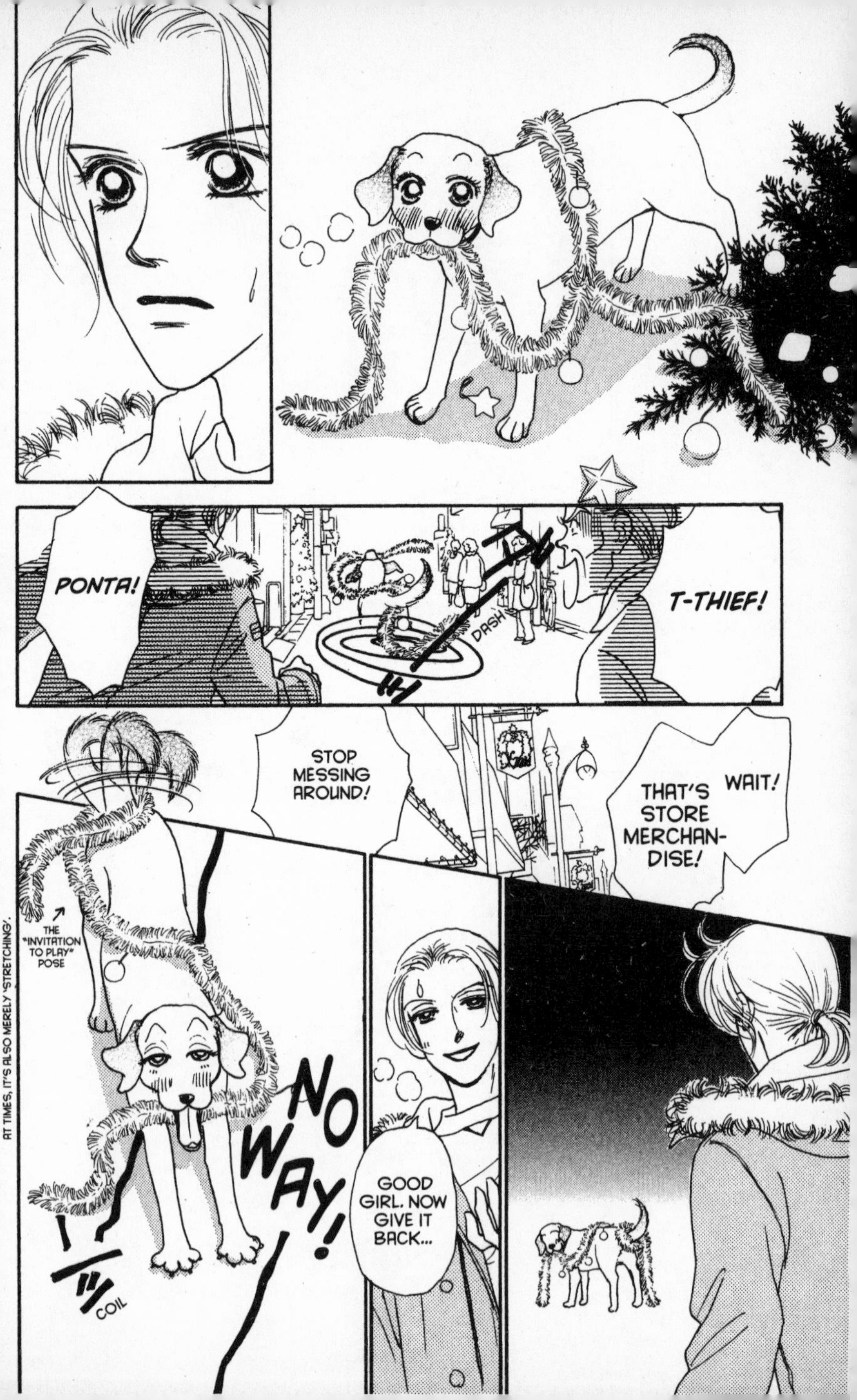
PONTA!
T-THIEF!
DASH
WAIT!
THAT'S STORE MERCHAN-DISE!
STOP MESSING AROUND!
GOOD GIRL. NOW GIVE IT BACK...
NO WAY!!
COIL
THE "INVITATION TO PLAY" POSE
AT TIMES, IT'S ALSO MERELY 'STRETCHING'.

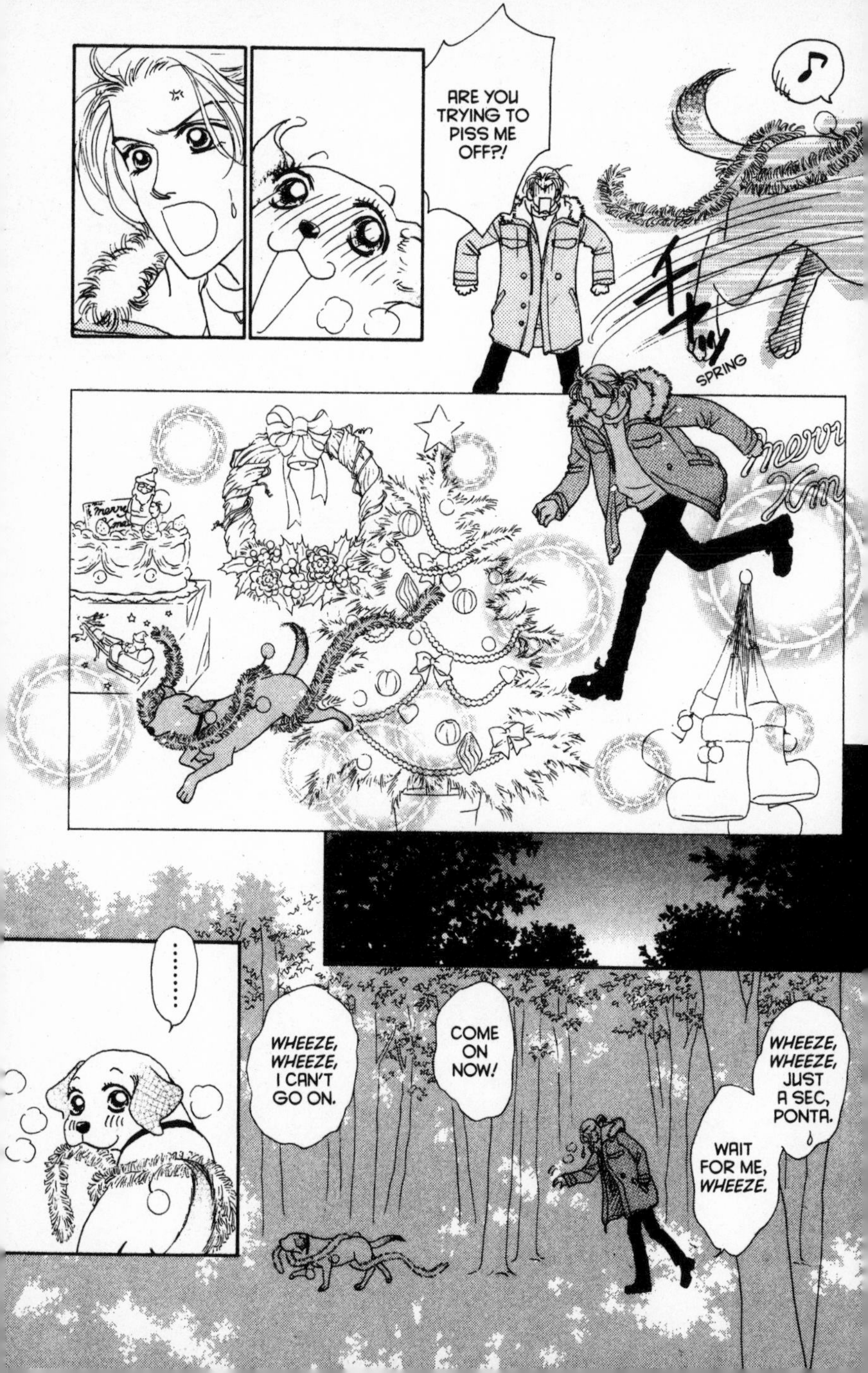
ARE YOU TRYING TO PISS ME OFF?!
SPRING
WHEEZE, WHEEZE, JUST A SEC, PONTA.
WAIT FOR ME, WHEEZE.
COME ON NOW!
WHEEZE, WHEEZE, I CAN'T GO ON.
......

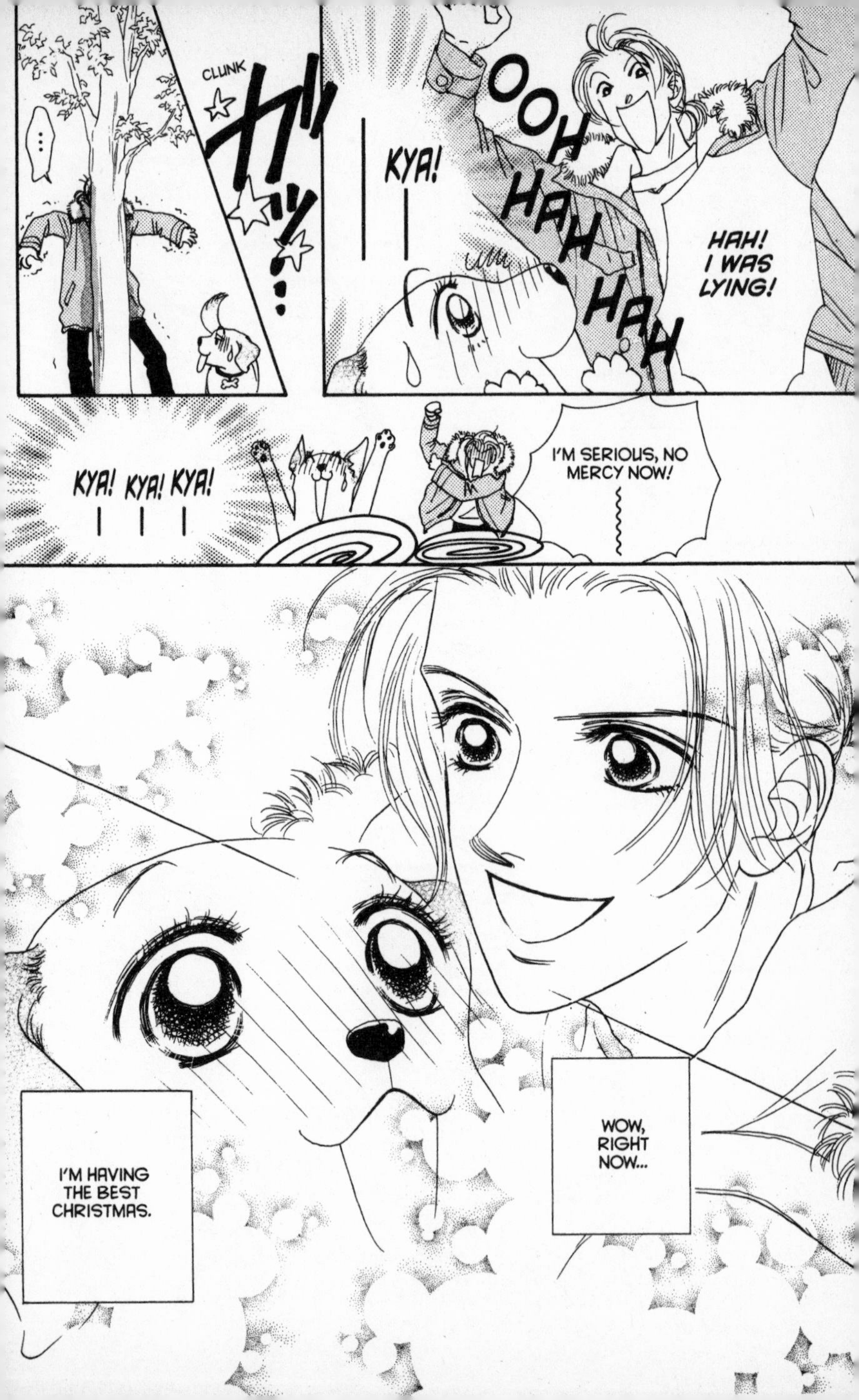
HAH! I WAS LYING!
OOH HAH HAH HAH
KYA!
CLUNK
...
I'M SERIOUS, NO MERCY NOW!
KYA! KYA! KYA!
WOW, RIGHT NOW...
I'M HAVING THE BEST CHRISTMAS.

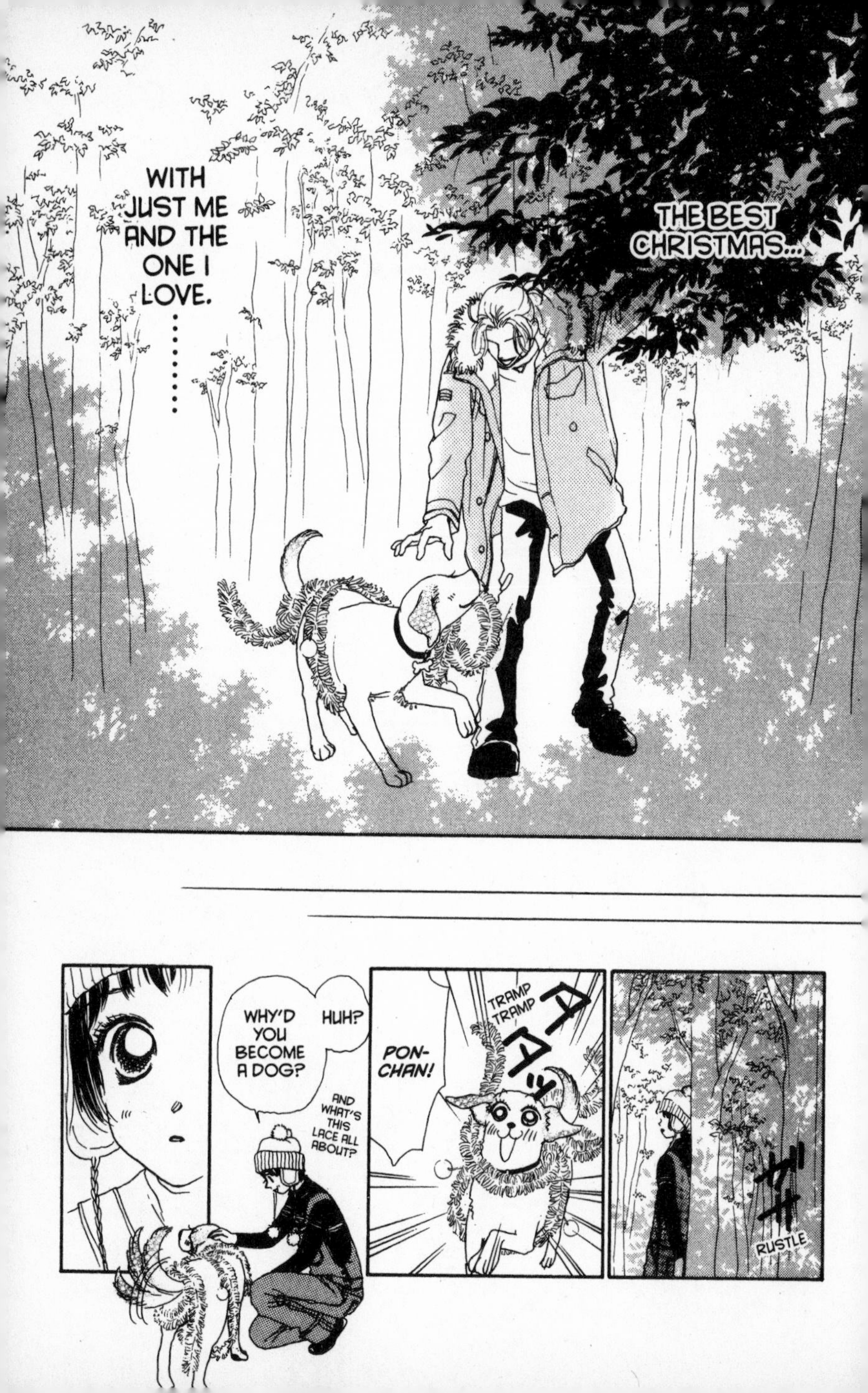
THE BEST CHRISTMAS...
WITH JUST ME AND THE ONE I LOVE.
......
RUSTLE
TRAMP TRAMP
PON-CHAN!
HUH?
WHY'D YOU BECOME A DOG?
AND WHAT'S THIS LACE ALL ABOUT?

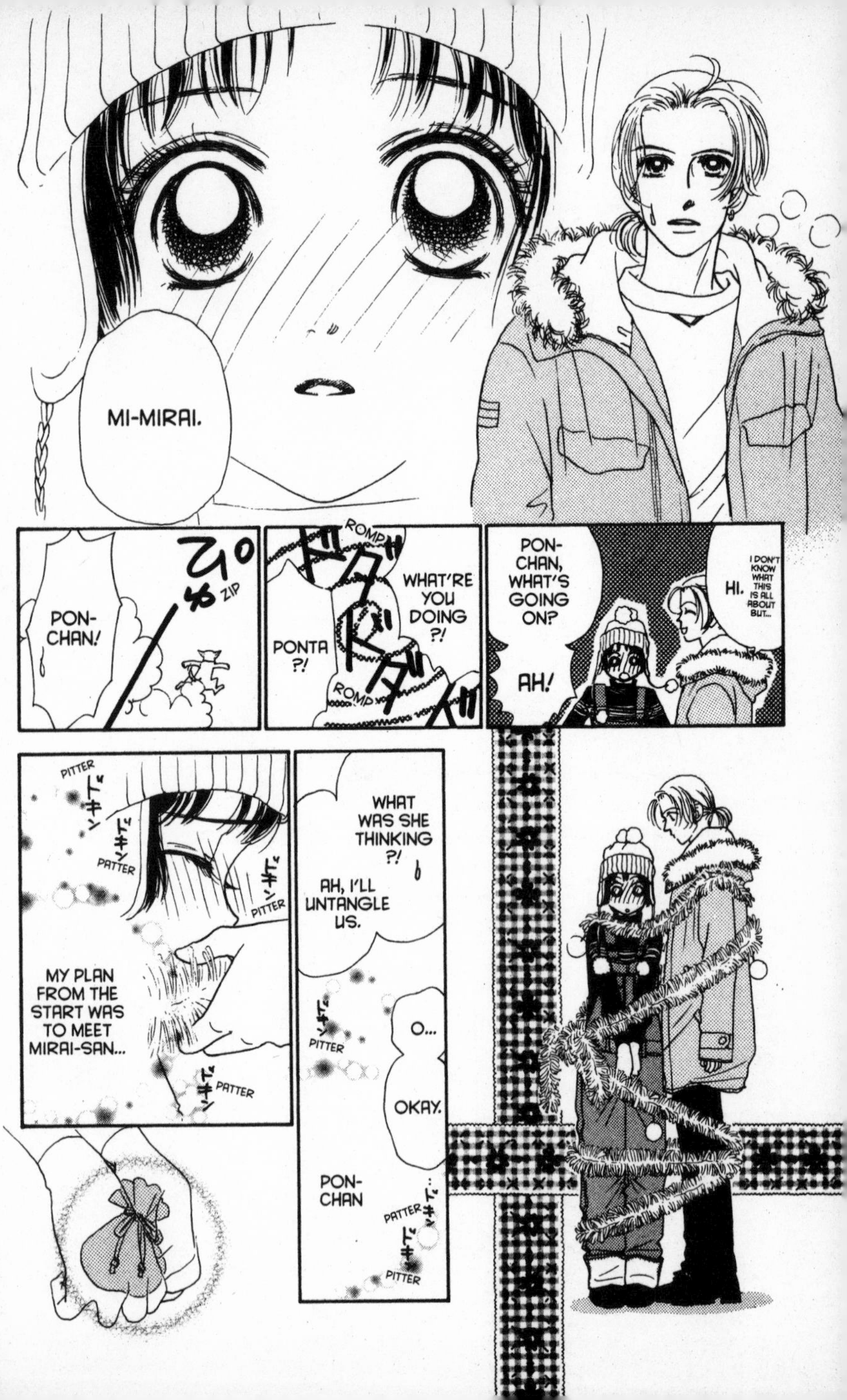
MI-MIRAI.
I DON'T KNOW WHAT THIS IS ALL ABOUT BUT...
HI.
PON-CHAN, WHAT'S GOING ON?
AH!
ROMP
WHAT'RE YOU DOING ?!
PONTA ?!
ROMP
ZIP
PON-CHAN!
WHAT WAS SHE THINKING ?!
AH, I'LL UNTANGLE US.
PITTER
O...
OKAY.
PON-CHAN
PATTER
PITTER
PITTER
PATTER
PITTER
MY PLAN FROM THE START WAS TO MEET MIRAI-SAN...
PATTER

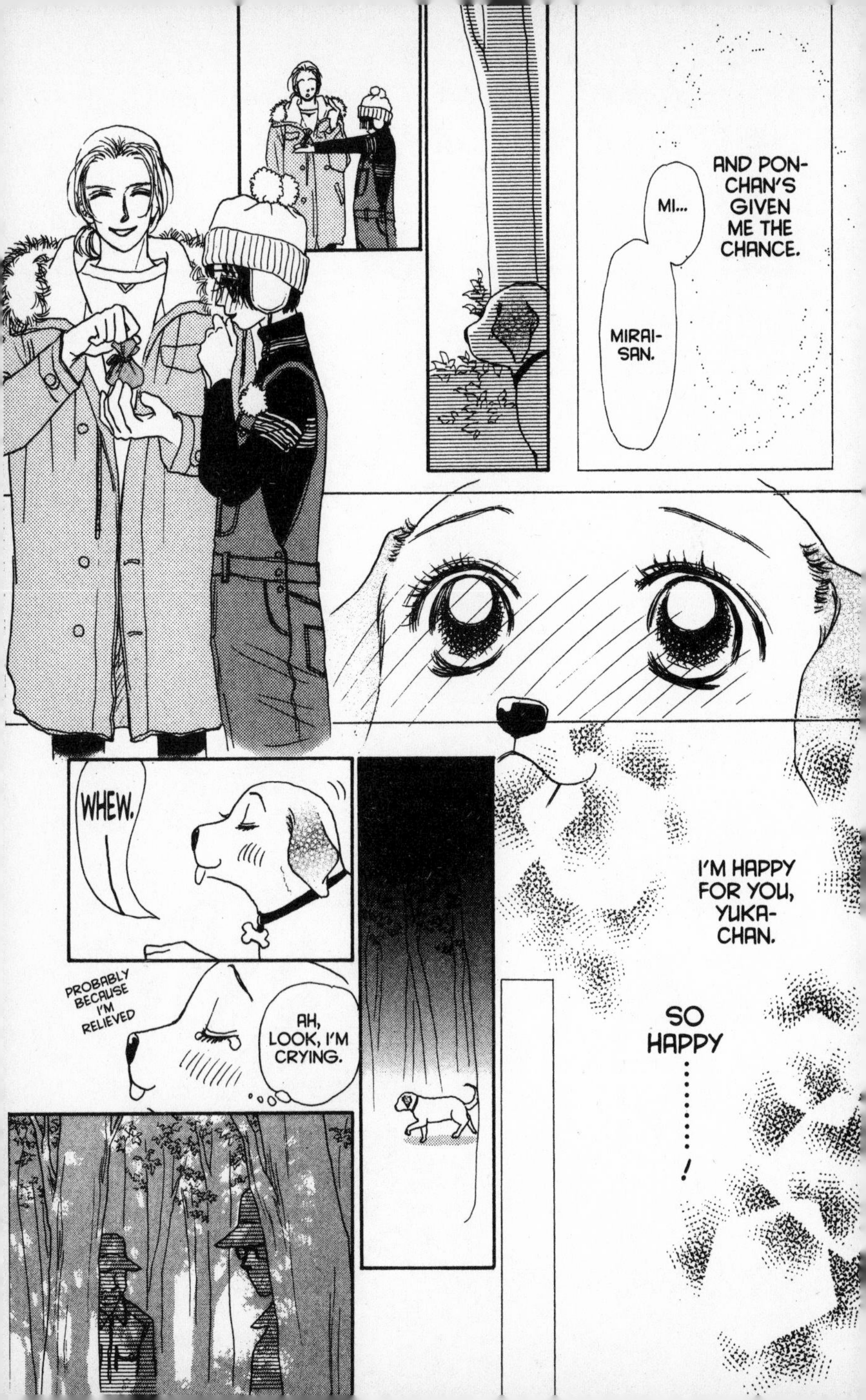
AND PON-CHAN'S GIVEN ME THE CHANCE.
MI...
MIRAI-SAN.
I'M HAPPY FOR YOU, YUKA-CHAN.
SO HAPPY ......!
WHEW.
AH, LOOK, I'M CRYING.
PROBABLY BECAUSE I'M RELIEVED

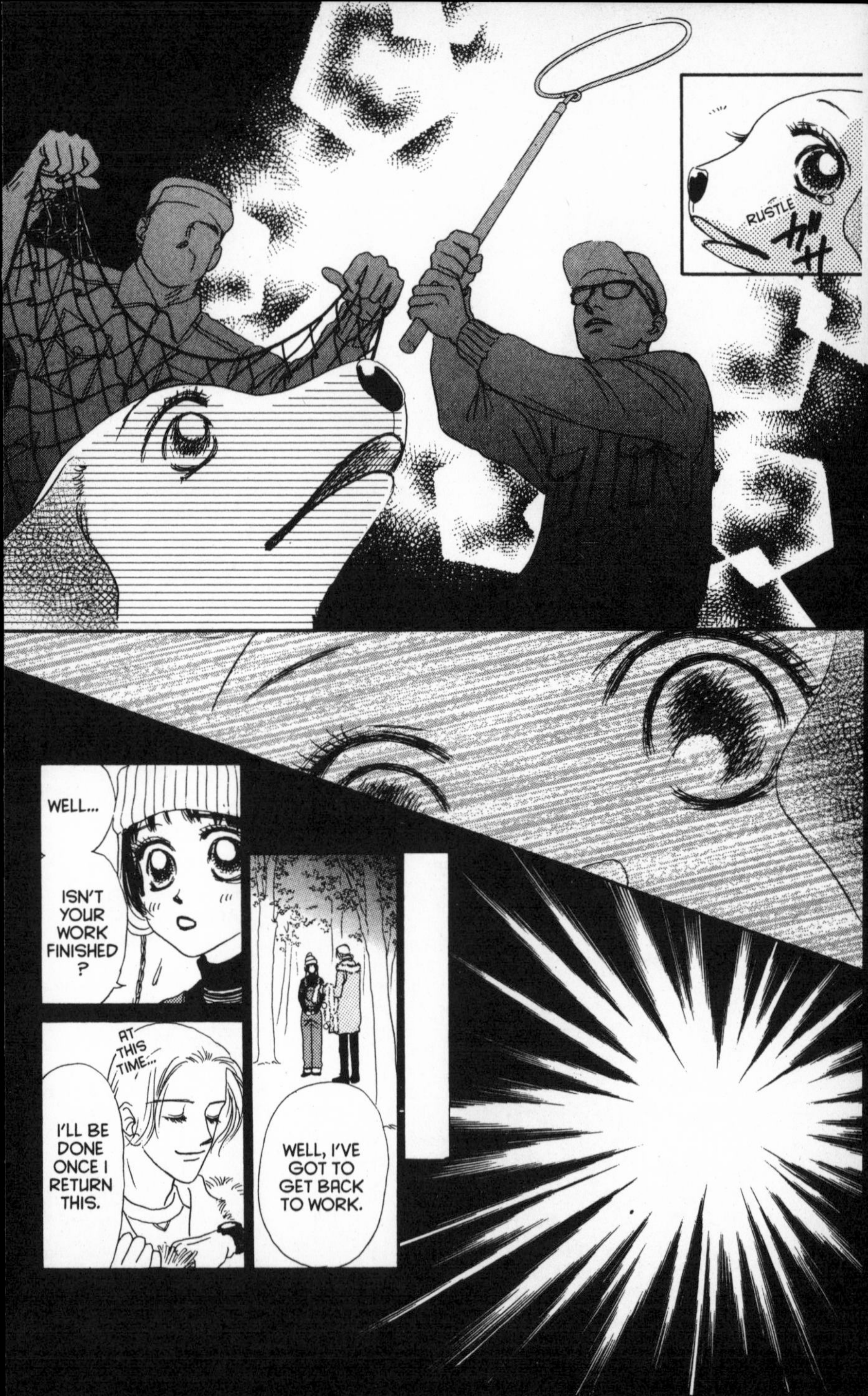
RUSTLE
ガサ
WELL, I'VE GOT TO GET BACK TO WORK.
WELL...
ISN'T YOUR WORK FINISHED?
AT THIS TIME...
I'LL BE DONE ONCE I RETURN THIS.

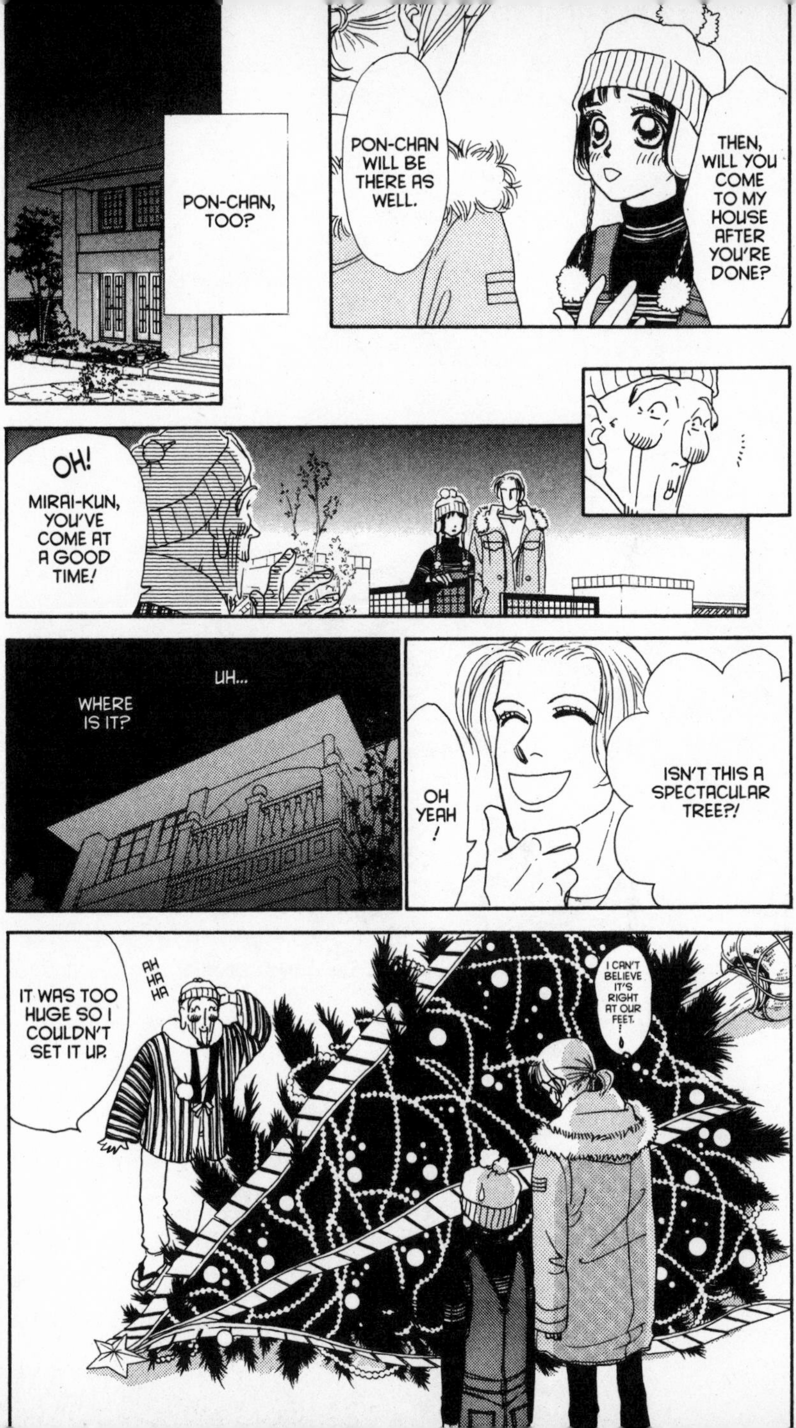
THEN, WILL YOU COME TO MY HOUSE AFTER YOU'RE DONE?
PON-CHAN WILL BE THERE AS WELL.
PON-CHAN, TOO?
OH!
MIRAI-KUN, YOU'VE COME AT A GOOD TIME!
ISN'T THIS A SPECTACULAR TREE?!
OH YEAH!
UH...
WHERE IS IT?
I CAN'T BELIEVE IT'S RIGHT AT OUR FEET.
AH HA HA
IT WAS TOO HUGE SO I COULDN'T SET IT UP.

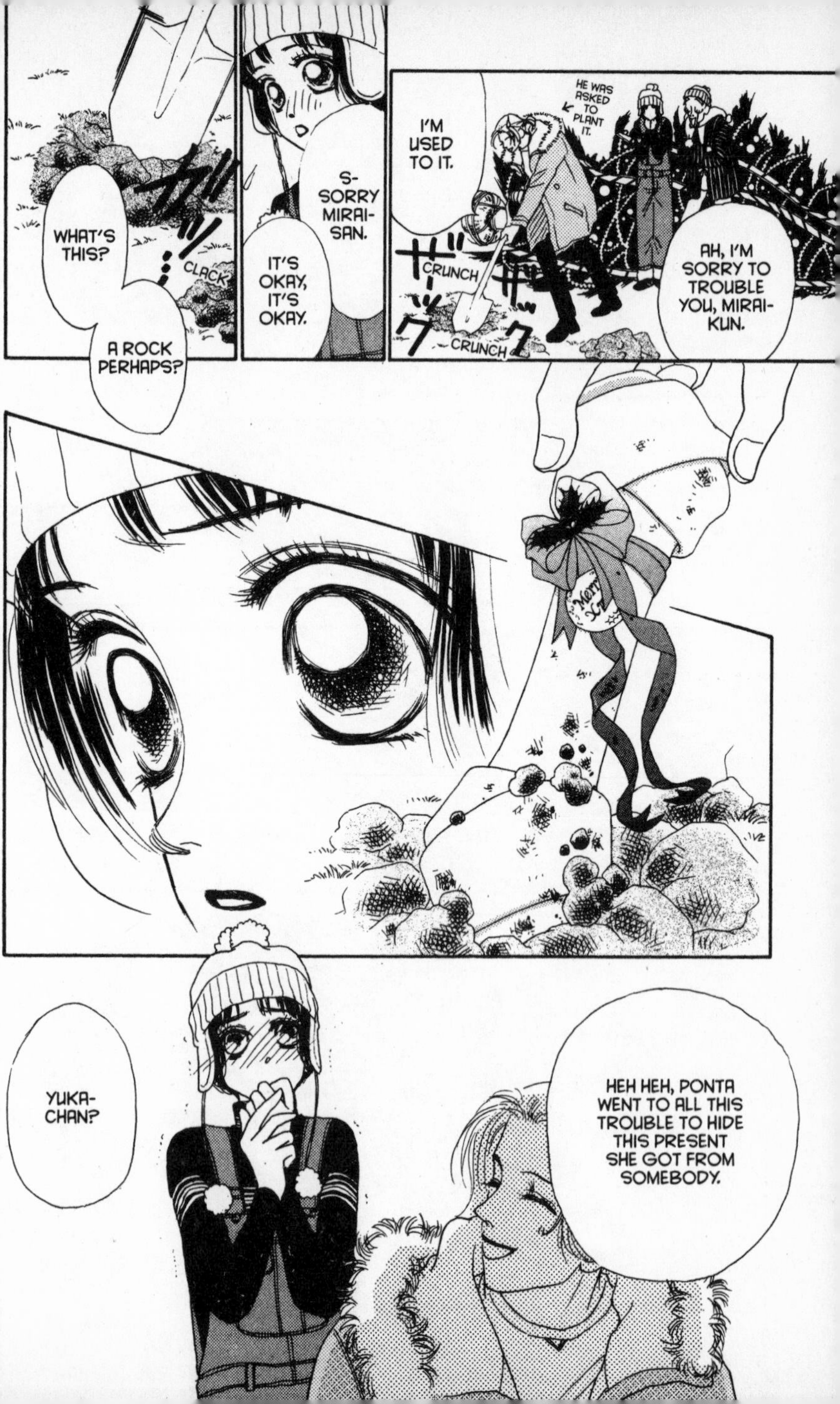
AH, I'M SORRY TO TROUBLE YOU, MIRAI-KUN.
I'M USED TO IT.
HE WAS ASKED TO PLANT IT.
CRUNCH
CRUNCH
S-SORRY MIRAI-SAN.
IT'S OKAY, IT'S OKAY.
WHAT'S THIS?
CLACK
A ROCK PERHAPS?
HEH HEH, PONTA WENT TO ALL THIS TROUBLE TO HIDE THIS PRESENT SHE GOT FROM SOMEBODY.
YUKA-CHAN?

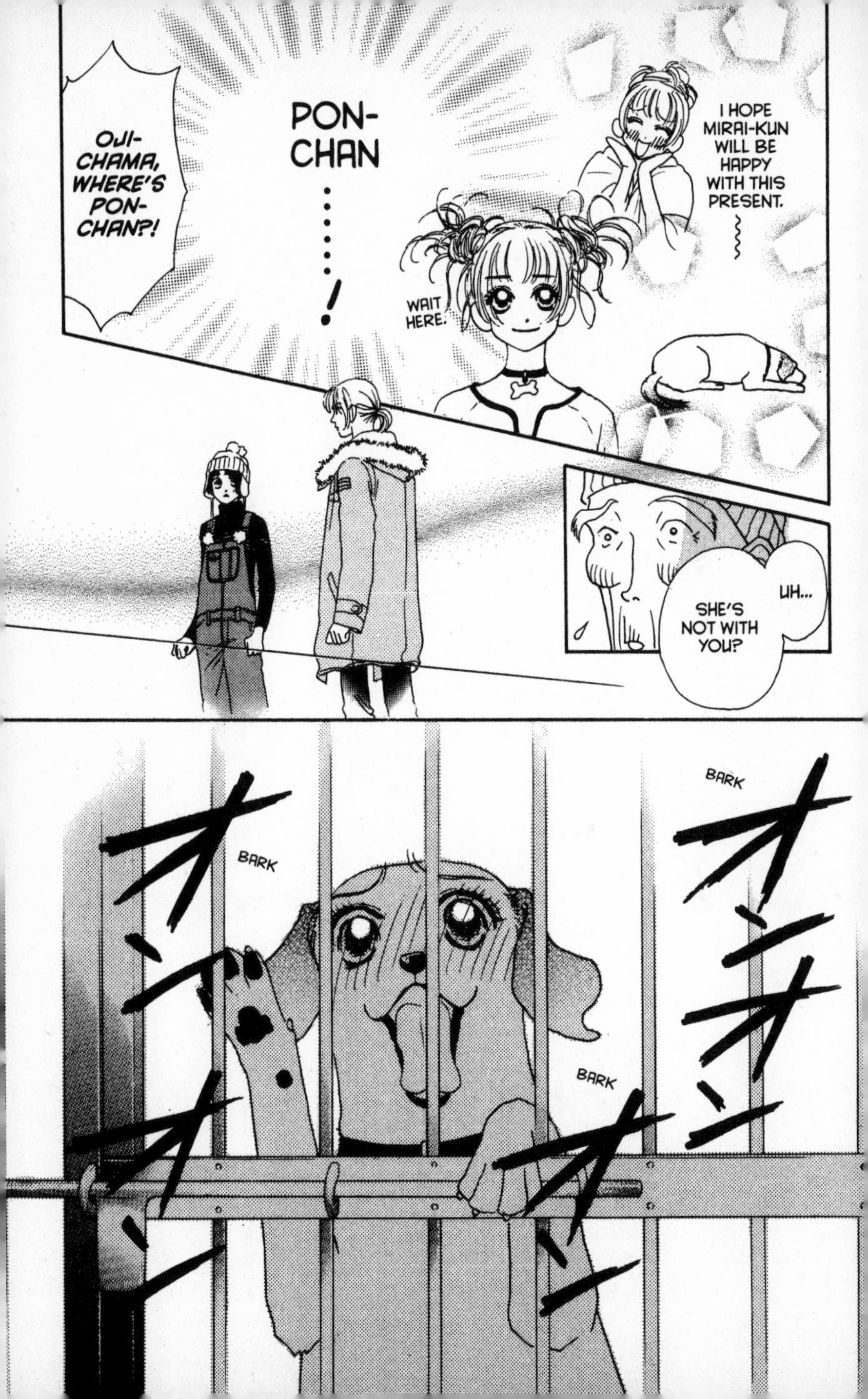
I HOPE MIRAI-KUN WILL BE HAPPY WITH THIS PRESENT. ~
WAIT HERE.
PON-CHAN ......!
OJI-CHAMA, WHERE'S PON-CHAN?!
UH...
SHE'S NOT WITH YOU?
BARK
BARK
BARK

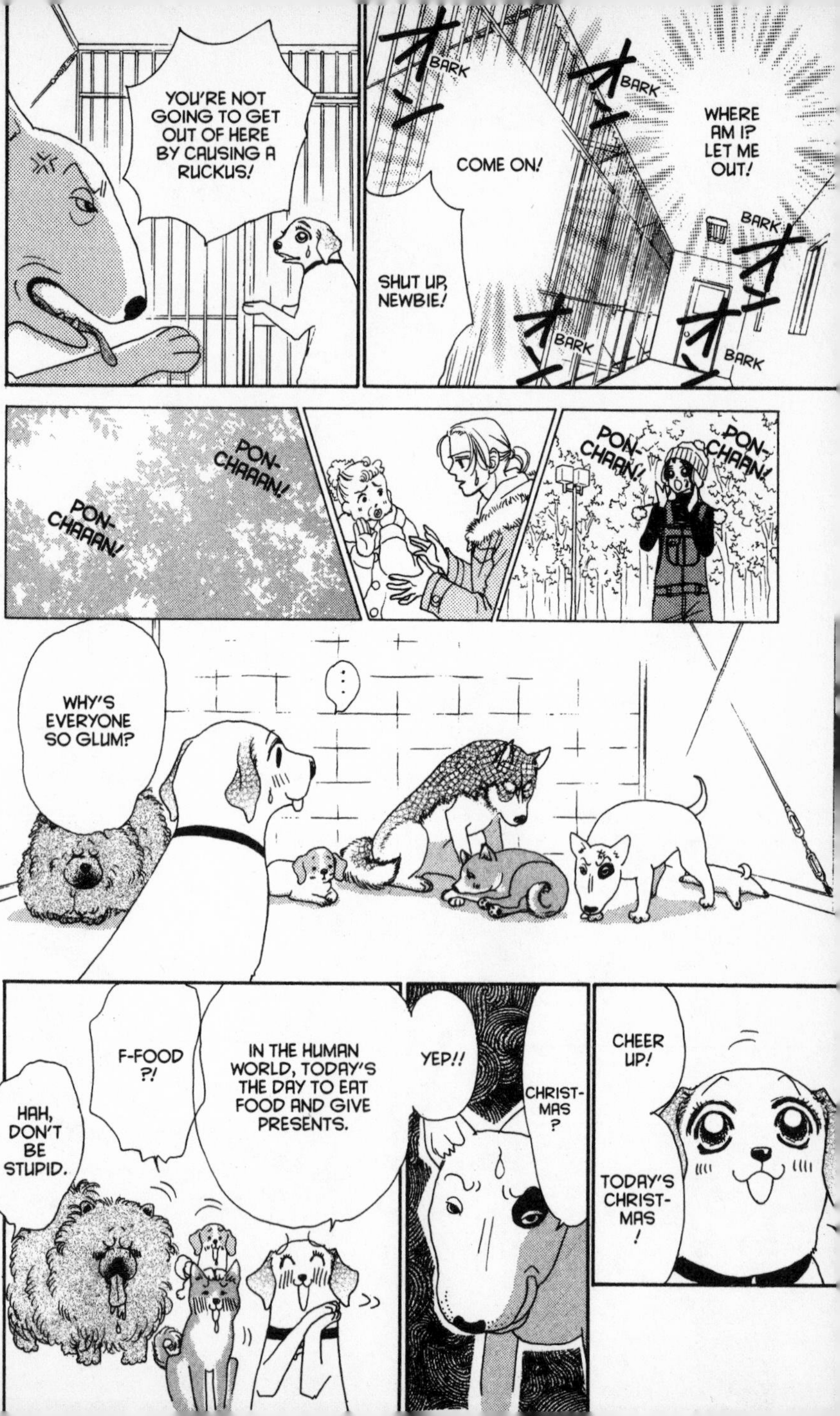
WHERE AM I? LET ME OUT!
BARK
BARK
BARK
BARK
BARK
SHUT UP, NEWBIE!
COME ON!
YOU'RE NOT GOING TO GET OUT OF HERE BY CAUSING A RUCKUS!
PON-CHAAAN!
PON-CHAAAN!
PON-CHAAAN!
PON-CHAAAN!
WHY'S EVERYONE SO GLUM?
...
CHEER UP!
TODAY'S CHRISTMAS!
CHRISTMAS?
YEP!!
IN THE HUMAN WORLD, TODAY'S THE DAY TO EAT FOOD AND GIVE PRESENTS.
F-FOOD?!
HAH, DON'T BE STUPID.

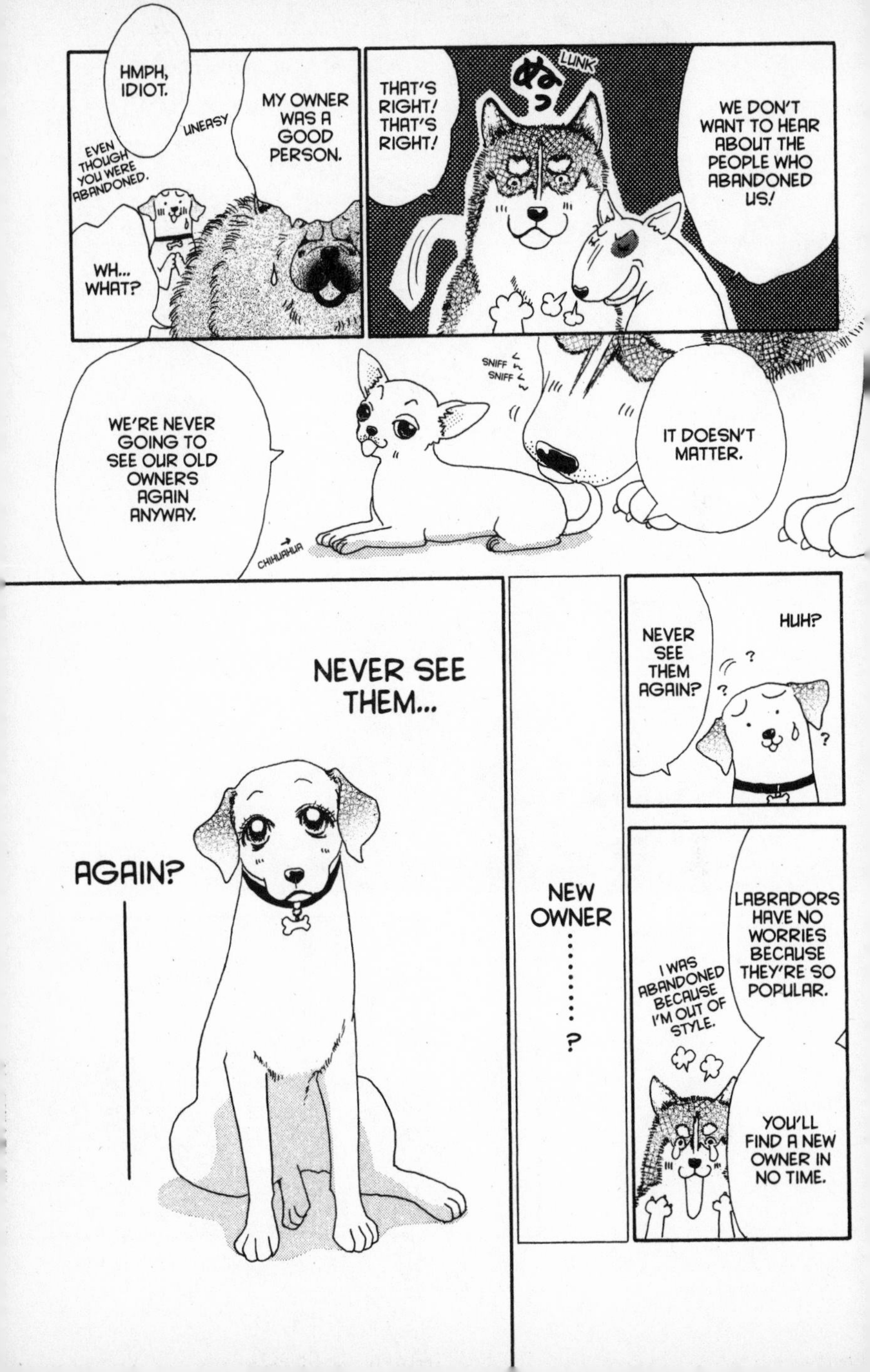
WE DON'T WANT TO HEAR ABOUT THE PEOPLE WHO ABANDONED US!
LUNK
ぬっ
THAT'S RIGHT! THAT'S RIGHT!
MY OWNER WAS A GOOD PERSON.
UNEASY
HMPH, IDIOT.
EVEN THOUGH YOU WERE ABANDONED.
WH... WHAT?
IT DOESN'T MATTER.
SNIFF SNIFF
WE'RE NEVER GOING TO SEE OUR OLD OWNERS AGAIN ANYWAY.
CHIHUAHUA
HUH?
NEVER SEE THEM AGAIN?
LABRADORS HAVE NO WORRIES BECAUSE THEY'RE SO POPULAR.
I WAS ABANDONED BECAUSE I'M OUT OF STYLE.
YOU'LL FIND A NEW OWNER IN NO TIME.
NEW OWNER ....?
NEVER SEE THEM...
AGAIN?

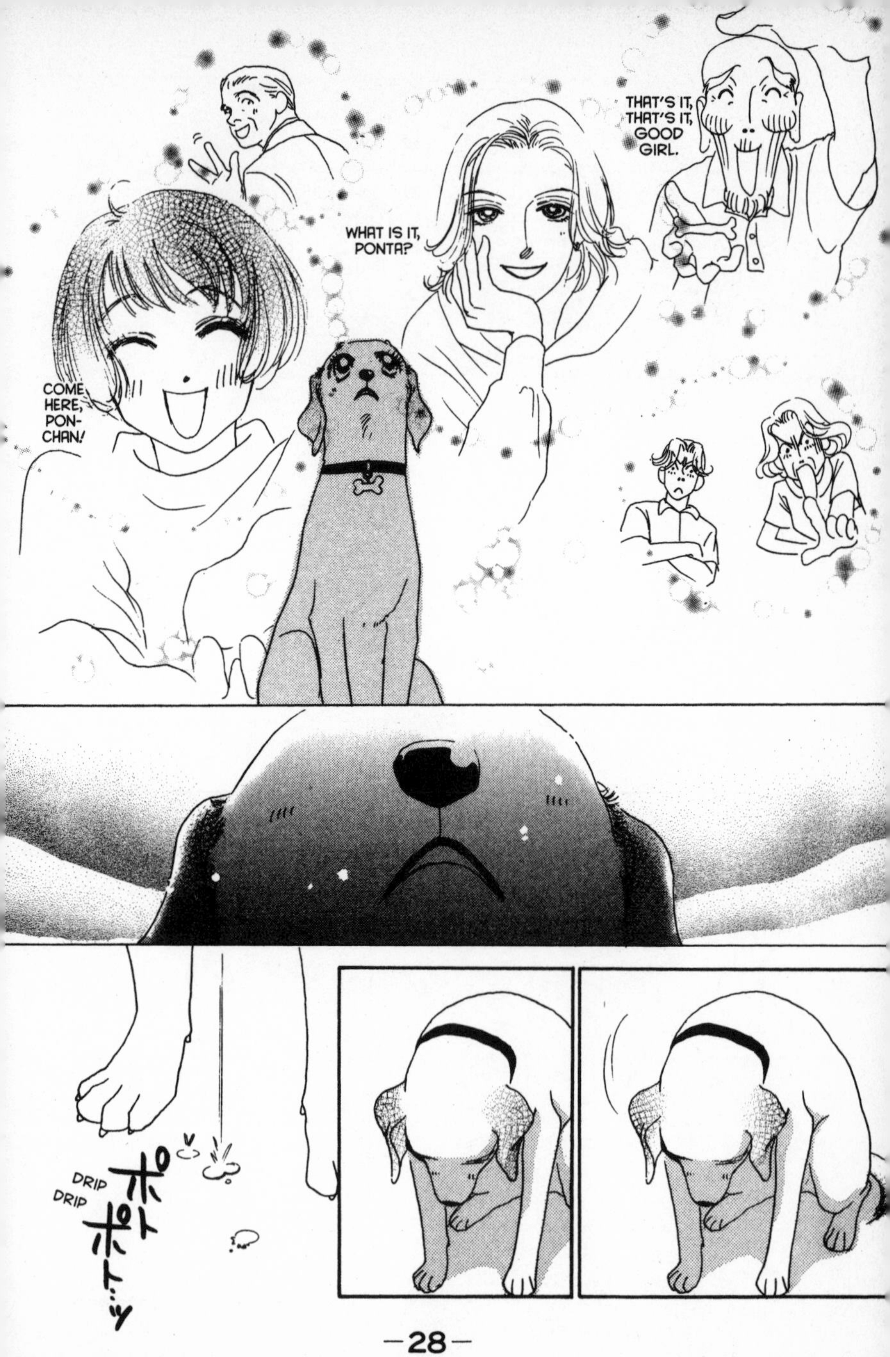
THAT'S IT, THAT'S IT, GOOD GIRL.
WHAT IS IT, PONTA?
COME HERE, PON-CHAN!
DRIP DRIP
ポトポト…ッ

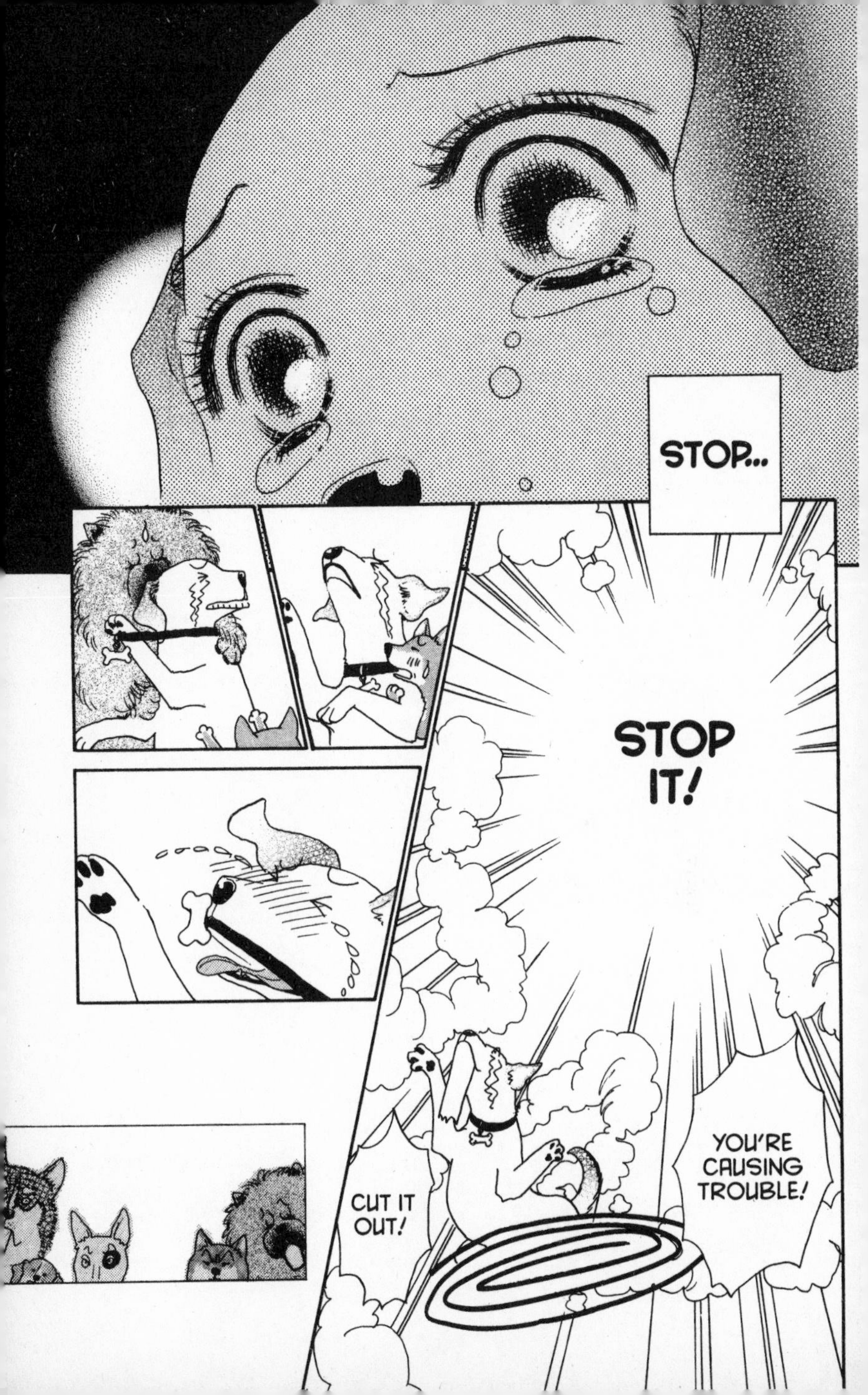
STOP...
STOP IT!
YOU'RE CAUSING TROUBLE!
CUT IT OUT!

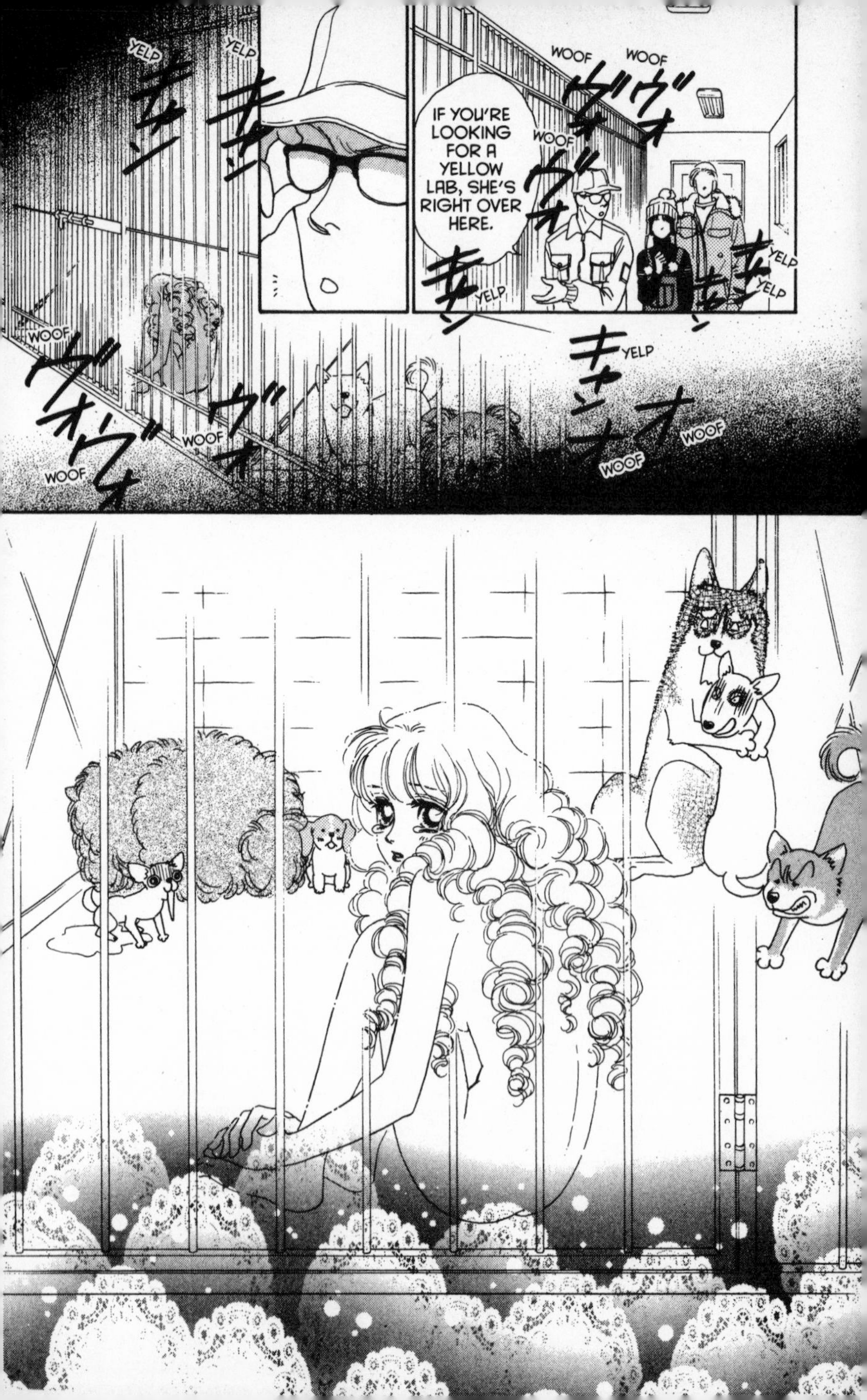
WOOF WOOF
WOOF
IF YOU'RE LOOKING FOR A YELLOW LAB, SHE'S RIGHT OVER HERE.
YELP YELP
YELP
YELP
WOOF WOOF
YELP YELP
WOOF
WOOF
WOOF

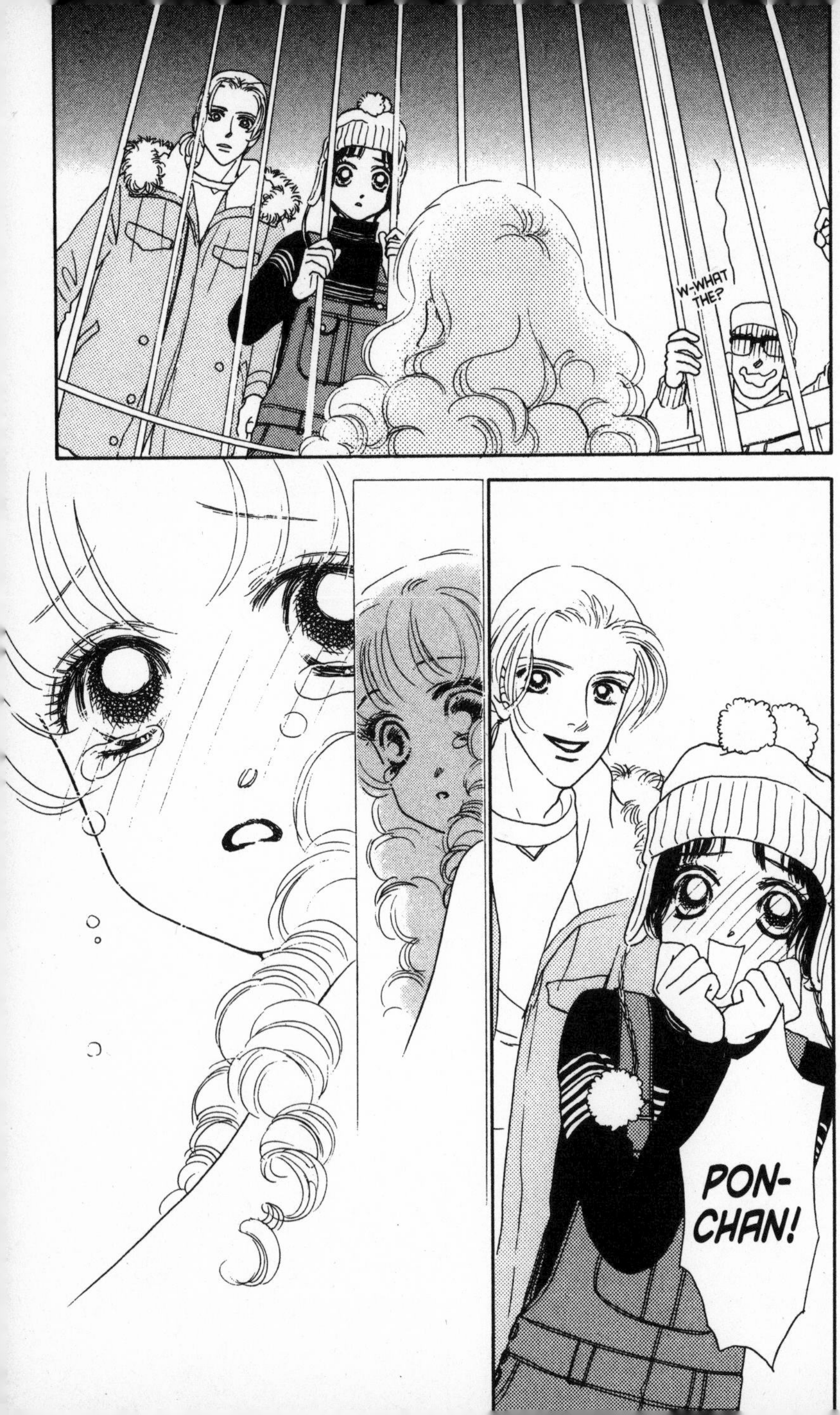
W-WHAT THE?
PON-CHAN!

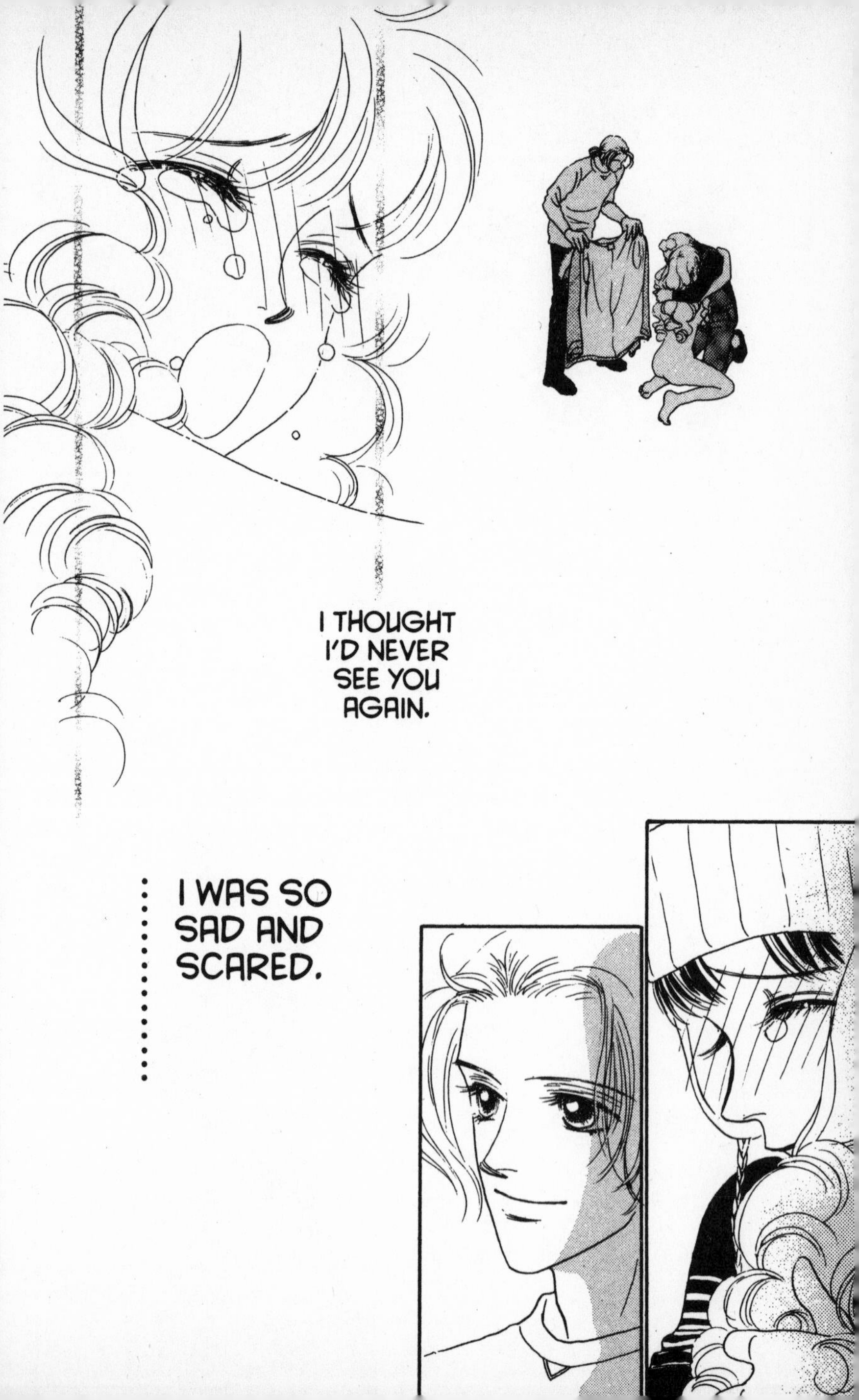
I THOUGHT I'D NEVER SEE YOU AGAIN.
.... I WAS SO SAD AND SCARED.

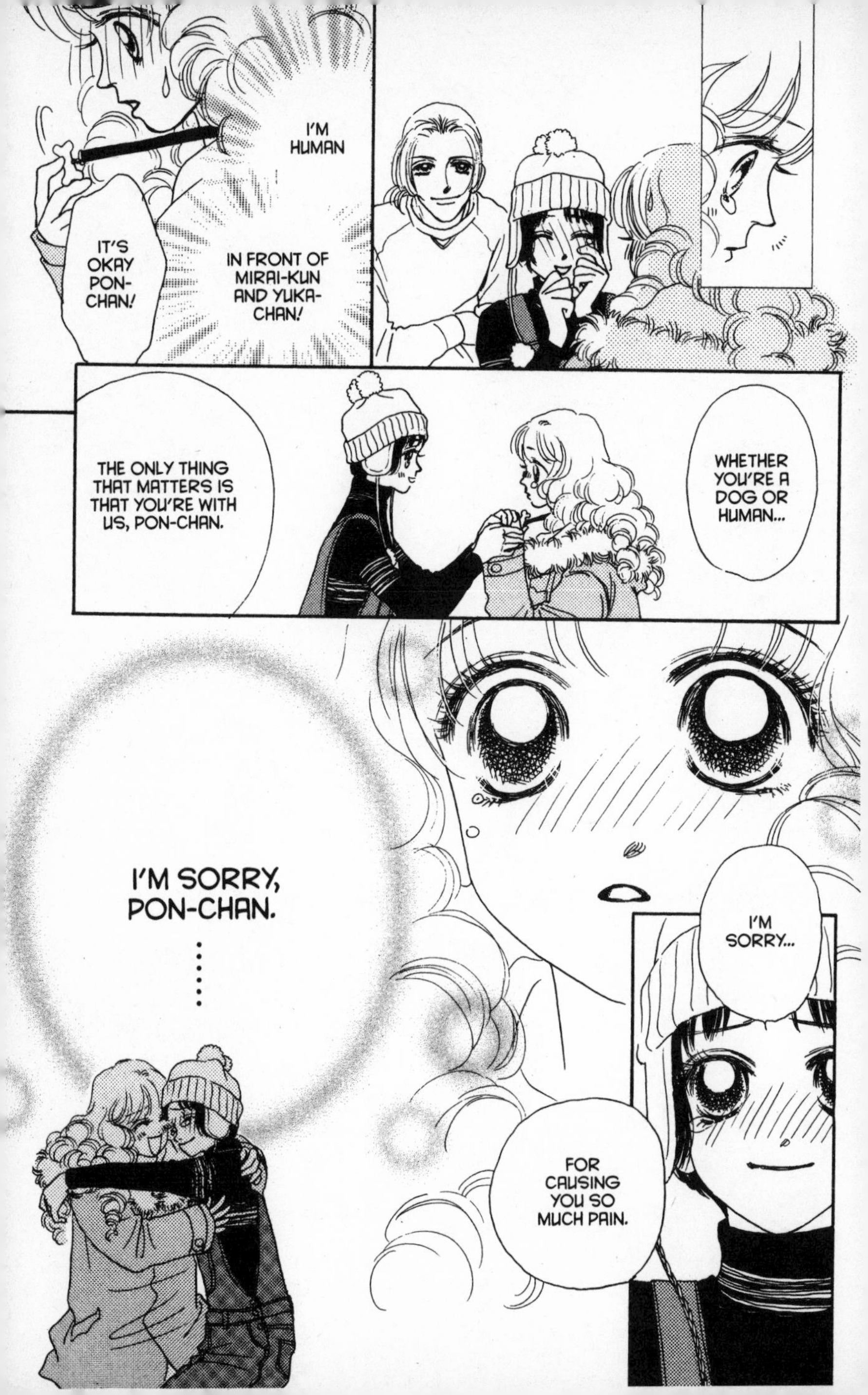
I'M HUMAN
IN FRONT OF MIRAI-KUN AND YUKA-CHAN!
IT'S OKAY PON-CHAN!
WHETHER YOU'RE A DOG OR HUMAN...
THE ONLY THING THAT MATTERS IS THAT YOU'RE WITH US, PON-CHAN.
I'M SORRY...
FOR CAUSING YOU SO MUCH PAIN.
I'M SORRY, PON-CHAN.
......

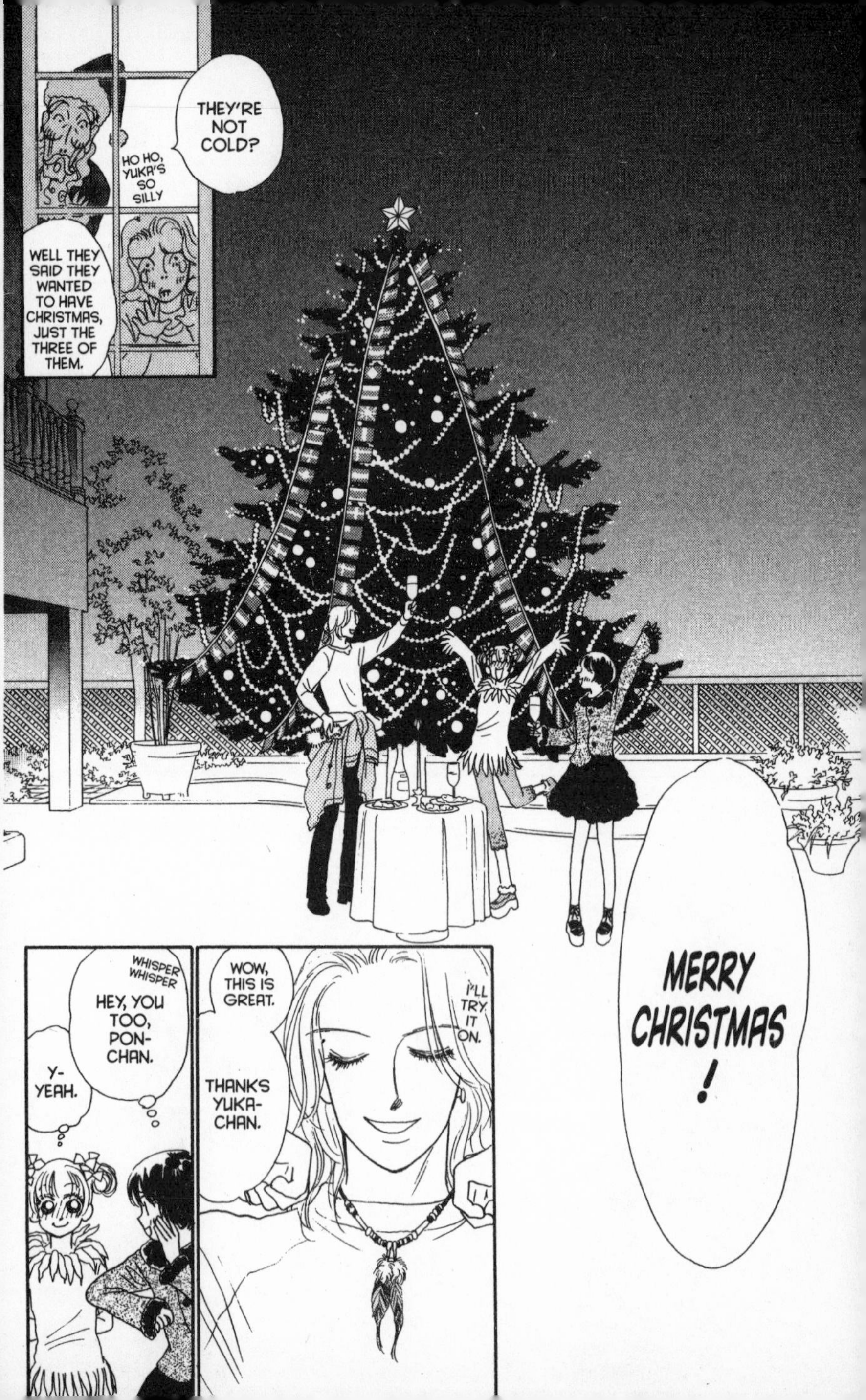
THEY'RE NOT COLD?
HO HO, YUKA'S SO SILLY
WELL THEY SAID THEY WANTED TO HAVE CHRISTMAS, JUST THE THREE OF THEM.
MERRY CHRISTMAS!
I'LL TRY IT ON.
WOW, THIS IS GREAT.
THANKS YUKA-CHAN.
WHISPER WHISPER
HEY, YOU TOO, PON-CHAN.
Y-YEAH.

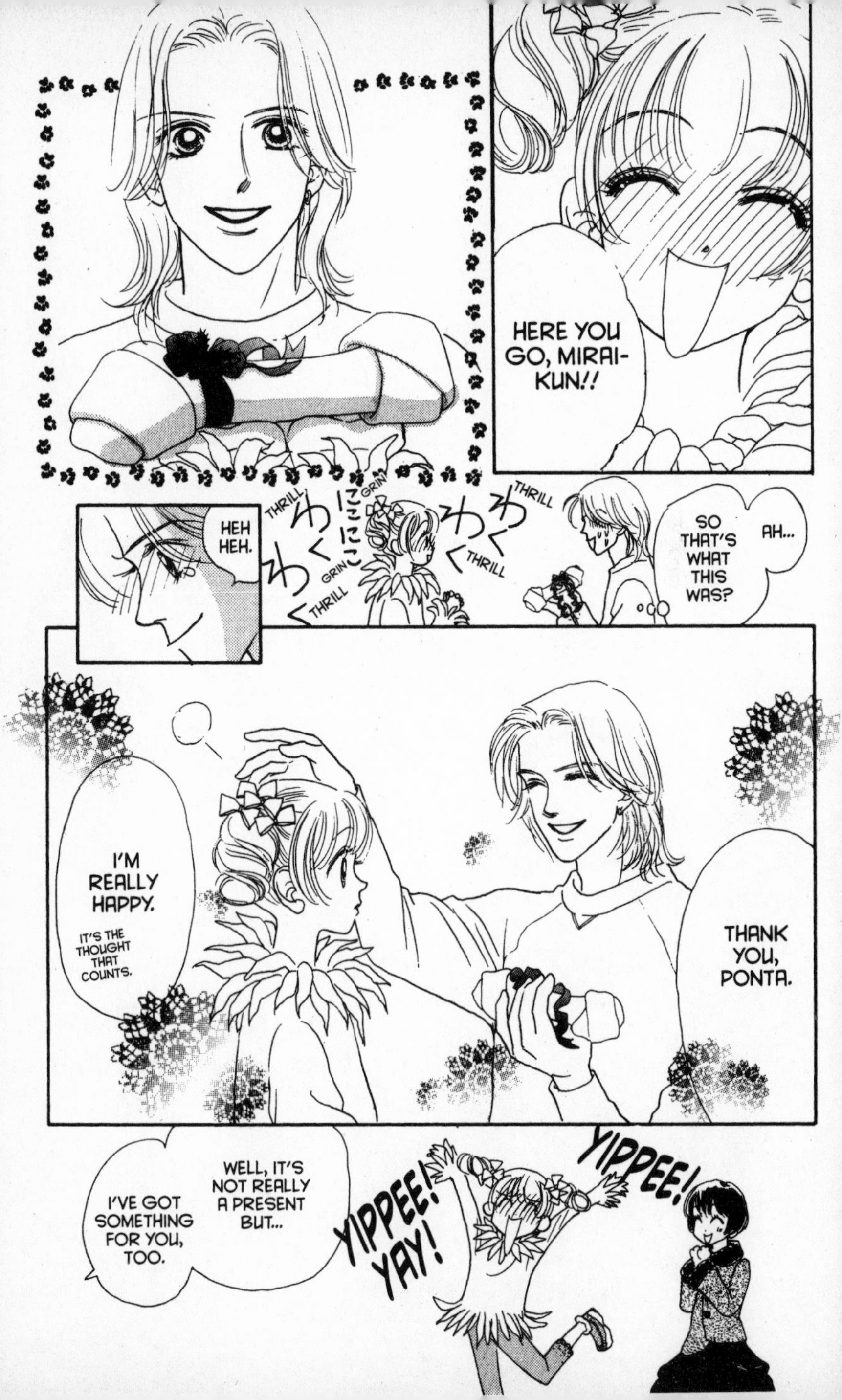
HERE YOU GO, MIRAI-KUN!!
AH...
SO THAT'S WHAT THIS WAS?
わくわく THRILL THRILL
にこにこ GRIN GRIN
わくわく THRILL THRILL
HEH HEH.
THANK YOU, PONTA.
I'M REALLY HAPPY.
IT'S THE THOUGHT THAT COUNTS.
YIPPEE!
YIPPEE! YAY!
WELL, IT'S NOT REALLY A PRESENT BUT...
I'VE GOT SOMETHING FOR YOU, TOO.

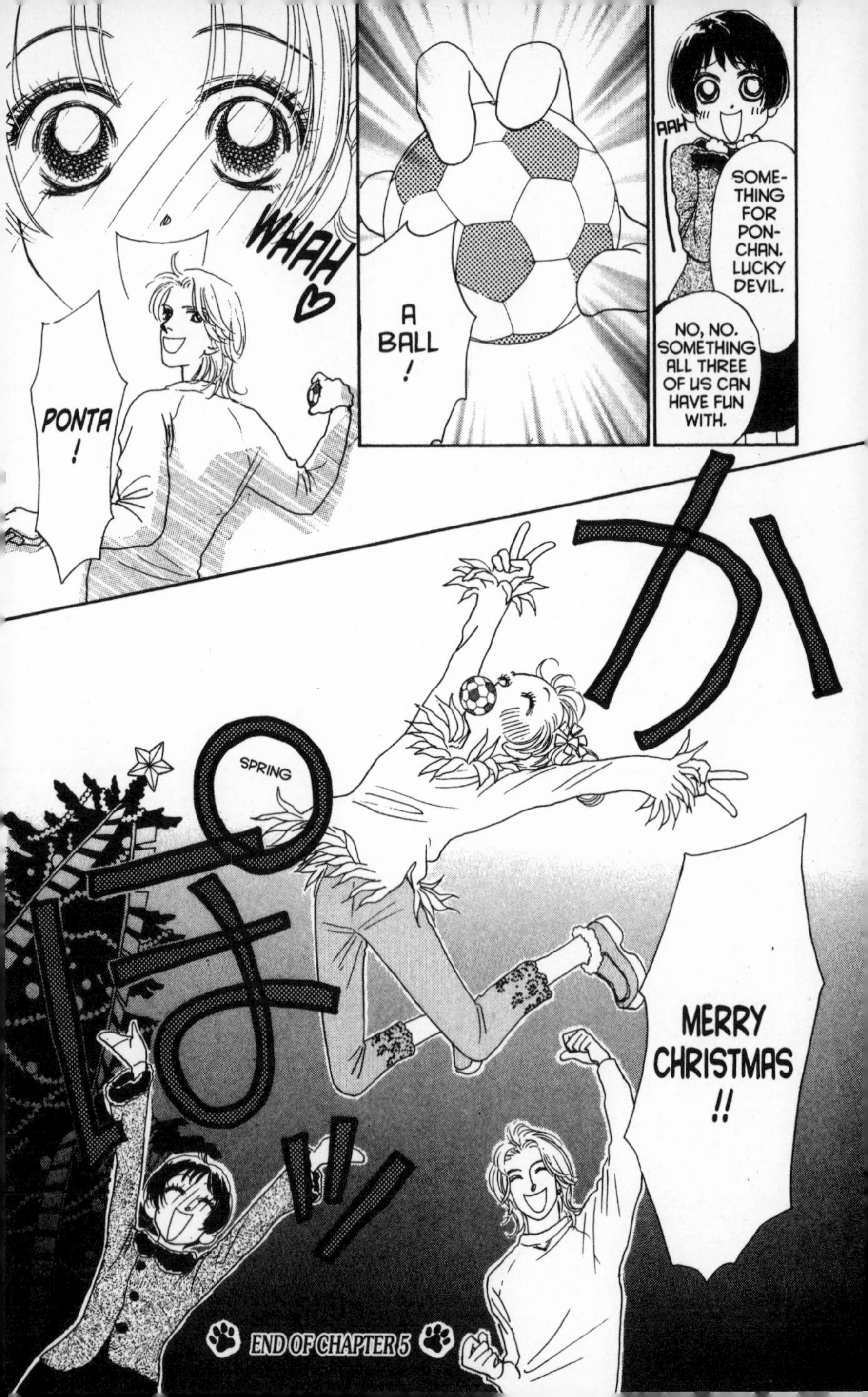
AAH
SOMETHING FOR PON-CHAN. LUCKY DEVIL.
NO, NO. SOMETHING ALL THREE OF US CAN HAVE FUN WITH.
A BALL!
WHAH ♥
PONTA!
かぽッ
SPRING
MERRY CHRISTMAS !!
END OF CHAPTER 5

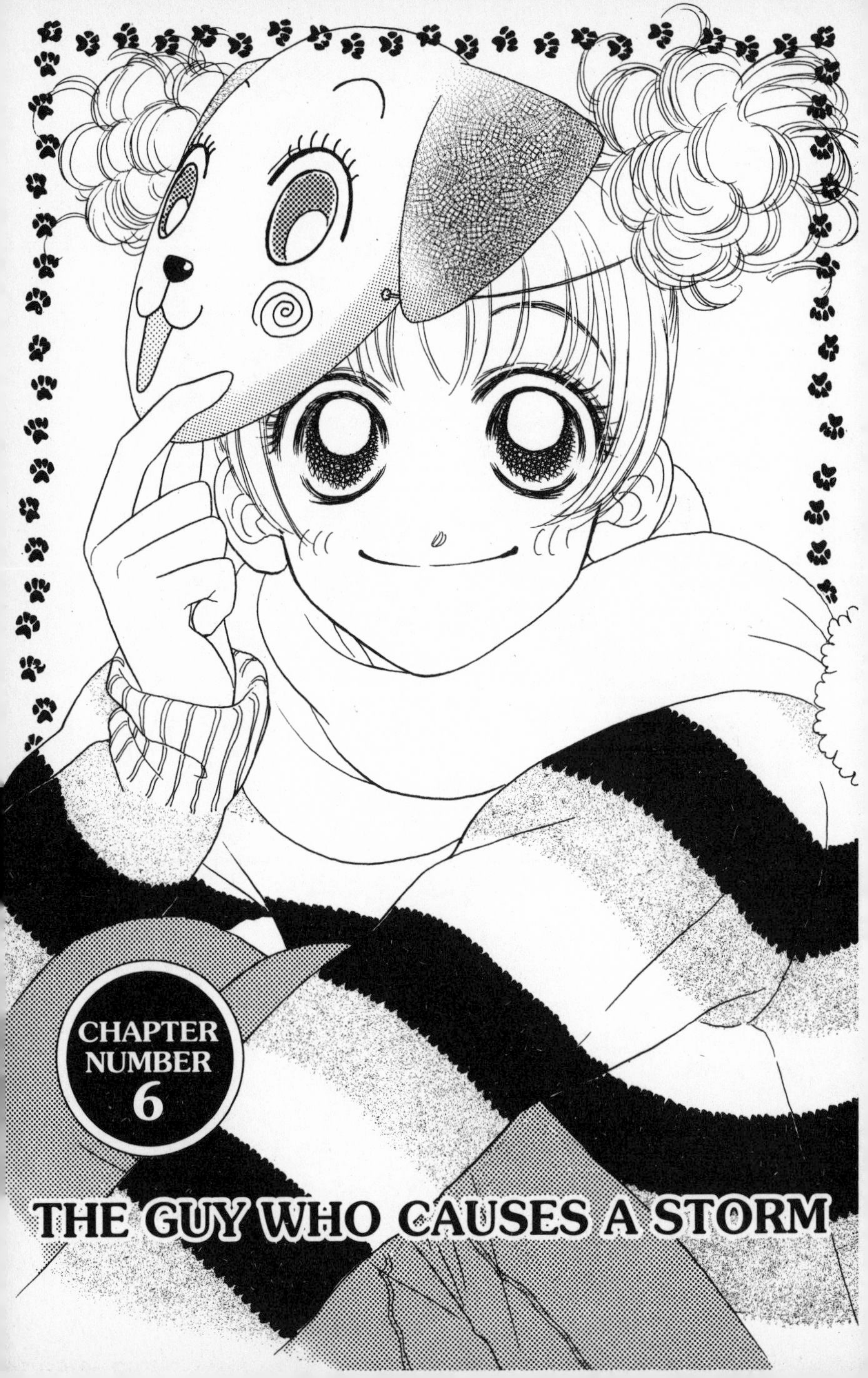
CHAPTER NUMBER 6
THE GUY WHO CAUSES A STORM

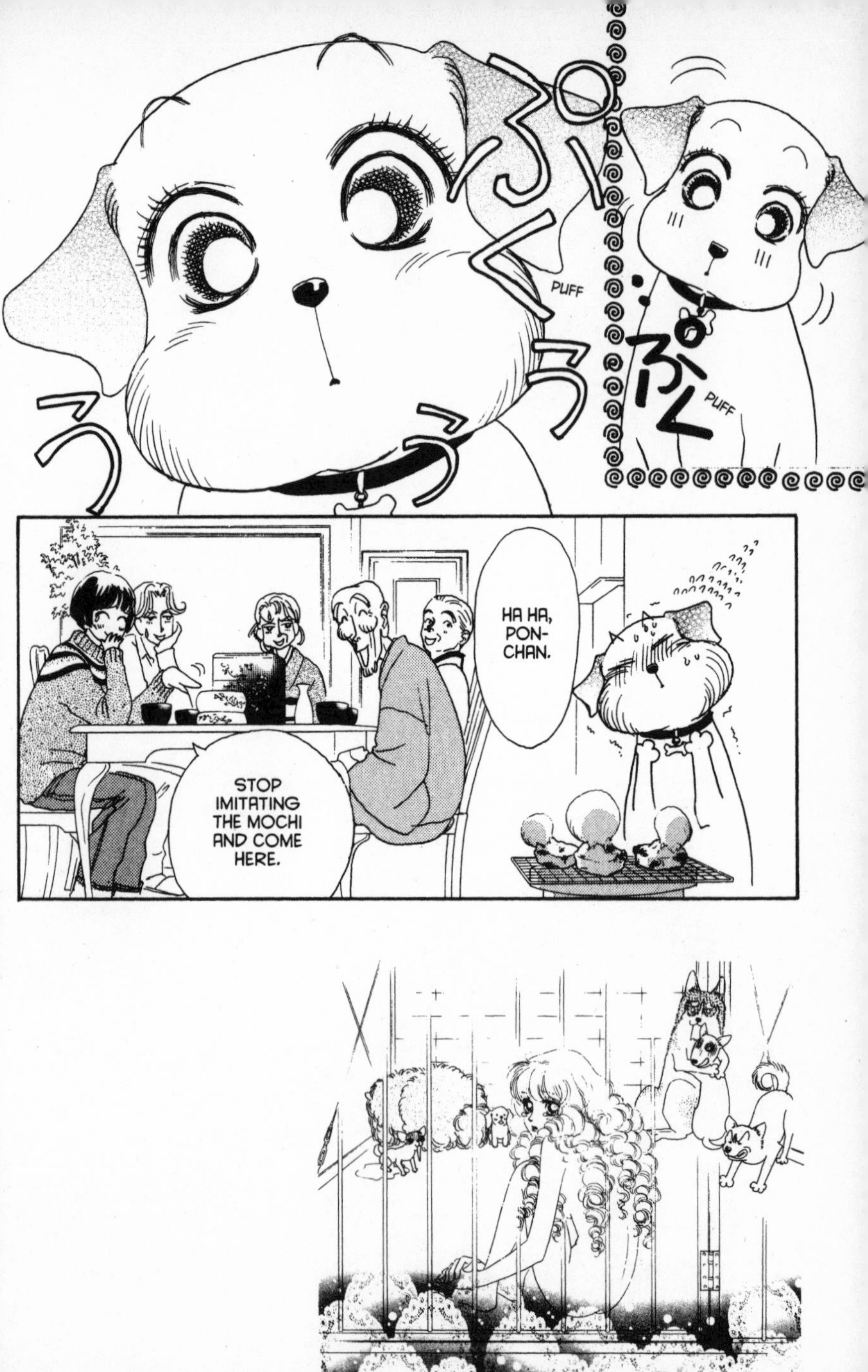
PUFF
ぷく
PUFF
HA HA, PON-CHAN.
STOP IMITATING THE MOCHI AND COME HERE.

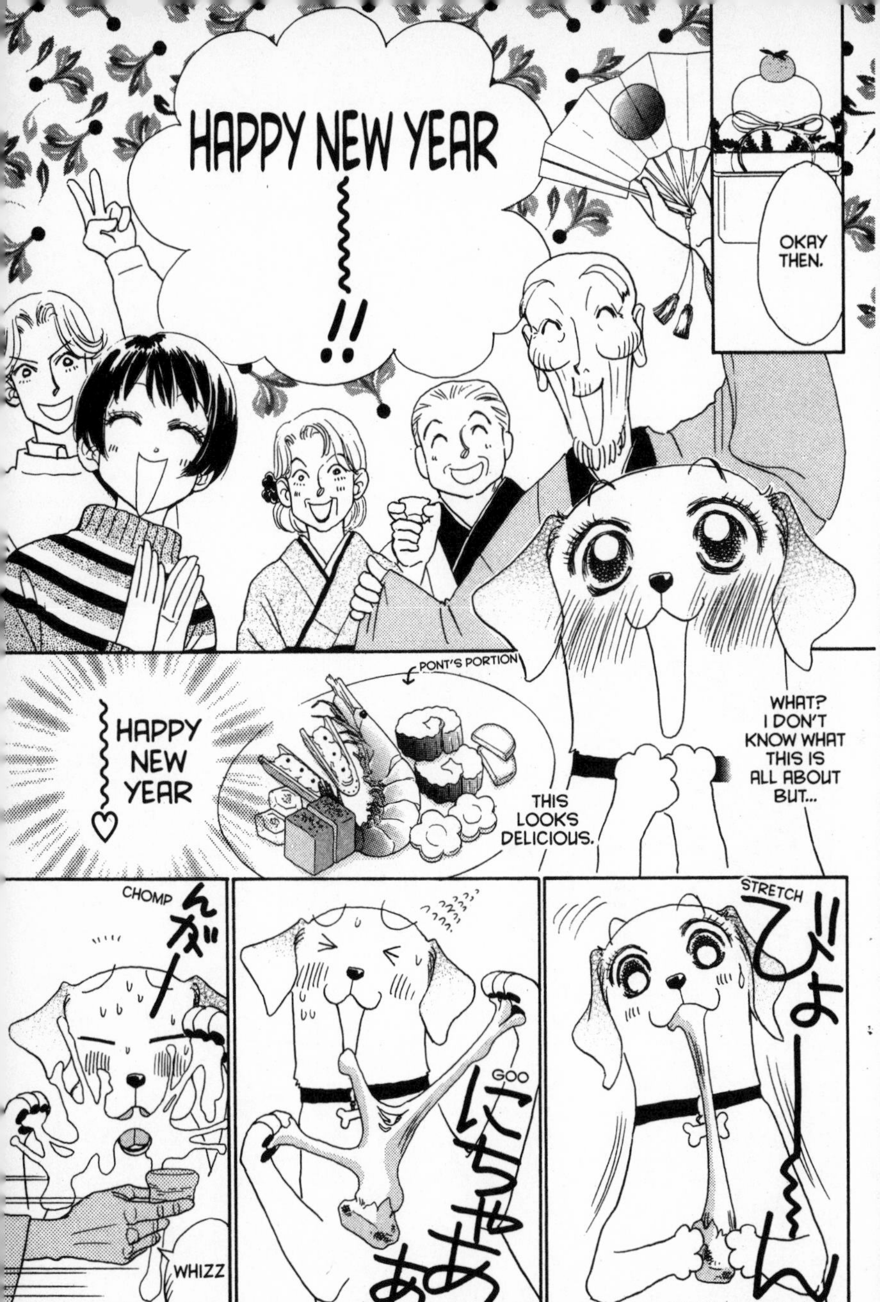
OKAY THEN.
HAPPY NEW YEAR ~~~!!
WHAT? I DON'T KNOW WHAT THIS IS ALL ABOUT BUT...
THIS LOOKS DELICIOUS.
PONT'S PORTION
HAPPY NEW YEAR ♡
STRETCH
びょーん
GOO
にちゃあ
CHOMP
んが
WHIZZ

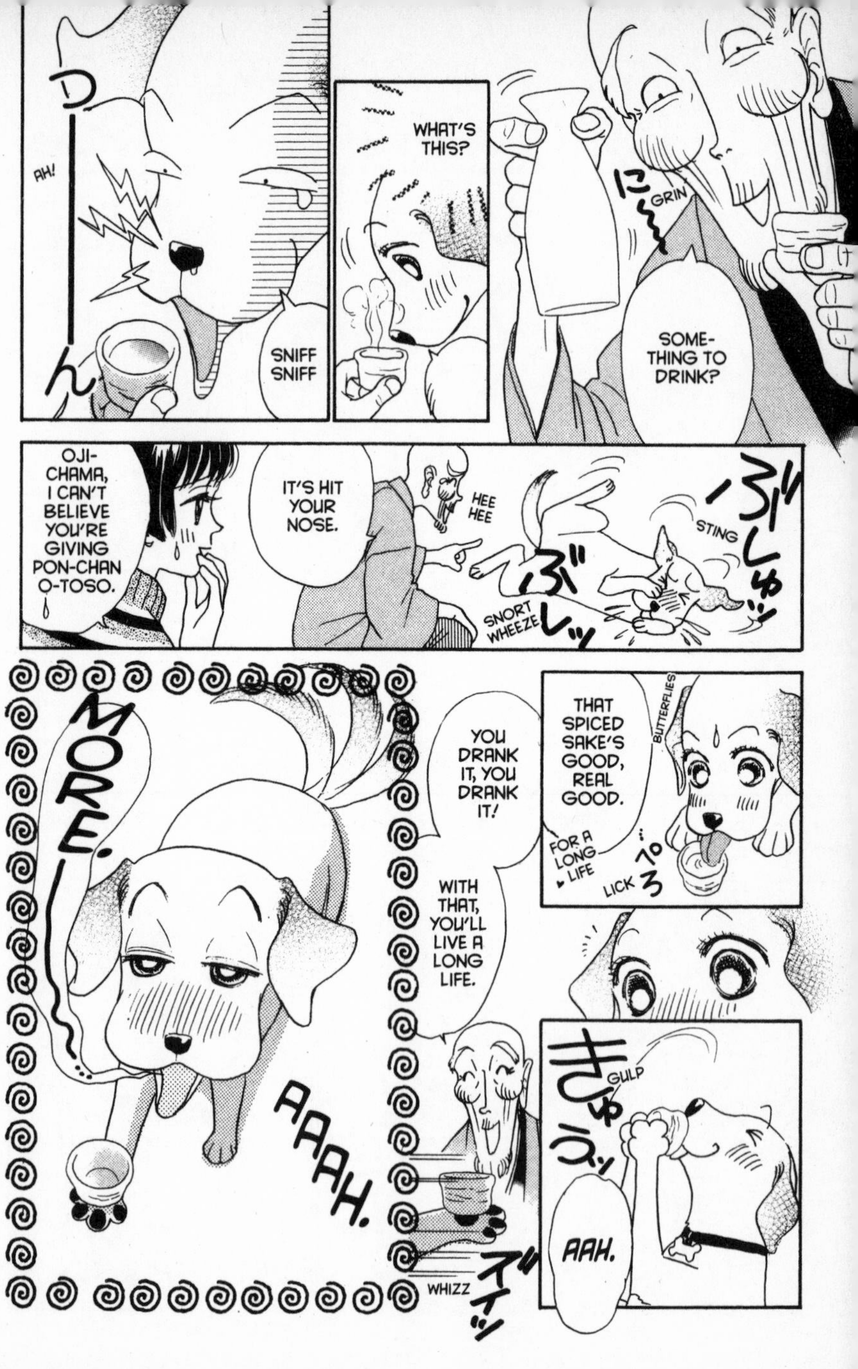

SOME-THING TO DRINK?
にっ
GRIN
WHAT'S THIS?
SNIFF SNIFF
AH!
つーん
ぷしゅっ
STING
ぶレッ
SNORT WHEEZE
HEE HEE
IT'S HIT YOUR NOSE.
OJI-CHAMA, I CAN'T BELIEVE YOU'RE GIVING PON-CHAN O-TOSO.
THAT SPICED SAKE'S GOOD, REAL GOOD.
BUTTERFLIES
FOR A LONG LIFE
ぺろ
LICK
きゅうっ
GULP
AAH.
YOU DRANK IT, YOU DRANK IT!
WITH THAT, YOU'LL LIVE A LONG LIFE.
ズイッ
WHIZZ
MORE.
AAAH.

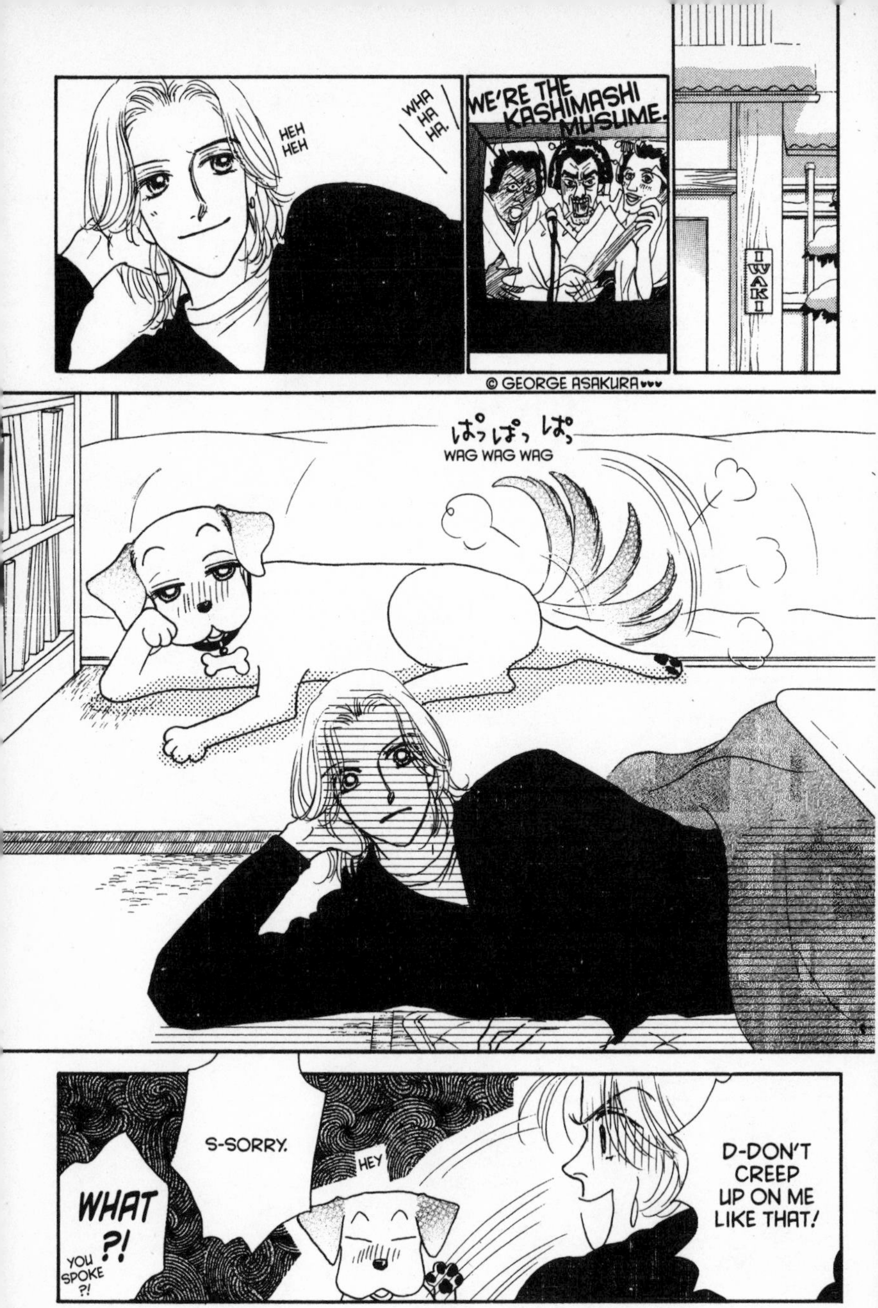
WHA HA HA.
HEH HEH
WE'RE THE KASHIMASHI MUSUME.
IWAKI
© GEORGE ASAKURA•••
ぱっぱっぱっ
WAG WAG WAG
D-DON'T CREEP UP ON ME LIKE THAT!
HEY
S-SORRY.
WHAT ?!
YOU SPOKE ?!

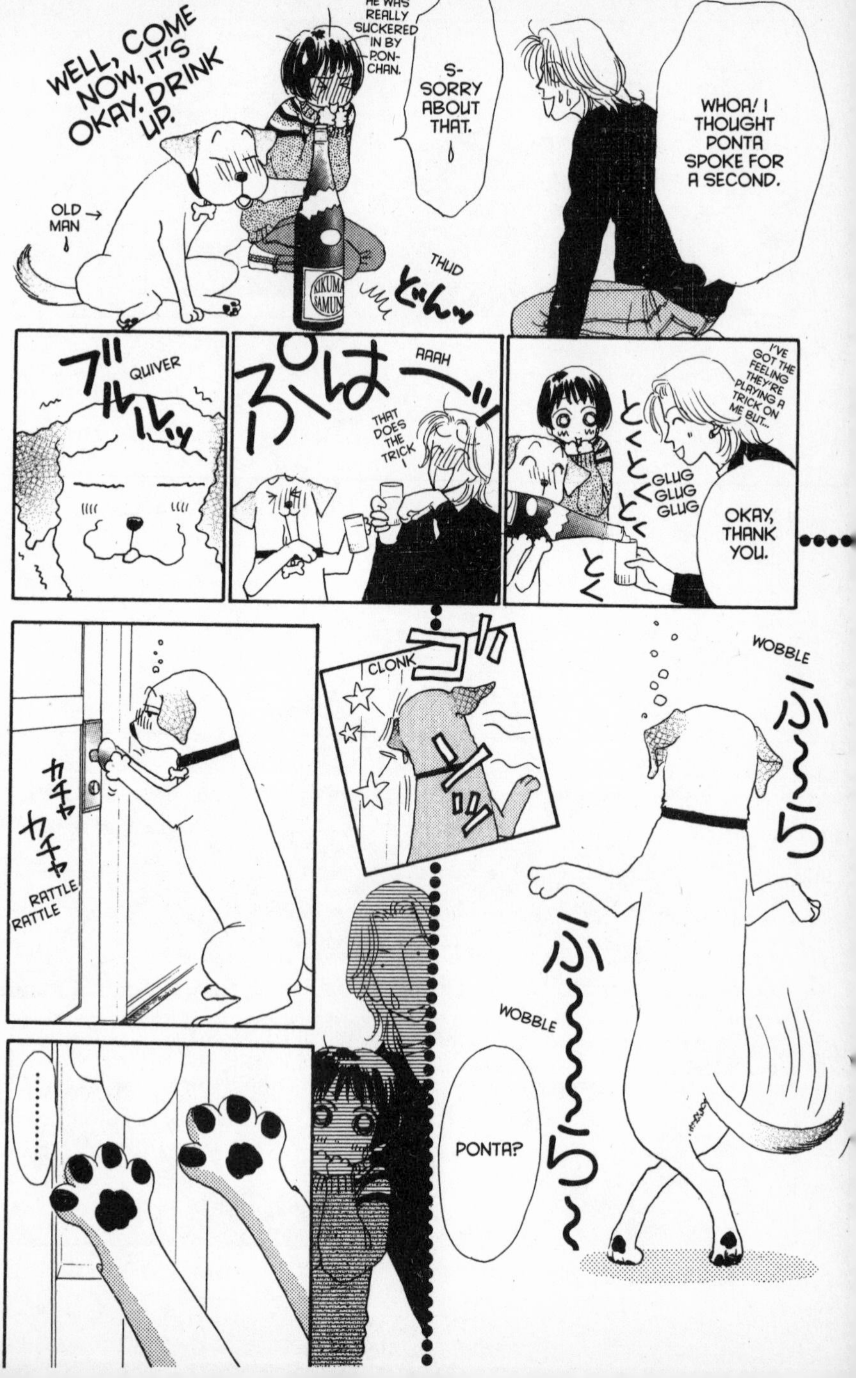

WHOA! I THOUGHT PONTA SPOKE FOR A SECOND.
S- SORRY ABOUT THAT.
HE WAS REALLY SUCKERED IN BY PON-CHAN.
WELL, COME NOW, IT'S OKAY. DRINK UP.
OLD MAN
THUD
どんッ
I'VE GOT THE FEELING THEY'RE PLAYING A TRICK ON ME BUT...
OKAY, THANK YOU.
とくとくとくとく
GLUG GLUG GLUG
ぷはーッ
AAAH
THAT DOES THE TRICK
ブルルッ
QUIVER
WOBBLE
ふ〜ら
ふ〜〜ら〜
WOBBLE
PONTA?
ゴッ
CLONK
カチャカチャ
RATTLE RATTLE
......

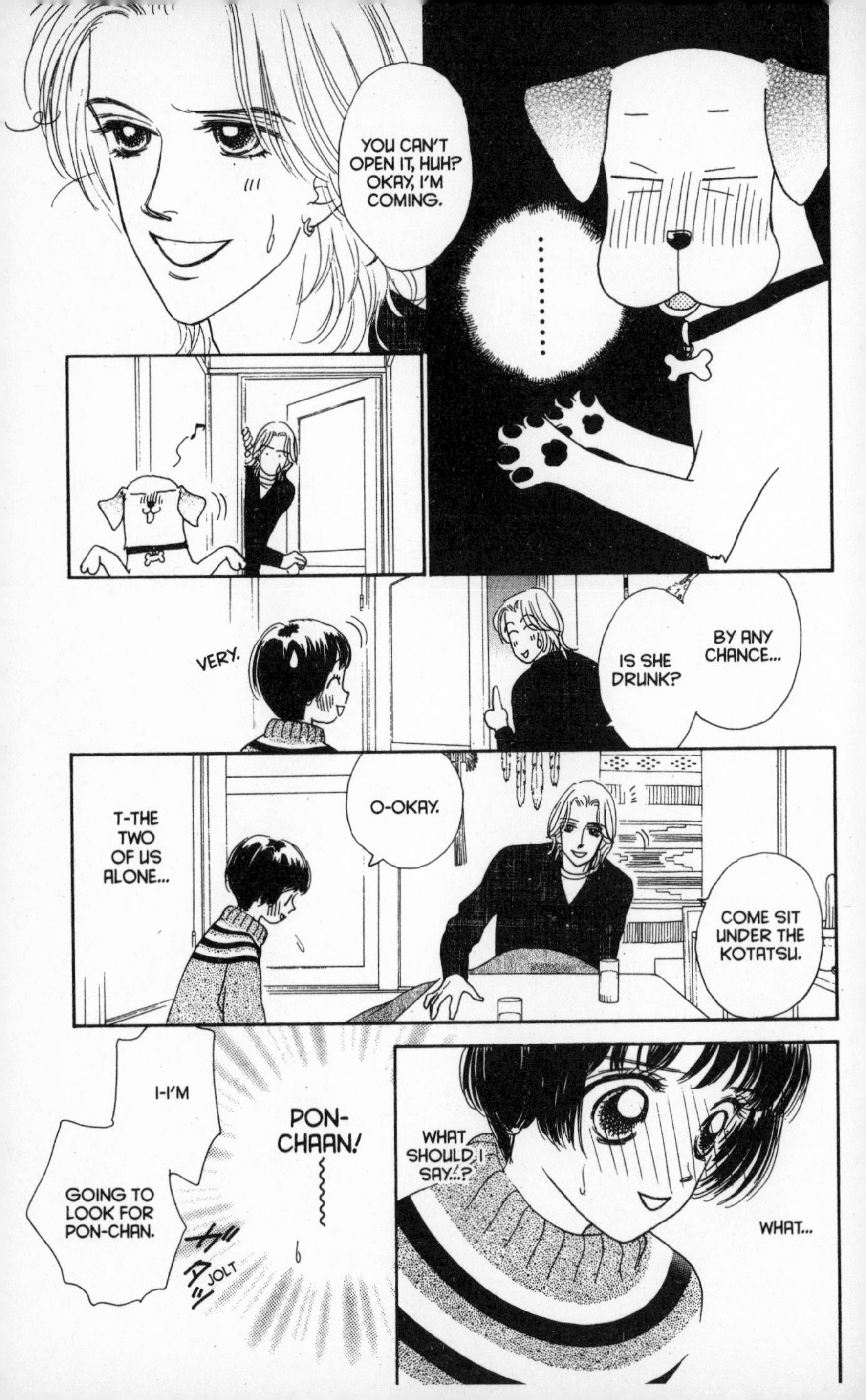
......
YOU CAN'T OPEN IT, HUH? OKAY, I'M COMING.
BY ANY CHANCE...
IS SHE DRUNK?
VERY.
COME SIT UNDER THE KOTATSU.
O-OKAY.
T-THE TWO OF US ALONE...
WHAT...
WHAT SHOULD I SAY...?
PON-CHAAN!
JOLT
I-I'M
GOING TO LOOK FOR PON-CHAN.

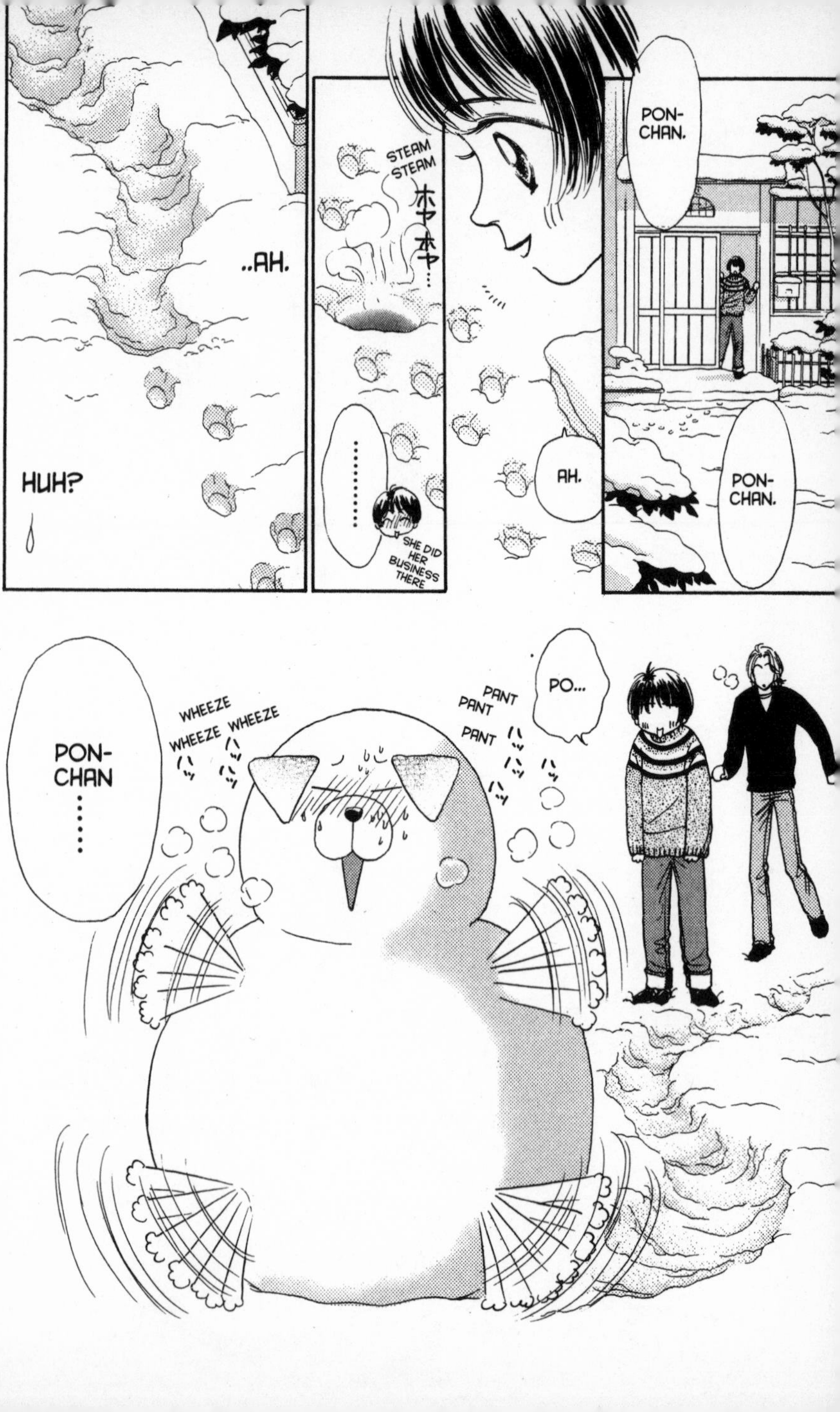
PON-CHAN.
PON-CHAN.
AH.
STEAM STEAM
ホヤホヤ…
……….
SHE DID HER BUSINESS THERE
..AH.
HUH?
PO...
PANT PANT PANT
ハッ ハッ ハッ ハッ
WHEEZE WHEEZE WHEEZE
ハッ ハッ
PON-CHAN……

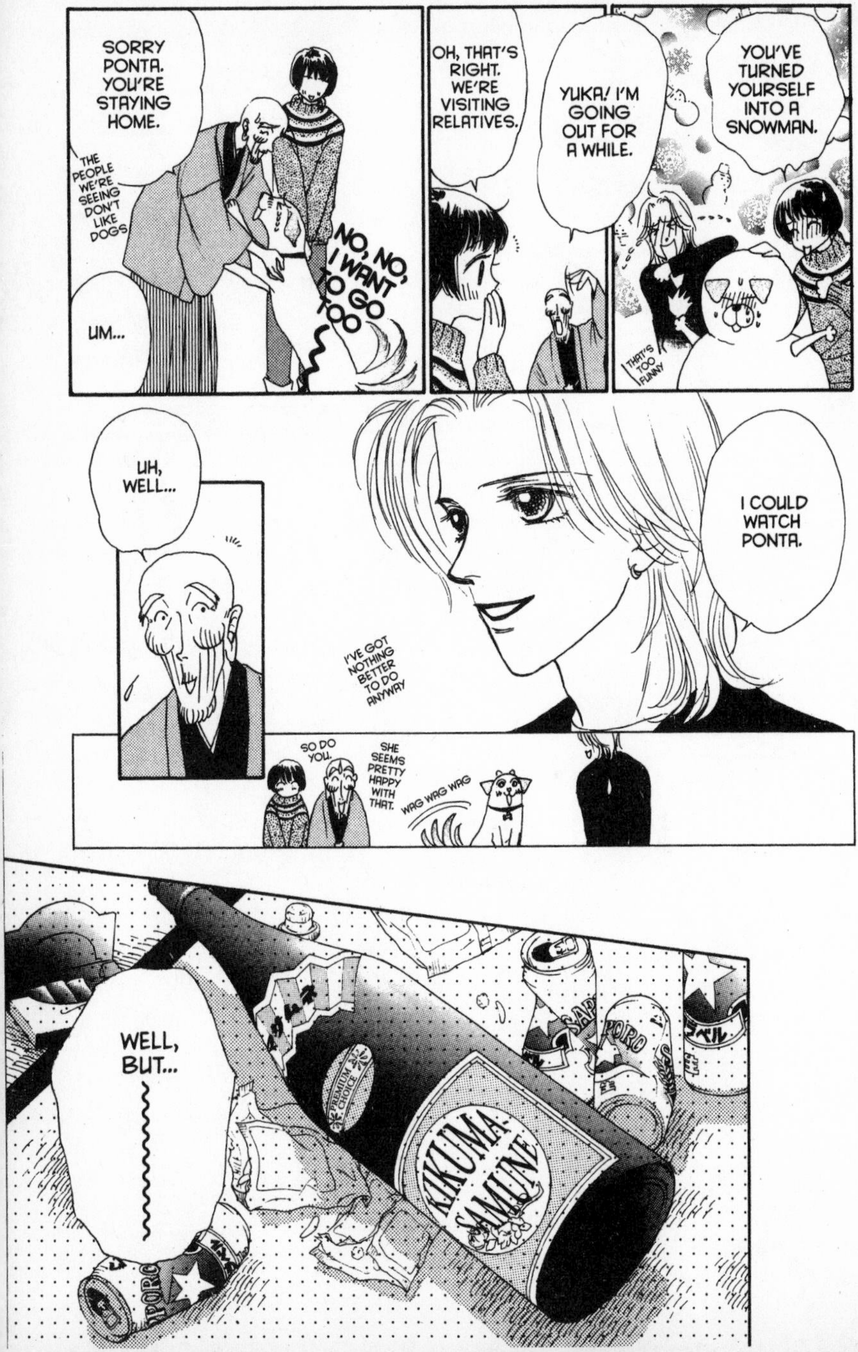
SORRY PONTA. YOU'RE STAYING HOME.
THE PEOPLE WE'RE SEEING DON'T LIKE DOGS
UM...
NO, NO, I WANT TO GO TOO
OH, THAT'S RIGHT. WE'RE VISITING RELATIVES.
YUKA! I'M GOING OUT FOR A WHILE.
YOU'VE TURNED YOURSELF INTO A SNOWMAN.
THAT'S TOO FUNNY
UH, WELL...
I COULD WATCH PONTA.
I'VE GOT NOTHING BETTER TO DO ANYWAY
SO DO YOU.
SHE SEEMS PRETTY HAPPY WITH THAT.
WAG WAG WAG
WELL, BUT...
PREMIUM CHOICE
KIKUMASAMUNE
SAPPORO

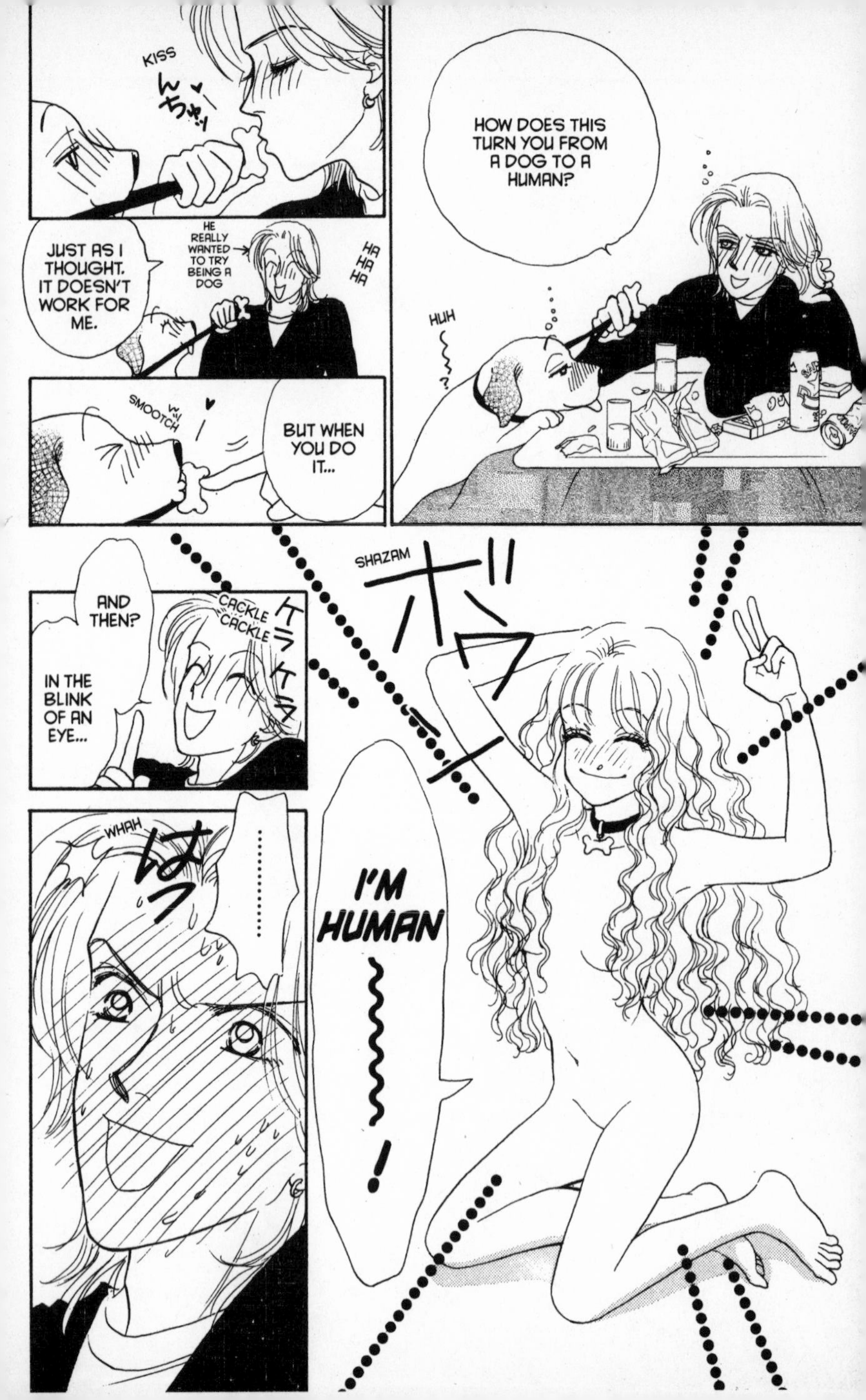
HOW DOES THIS TURN YOU FROM A DOG TO A HUMAN?
HUH
KISS
んちゅっ
JUST AS I THOUGHT. IT DOESN'T WORK FOR ME.
HE REALLY WANTED TO TRY BEING A DOG
HA HA HA
BUT WHEN YOU DO IT...
SMOOTCH
SHAZAM
ボワン
I'M HUMAN~!
AND THEN?
IN THE BLINK OF AN EYE...
CACKLE CACKLE
ケラケラ
WHAH
はっ
......

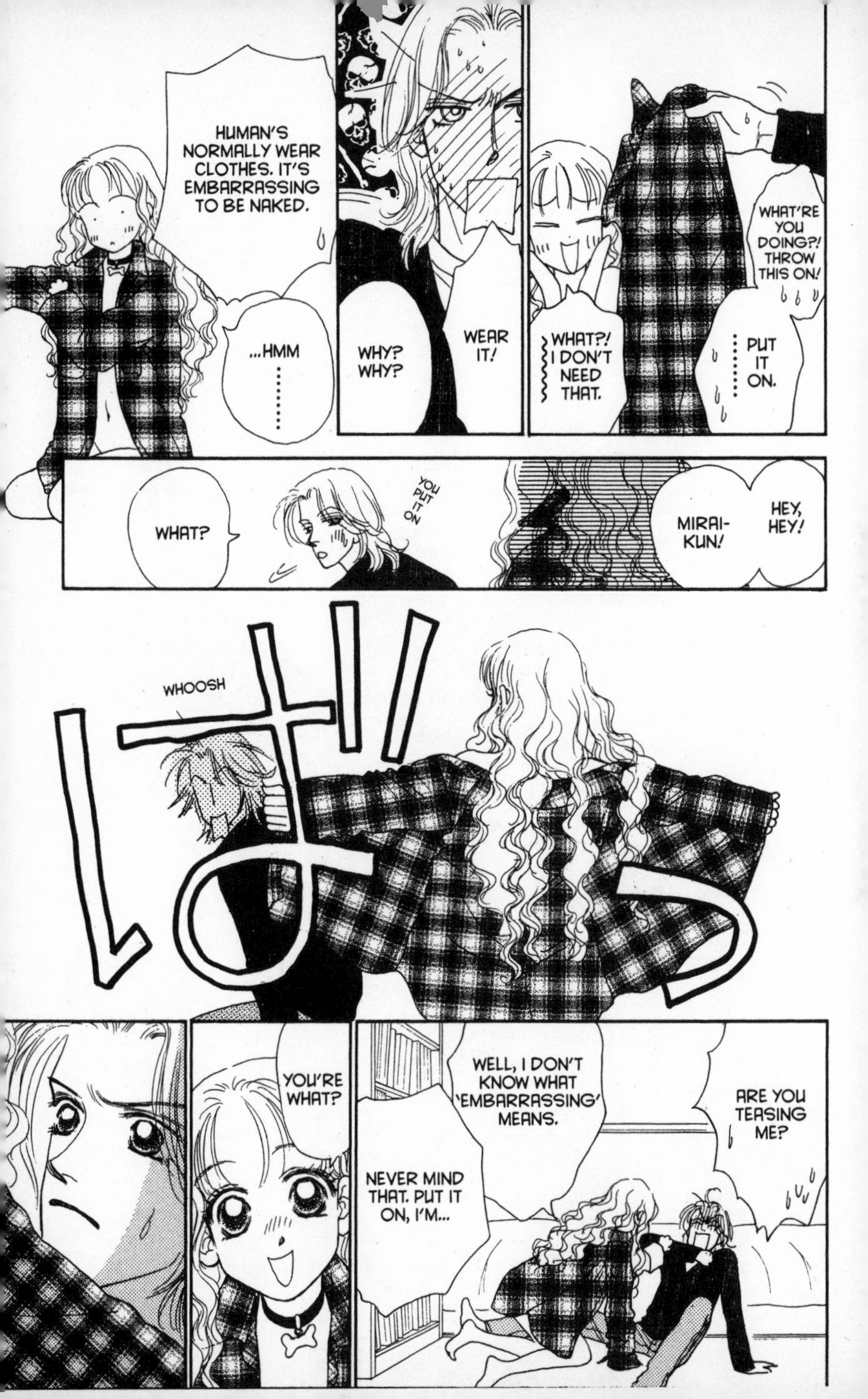
WHAT'RE YOU DOING?! THROW THIS ON!
...... PUT IT ON.
WHAT?! I DON'T NEED THAT.
WEAR IT!
WHY? WHY?
HUMAN'S NORMALLY WEAR CLOTHES. IT'S EMBARRASSING TO BE NAKED.
...HMM ......
HEY, HEY!
MIRAI-KUN!
YOU PUT IT ON
WHAT?
WHOOSH
ARE YOU TEASING ME?
WELL, I DON'T KNOW WHAT 'EMBARRASSING' MEANS.
NEVER MIND THAT. PUT IT ON, I'M...
YOU'RE WHAT?

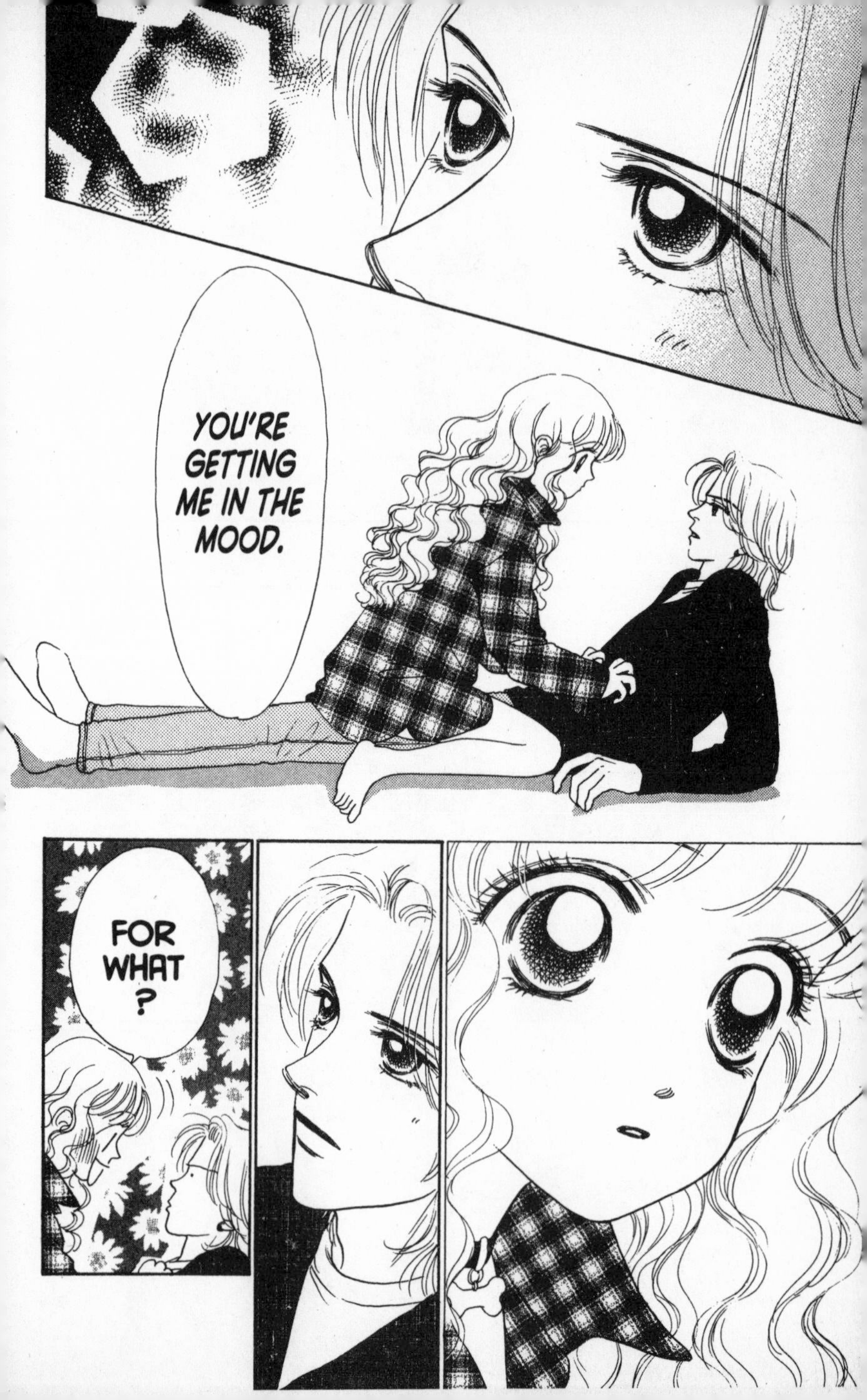
YOU'RE GETTING ME IN THE MOOD.
FOR WHAT ?

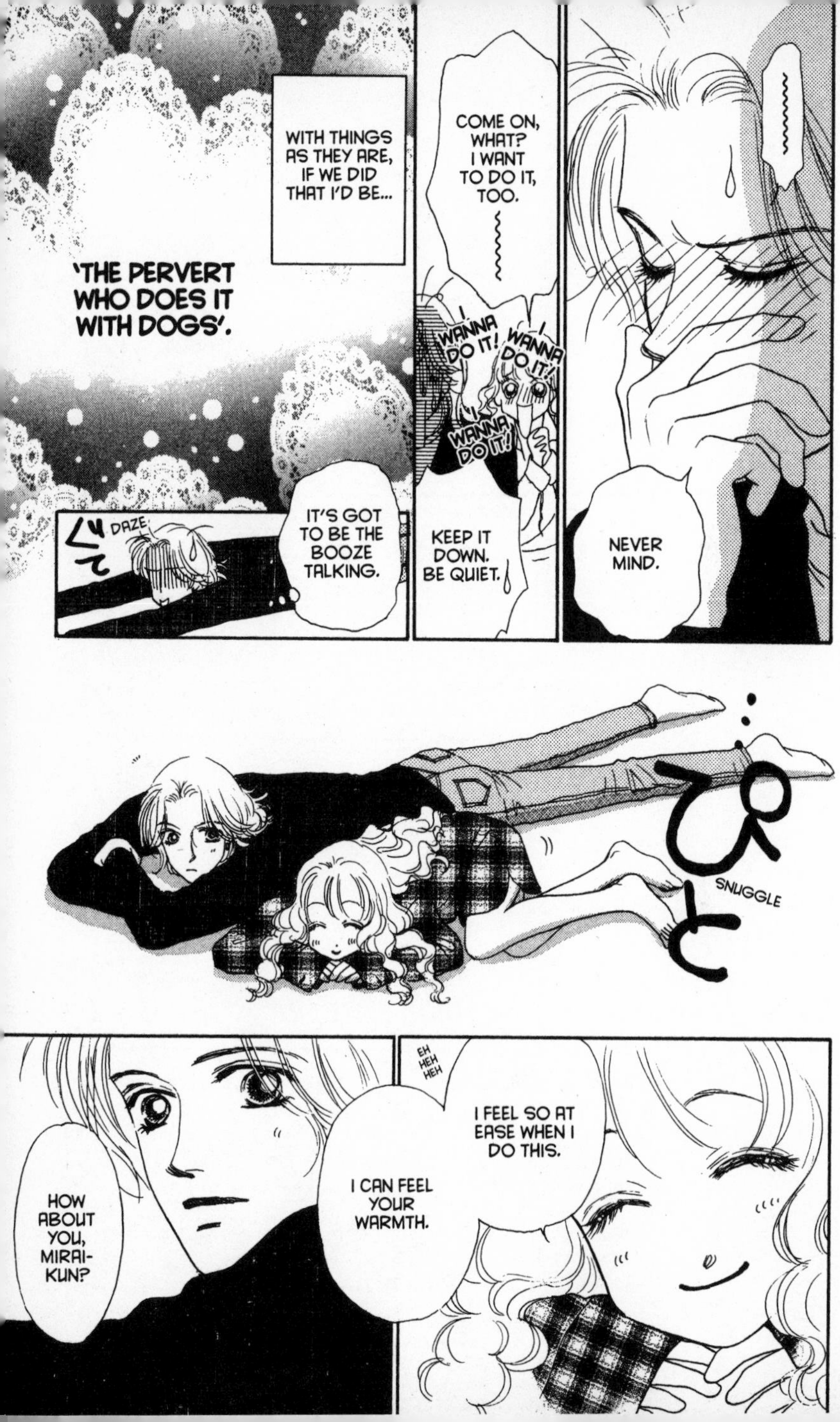
NEVER MIND.
COME ON, WHAT? I WANT TO DO IT, TOO.
I WANNA DO IT!
I WANNA DO IT!
I WANNA DO IT!
KEEP IT DOWN. BE QUIET.
WITH THINGS AS THEY ARE, IF WE DID THAT I'D BE...
'THE PERVERT WHO DOES IT WITH DOGS'.
DAZE
IT'S GOT TO BE THE BOOZE TALKING.
SNUGGLE
EH HEH HEH
I FEEL SO AT EASE WHEN I DO THIS.
I CAN FEEL YOUR WARMTH.
HOW ABOUT YOU, MIRAI-KUN?

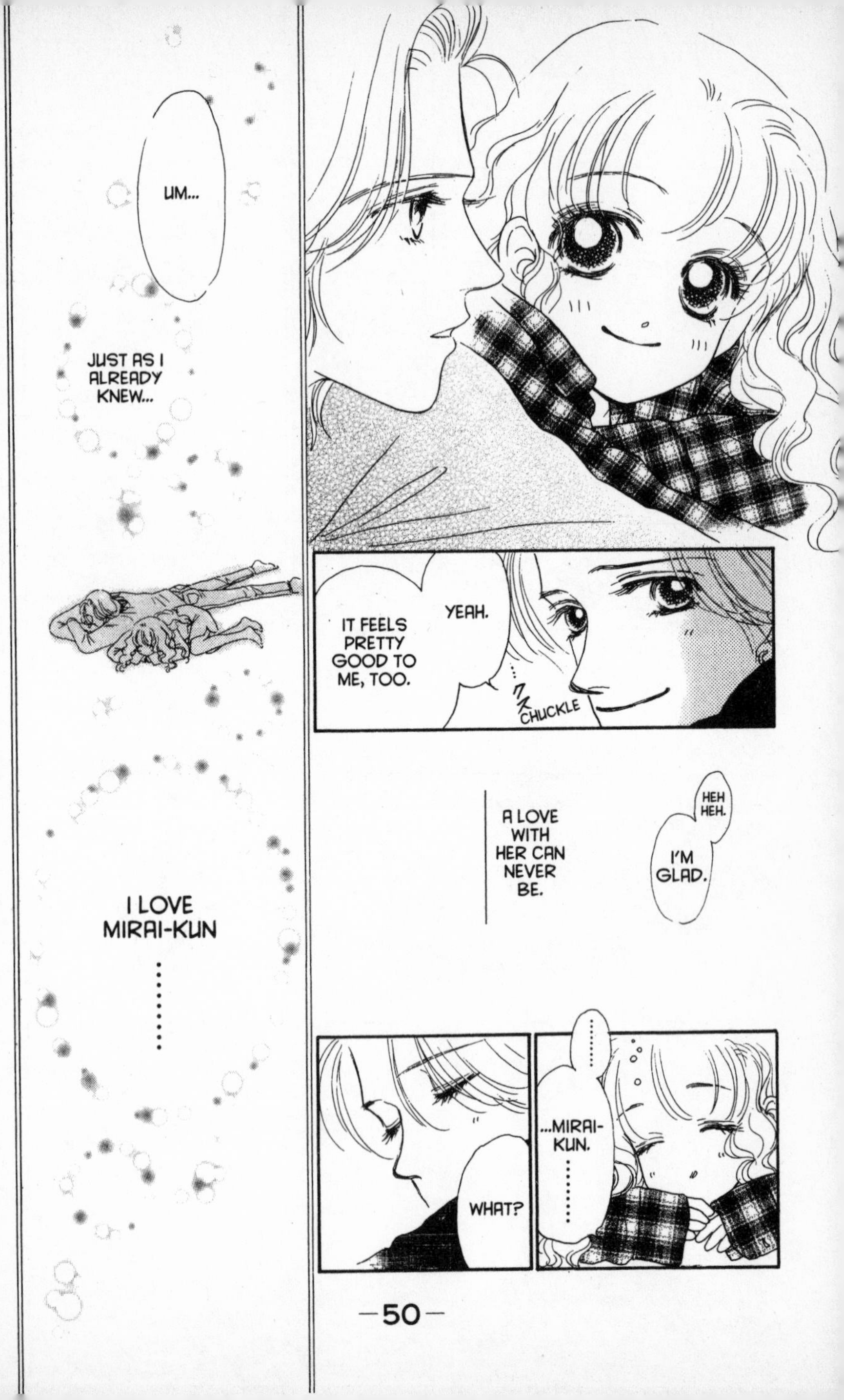

YEAH.
IT FEELS PRETTY GOOD TO ME, TOO.
... CHUCKLE
HEH HEH.
I'M GLAD.
A LOVE WITH HER CAN NEVER BE.
......
...MIRAI-KUN. ......
WHAT?
UM...
JUST AS I ALREADY KNEW...
I LOVE MIRAI-KUN ......

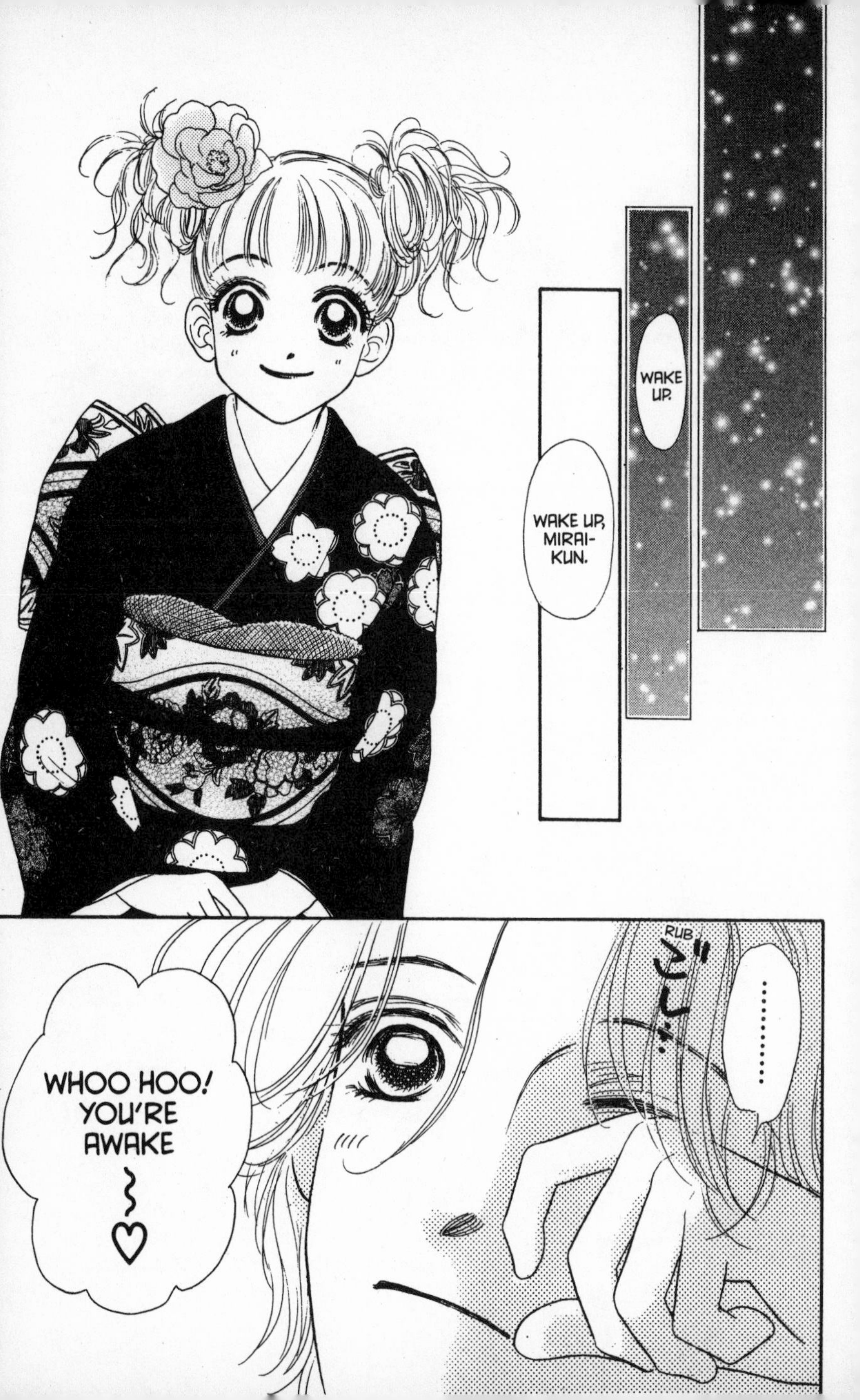
WAKE UP.
WAKE UP, MIRAI-KUN.
RUB
....
WHOO HOO! YOU'RE AWAKE ~ ♥

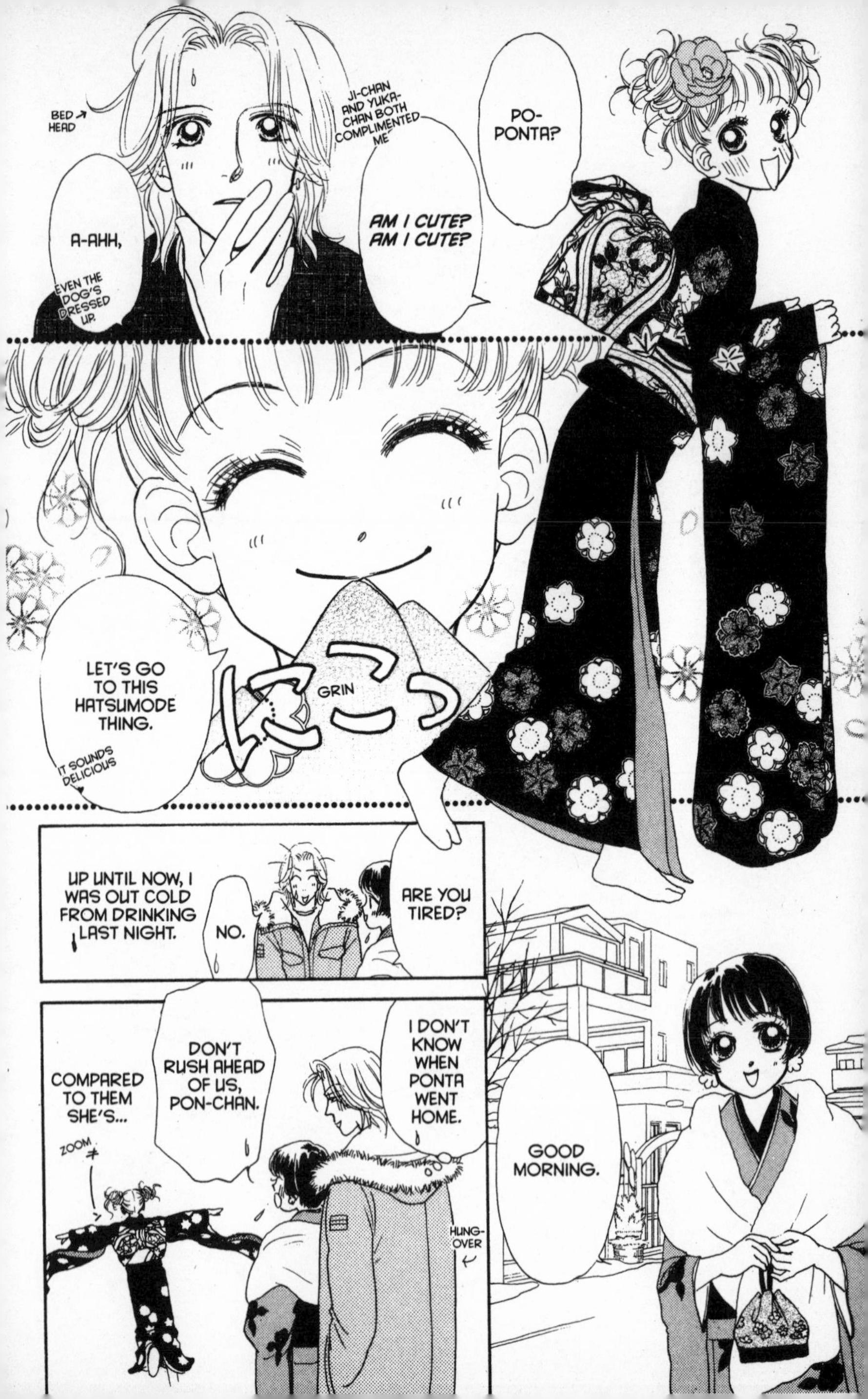
PO-PONTA?
JI-CHAN AND YUKA-CHAN BOTH COMPLIMENTED ME
AM I CUTE? AM I CUTE?
BED HEAD
A-AHH,
EVEN THE DOG'S DRESSED UP.
GRIN
LET'S GO TO THIS HATSUMODE THING.
IT SOUNDS DELICIOUS
GOOD MORNING.
ARE YOU TIRED?
NO.
UP UNTIL NOW, I WAS OUT COLD FROM DRINKING LAST NIGHT.
HUNG-OVER
I DON'T KNOW WHEN PONTA WENT HOME.
DON'T RUSH AHEAD OF US, PON-CHAN.
COMPARED TO THEM SHE'S...
ZOOM

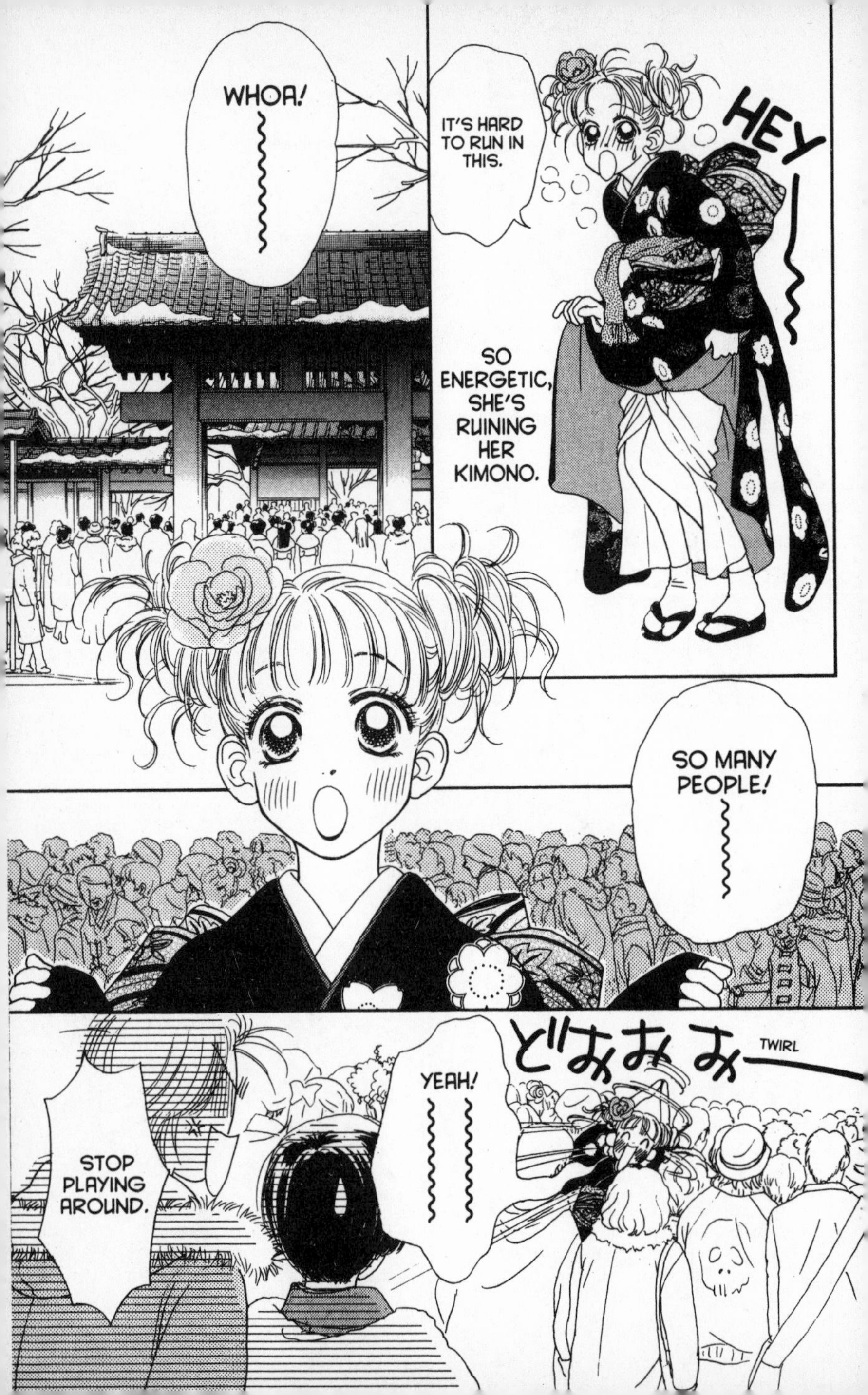

HEY
IT'S HARD TO RUN IN THIS.
SO ENERGETIC, SHE'S RUINING HER KIMONO.
WHOA!
SO MANY PEOPLE!
TWIRL
YEAH!
STOP PLAYING AROUND.

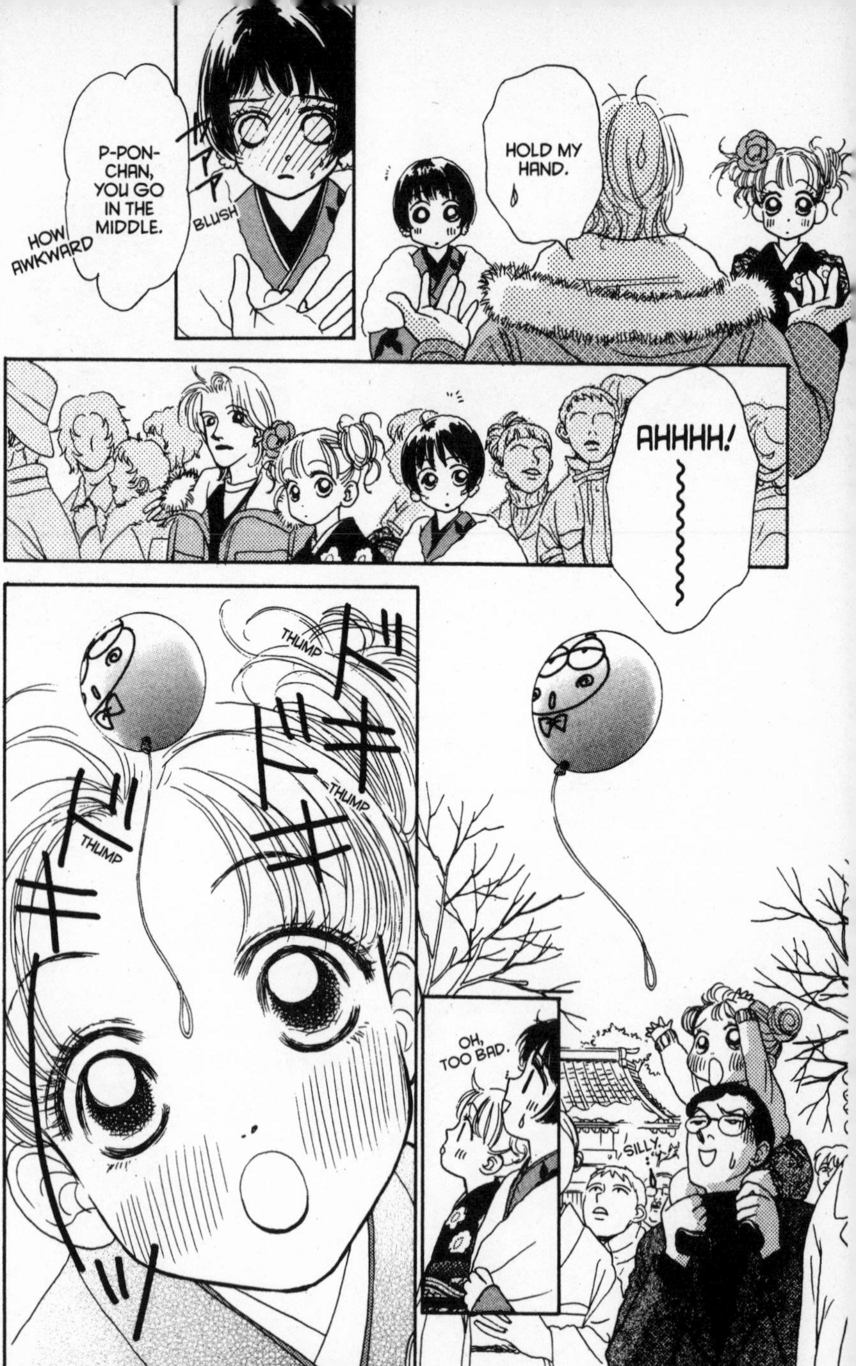
HOLD MY HAND.
P-PON-CHAN, YOU GO IN THE MIDDLE.
BLUSH
HOW AWKWARD
AHHHH!
OH, TOO BAD.
SILLY.
THUMP
THUMP
THUMP

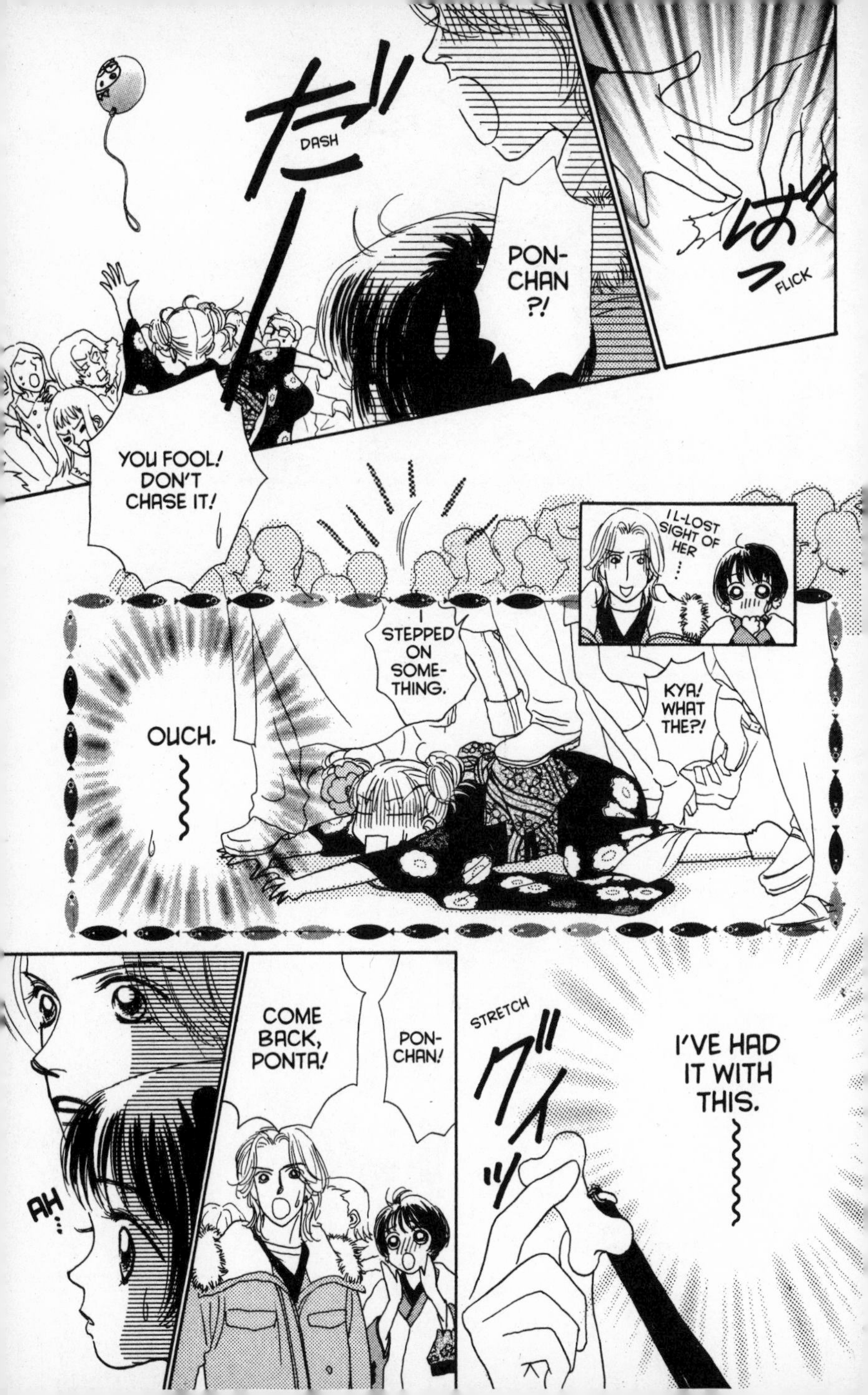

FLICK
PON-CHAN?!
DASH
YOU FOOL! DON'T CHASE IT!
I-I LOST SIGHT OF HER...
KYA! WHAT THE?!
I STEPPED ON SOME-THING.
OUCH.
I'VE HAD IT WITH THIS.
STRETCH
PON-CHAN!
COME BACK, PONTA!
AH...

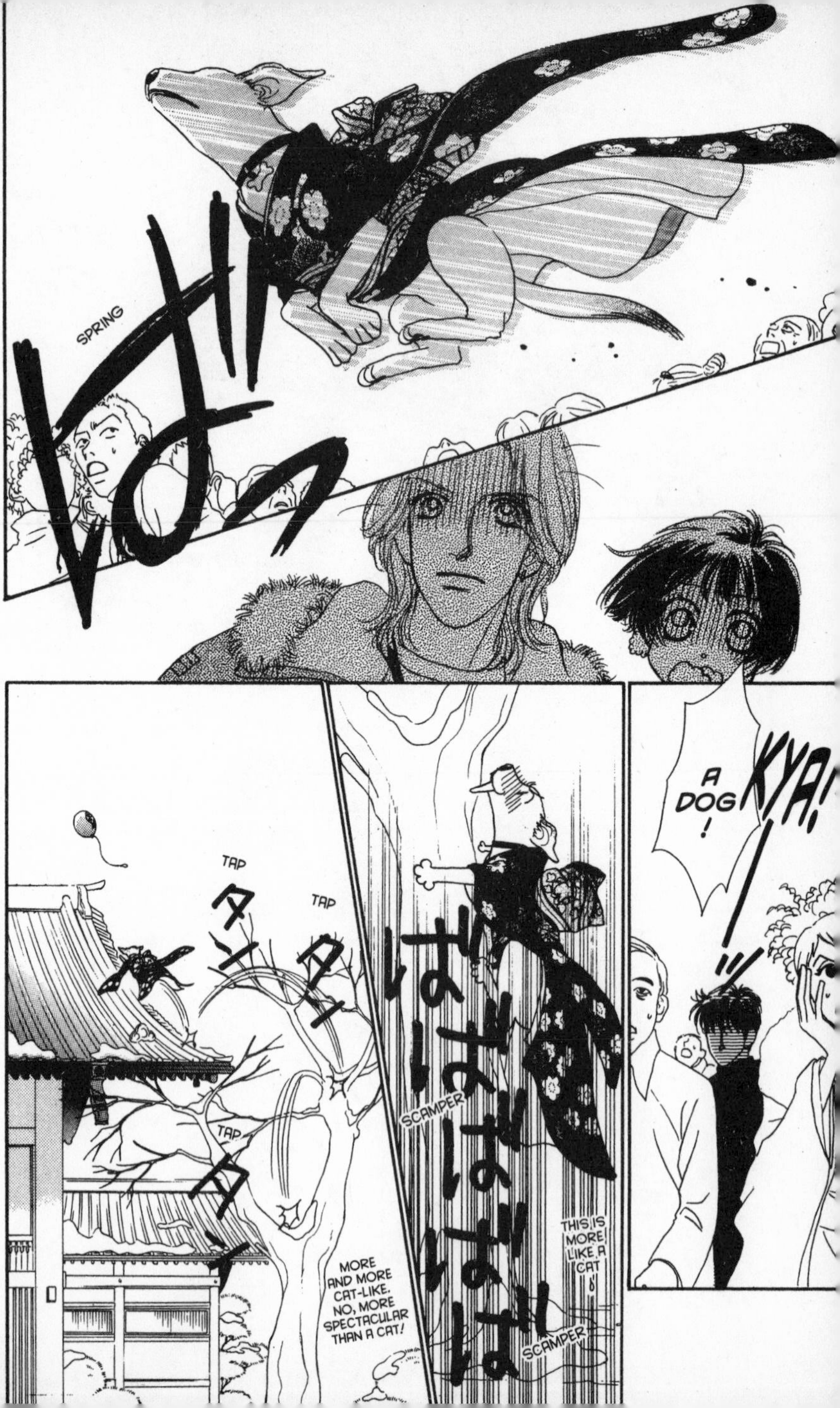

SPRING
A DOG!
KYA!!
THIS IS MORE LIKE A CAT ♪
SCAMPER
SCAMPER
TAP
TAP
TAP
MORE AND MORE CAT-LIKE. NO, MORE SPECTACULAR THAN A CAT!

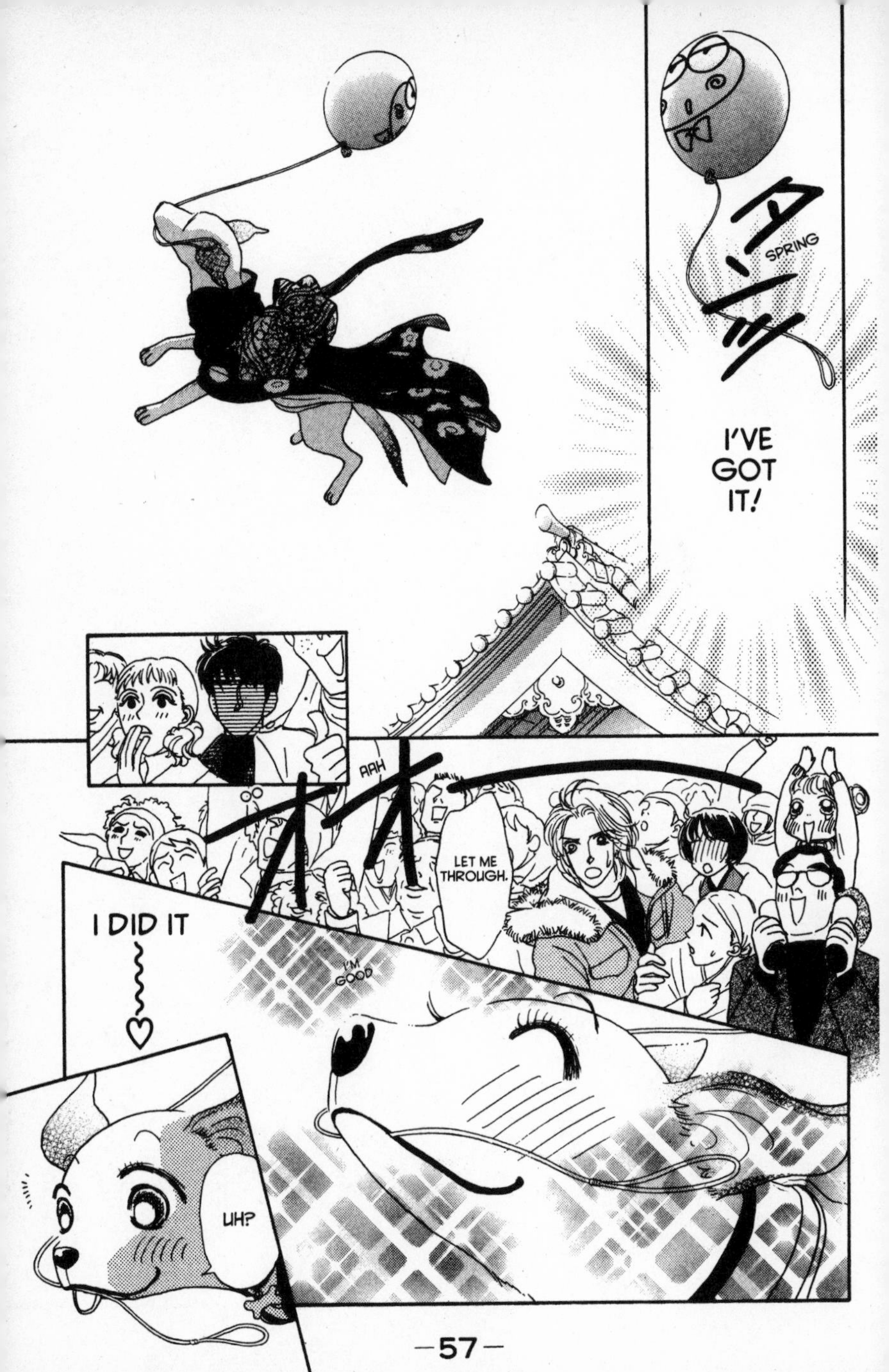
SPRING
I'VE GOT IT!
AAH
LET ME THROUGH.
I DID IT
I'M GOOD
UH?

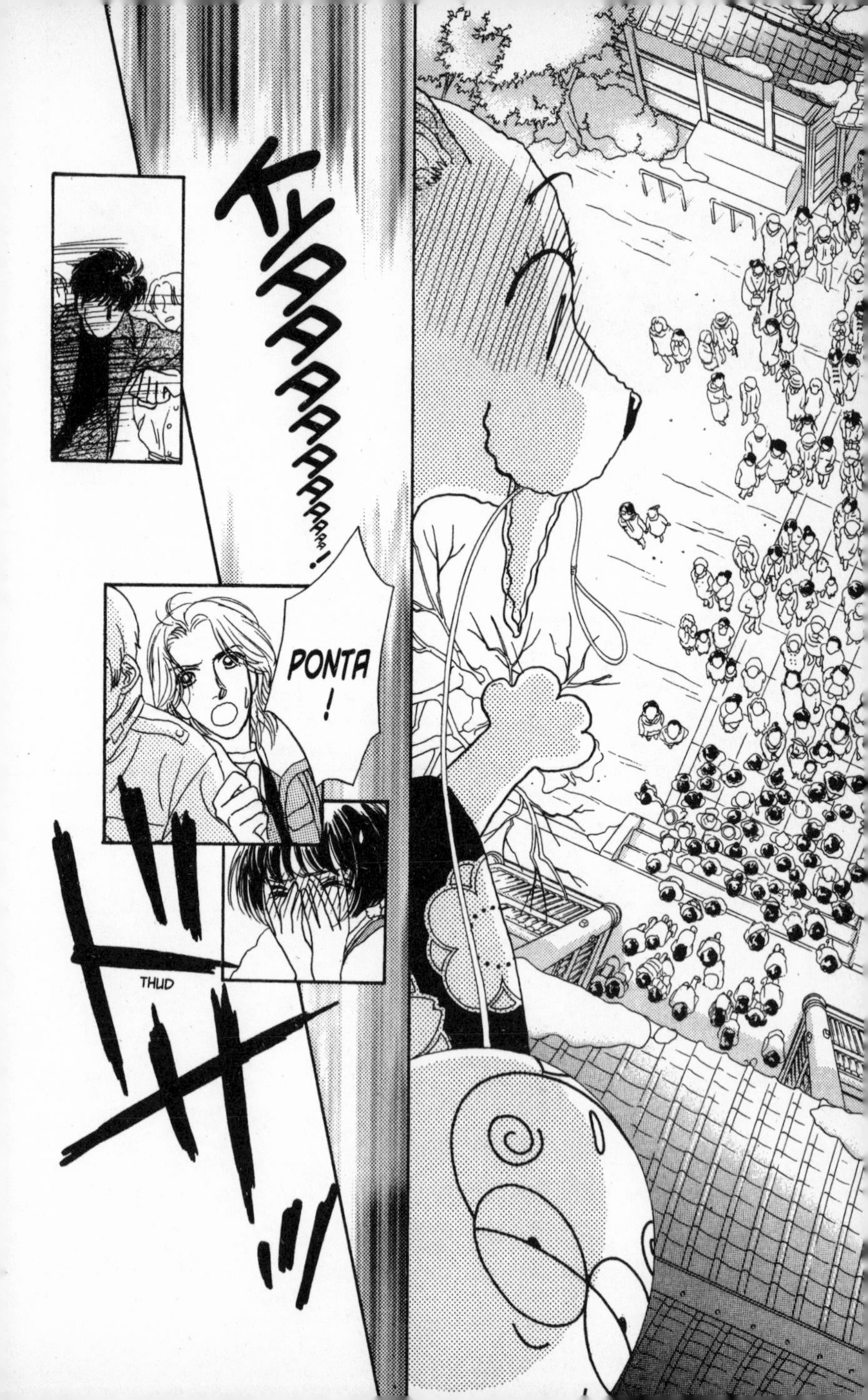
KYAAAAAAAAA!
PONTA!
THUD

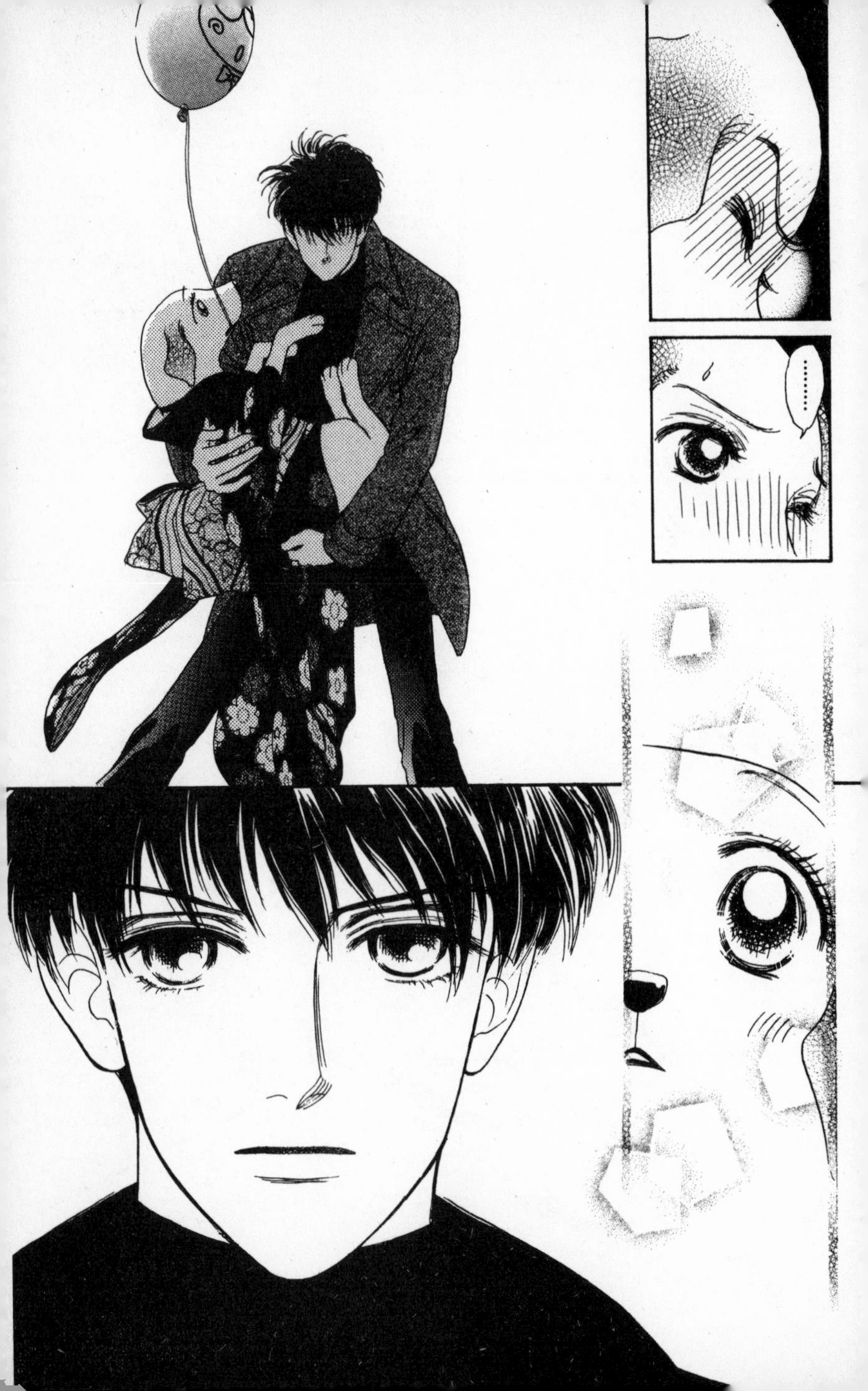
……

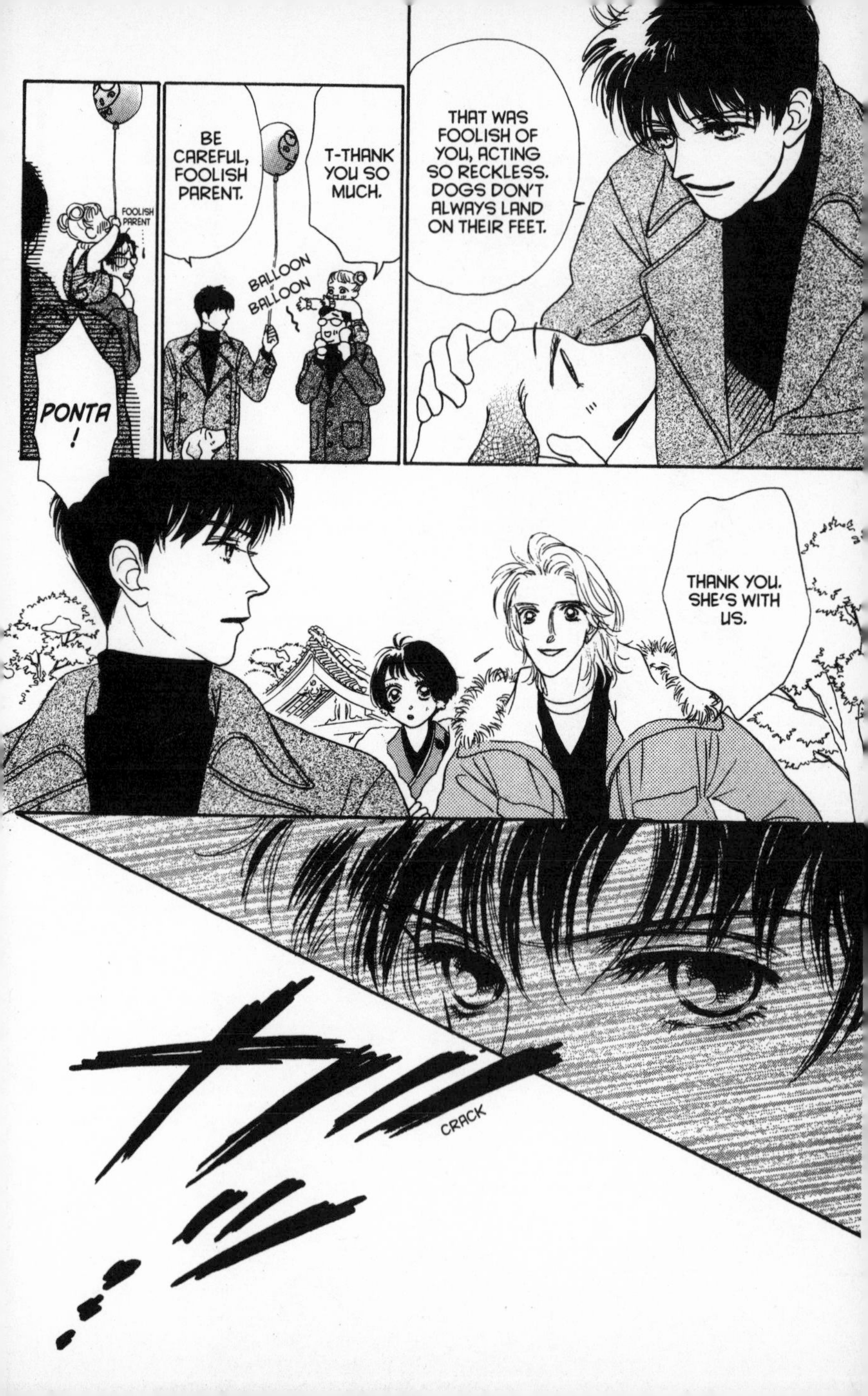
THAT WAS FOOLISH OF YOU, ACTING SO RECKLESS. DOGS DON'T ALWAYS LAND ON THEIR FEET.
T-THANK YOU SO MUCH.
BALLOON BALLOON
BE CAREFUL, FOOLISH PARENT.
FOOLISH PARENT
PONTA!
THANK YOU. SHE'S WITH US.
CRACK

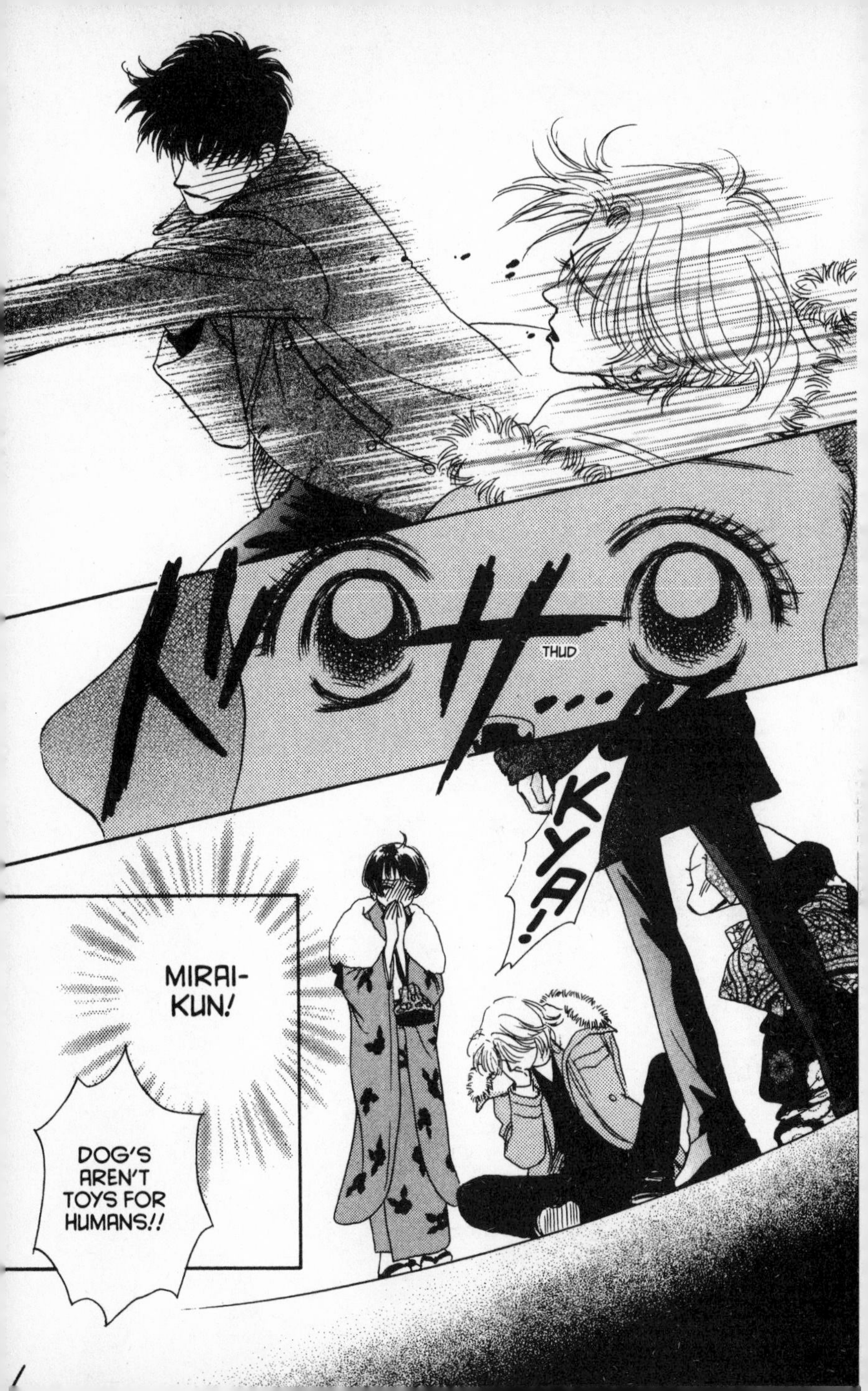
KYOTTT...
THUD
KYA!!
MIRAI-KUN!
DOG'S AREN'T TOYS FOR HUMANS!!

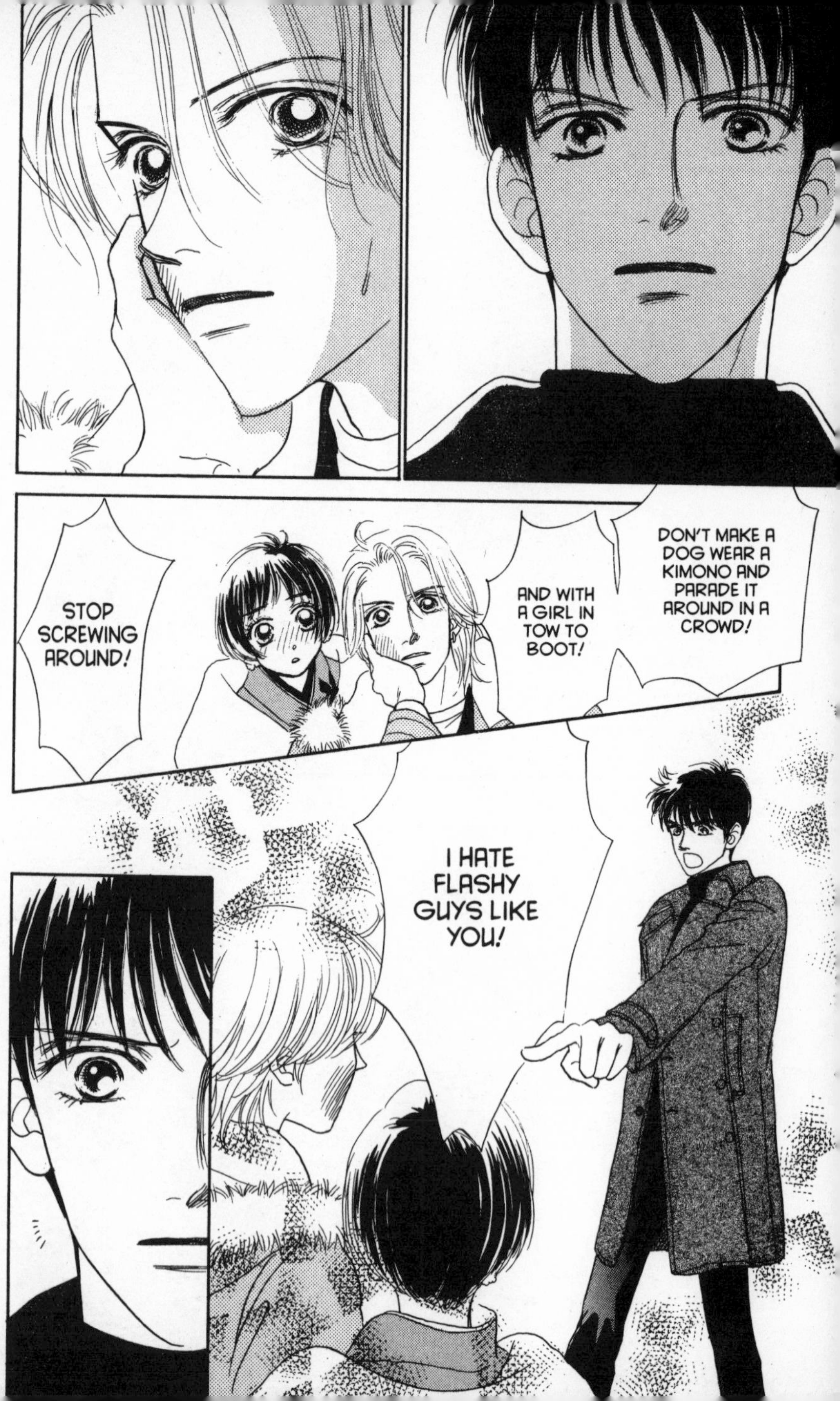
DON'T MAKE A DOG WEAR A KIMONO AND PARADE IT AROUND IN A CROWD!
AND WITH A GIRL IN TOW TO BOOT!
STOP SCREWING AROUND!
I HATE FLASHY GUYS LIKE YOU!

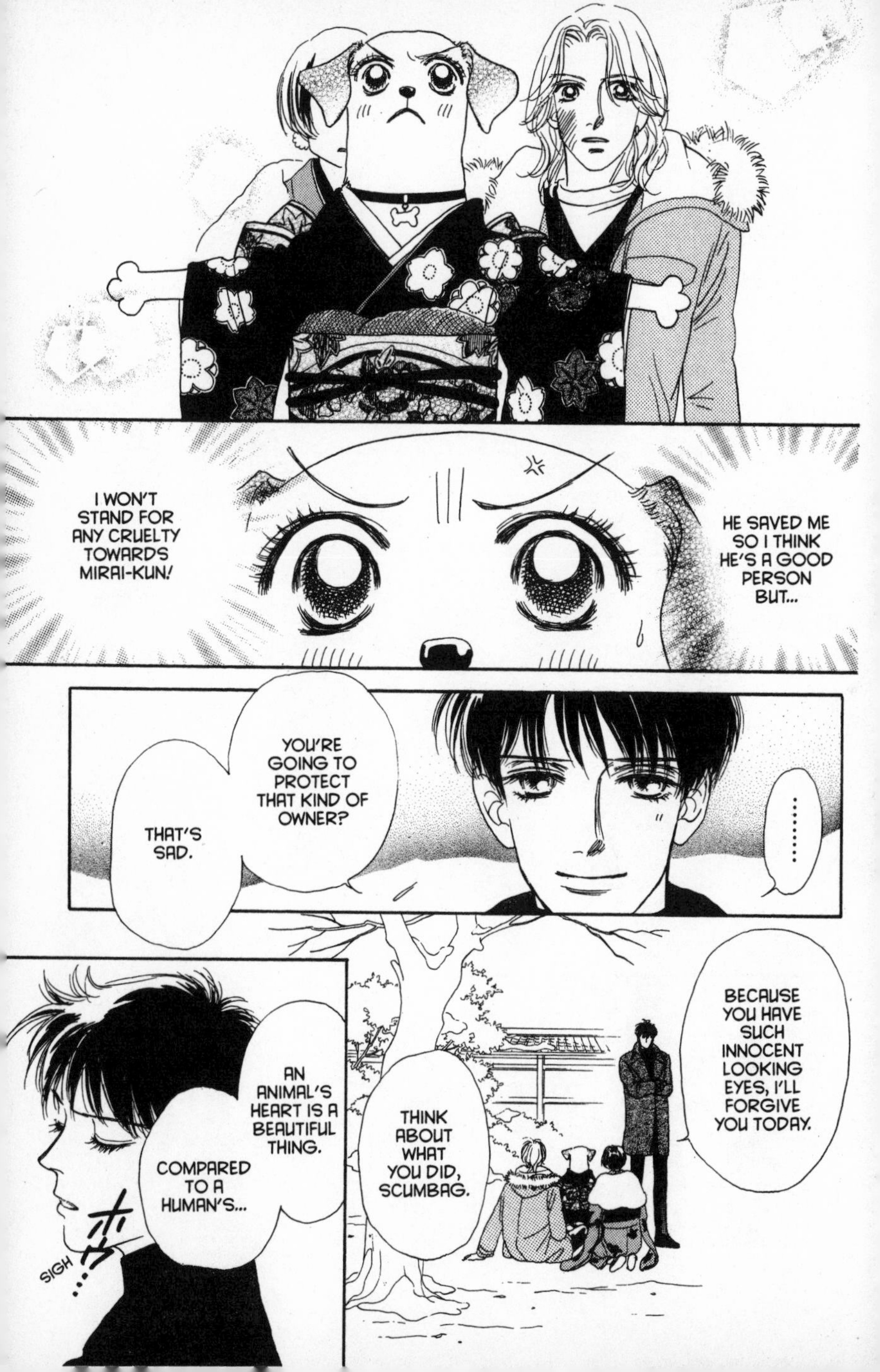
HE SAVED ME SO I THINK HE'S A GOOD PERSON BUT...
I WON'T STAND FOR ANY CRUELTY TOWARDS MIRAI-KUN!
......
YOU'RE GOING TO PROTECT THAT KIND OF OWNER?
THAT'S SAD.
BECAUSE YOU HAVE SUCH INNOCENT LOOKING EYES, I'LL FORGIVE YOU TODAY.
THINK ABOUT WHAT YOU DID, SCUMBAG.
AN ANIMAL'S HEART IS A BEAUTIFUL THING.
COMPARED TO A HUMAN'S...
SIGH...

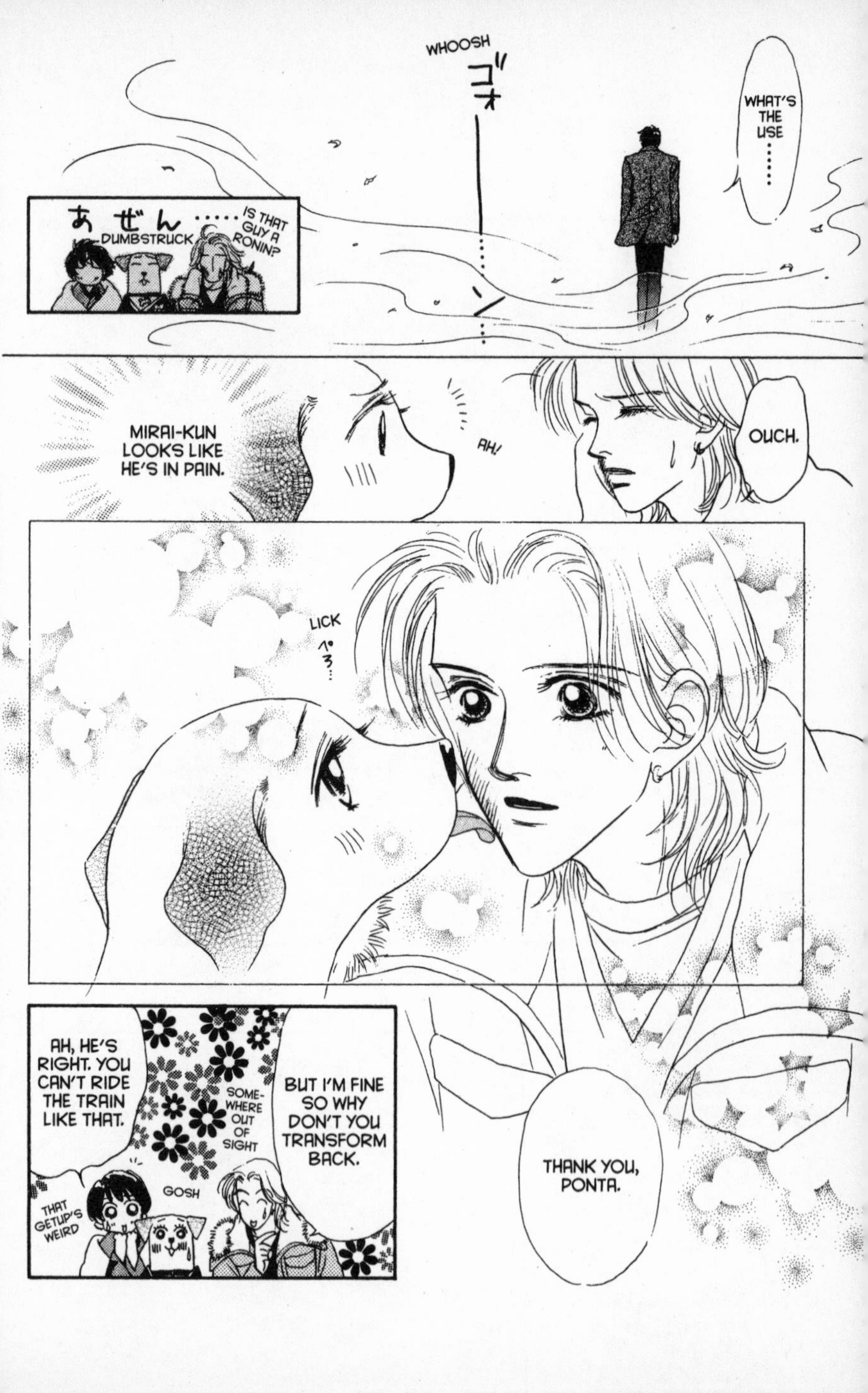
WHAT'S THE USE ......
WHOOSH
ゴォ
あぜん .....
DUMBSTRUCK
IS THAT GUY A RONIN?
OUCH.
AH!
MIRAI-KUN LOOKS LIKE HE'S IN PAIN.
LICK
ぺろ...
THANK YOU, PONTA.
BUT I'M FINE SO WHY DON'T YOU TRANSFORM BACK.
SOMEWHERE OUT OF SIGHT
AH, HE'S RIGHT. YOU CAN'T RIDE THE TRAIN LIKE THAT.
GOSH
THAT GETUP'S WEIRD

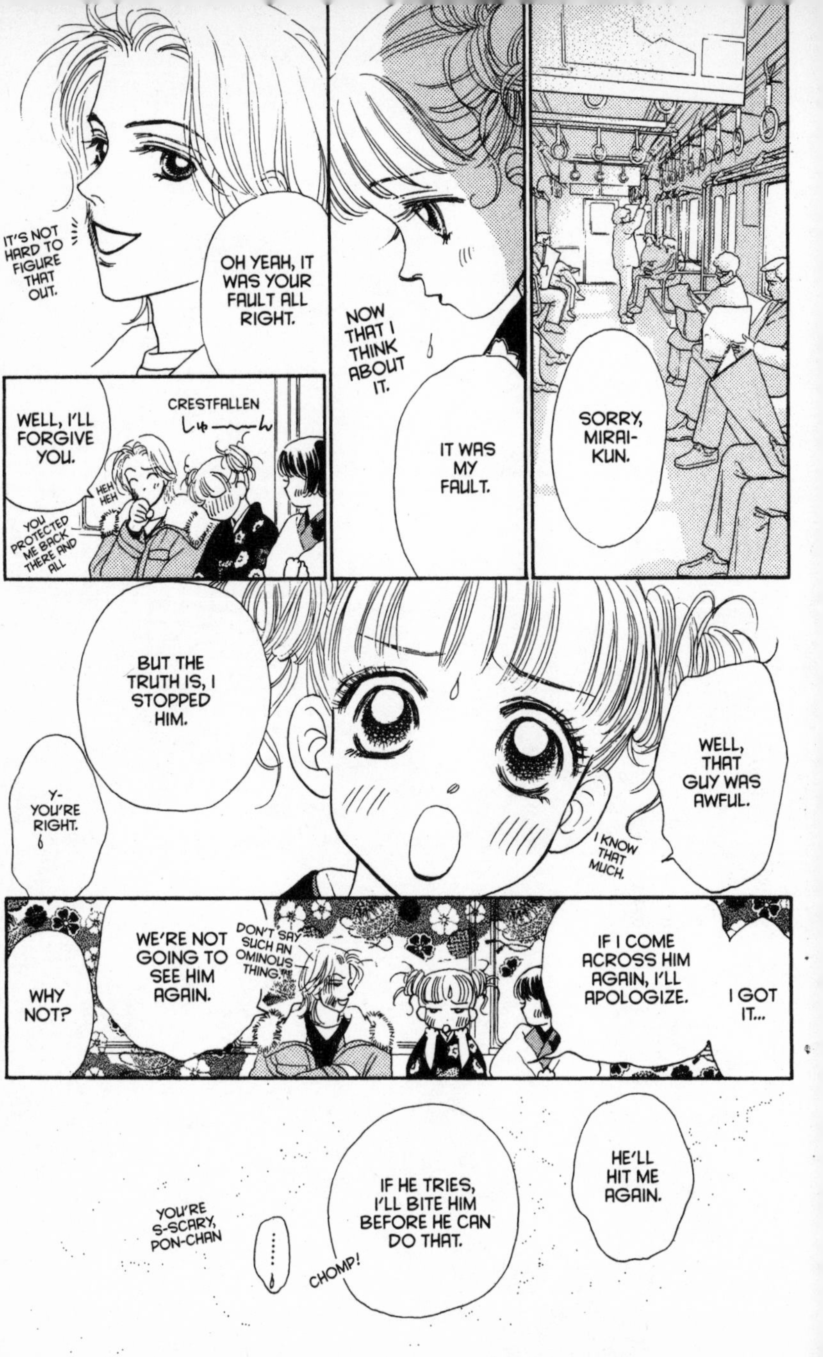
SORRY, MIRAI-KUN.
NOW THAT I THINK ABOUT IT.
IT WAS MY FAULT.
OH YEAH, IT WAS YOUR FAULT ALL RIGHT.
IT'S NOT HARD TO FIGURE THAT OUT.
WELL, I'LL FORGIVE YOU.
CRESTFALLEN
しゅ〜〜ん
HEH HEH
YOU PROTECTED ME BACK THERE AND ALL
WELL, THAT GUY WAS AWFUL.
I KNOW THAT MUCH.
BUT THE TRUTH IS, I STOPPED HIM.
Y-YOU'RE RIGHT.
I GOT IT...
IF I COME ACROSS HIM AGAIN, I'LL APOLOGIZE.
DON'T SAY SUCH AN OMINOUS THING.
WE'RE NOT GOING TO SEE HIM AGAIN.
WHY NOT?
HE'LL HIT ME AGAIN.
IF HE TRIES, I'LL BITE HIM BEFORE HE CAN DO THAT.
CHOMP!
......
YOU'RE S-SCARY, PON-CHAN

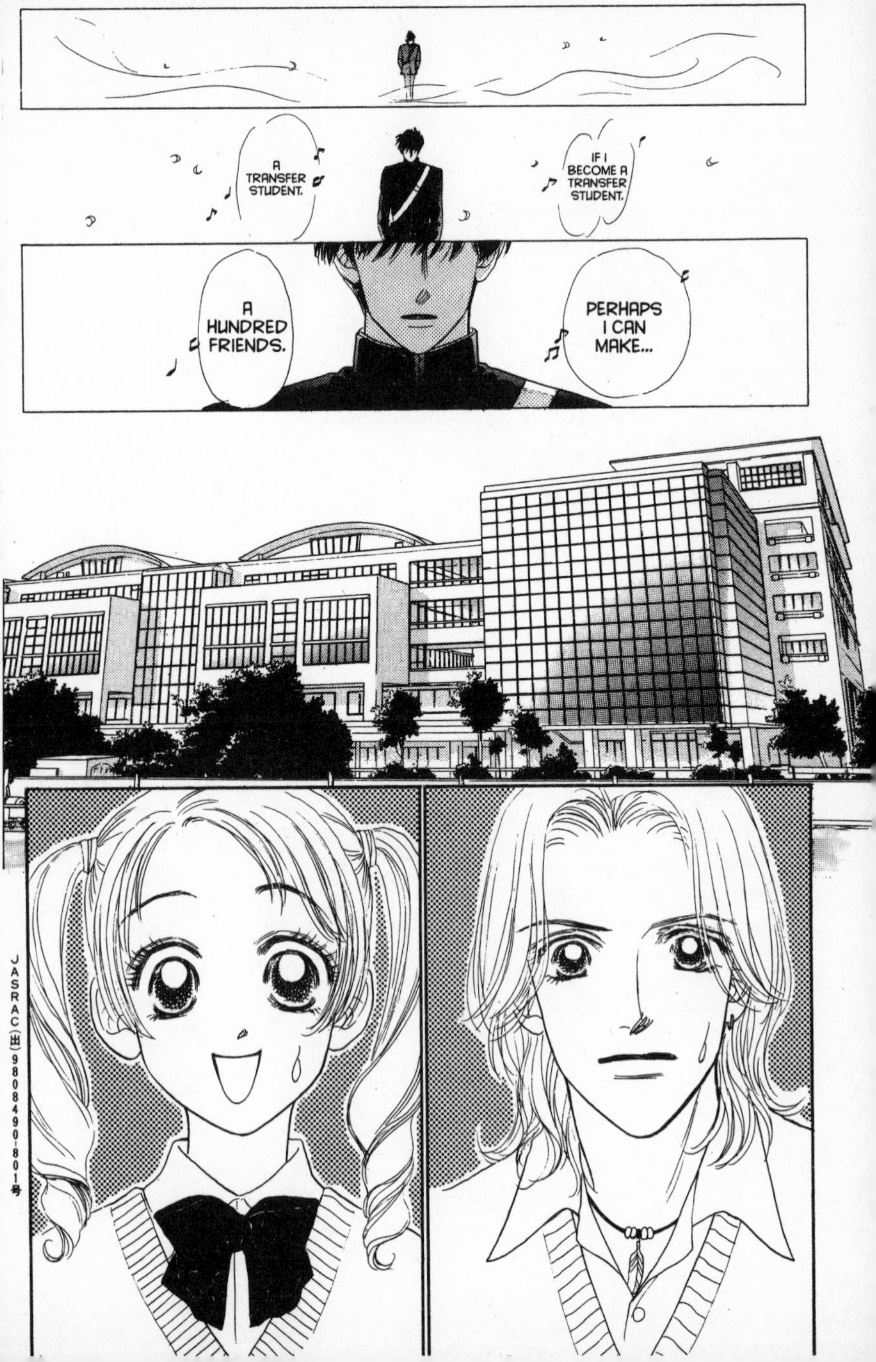
IF I BECOME A TRANSFER STUDENT.
A TRANSFER STUDENT.
PERHAPS I CAN MAKE...
A HUNDRED FRIENDS.

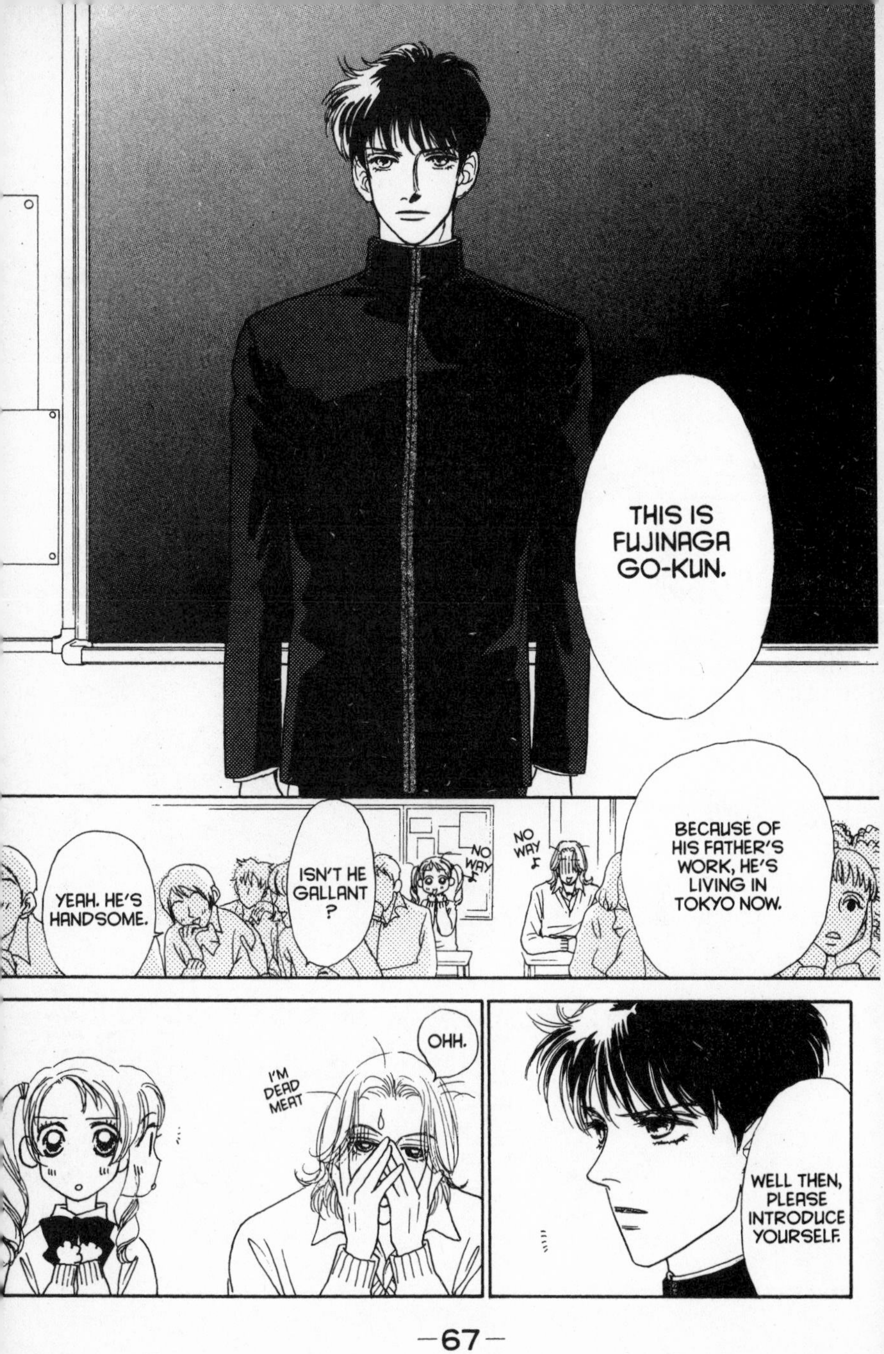
THIS IS FUJINAGA GO-KUN.
BECAUSE OF HIS FATHER'S WORK, HE'S LIVING IN TOKYO NOW.
NO WAY ♪
NO WAY ♪
ISN'T HE GALLANT ?
YEAH. HE'S HANDSOME.
WELL THEN, PLEASE INTRODUCE YOURSELF.
OHH.
I'M DEAD MEAT

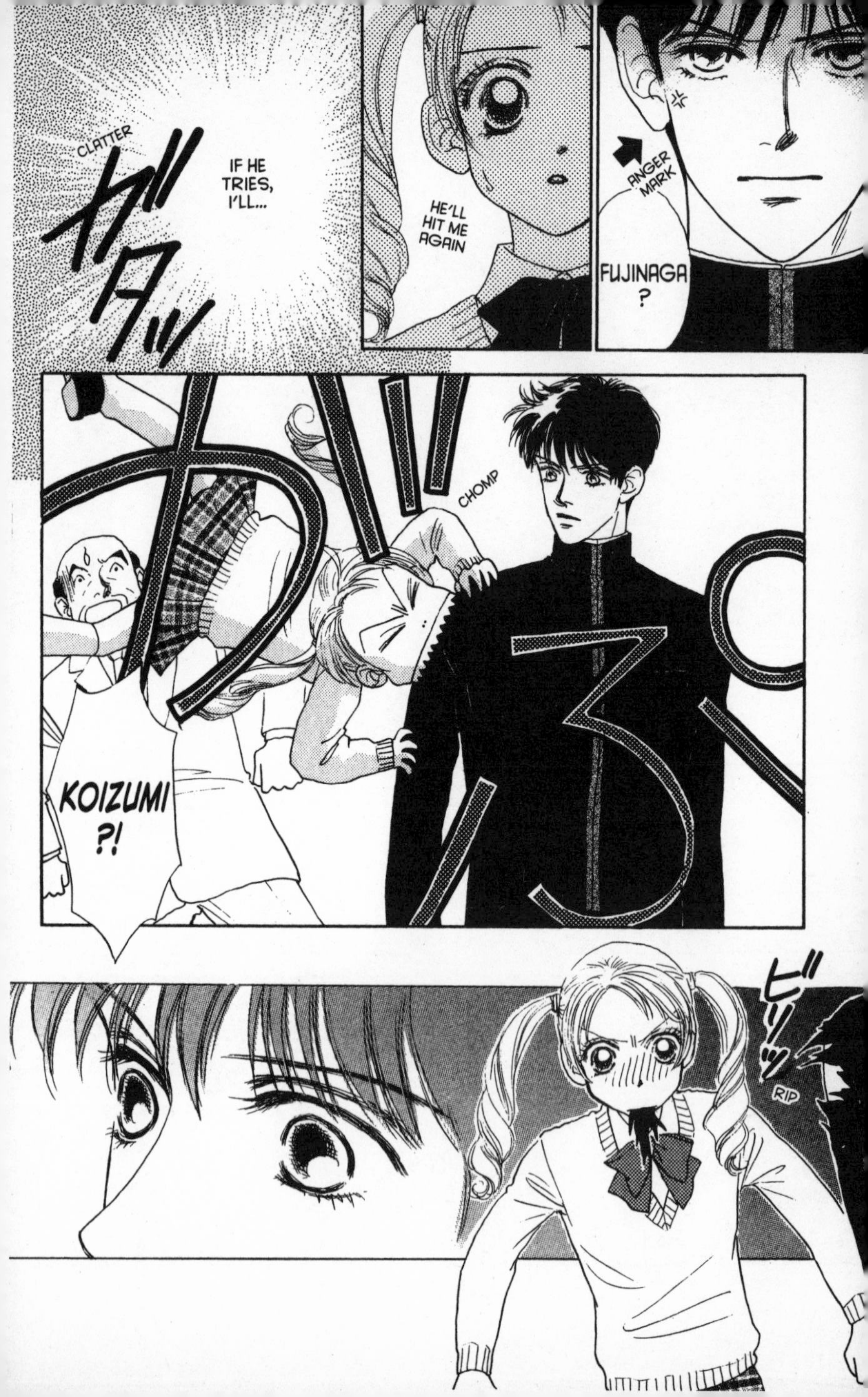
ANGER MARK
FUJINAGA ?
HE'LL HIT ME AGAIN
CLATTER
IF HE TRIES, I'LL...
CHOMP
KOIZUMI ?!
RIP

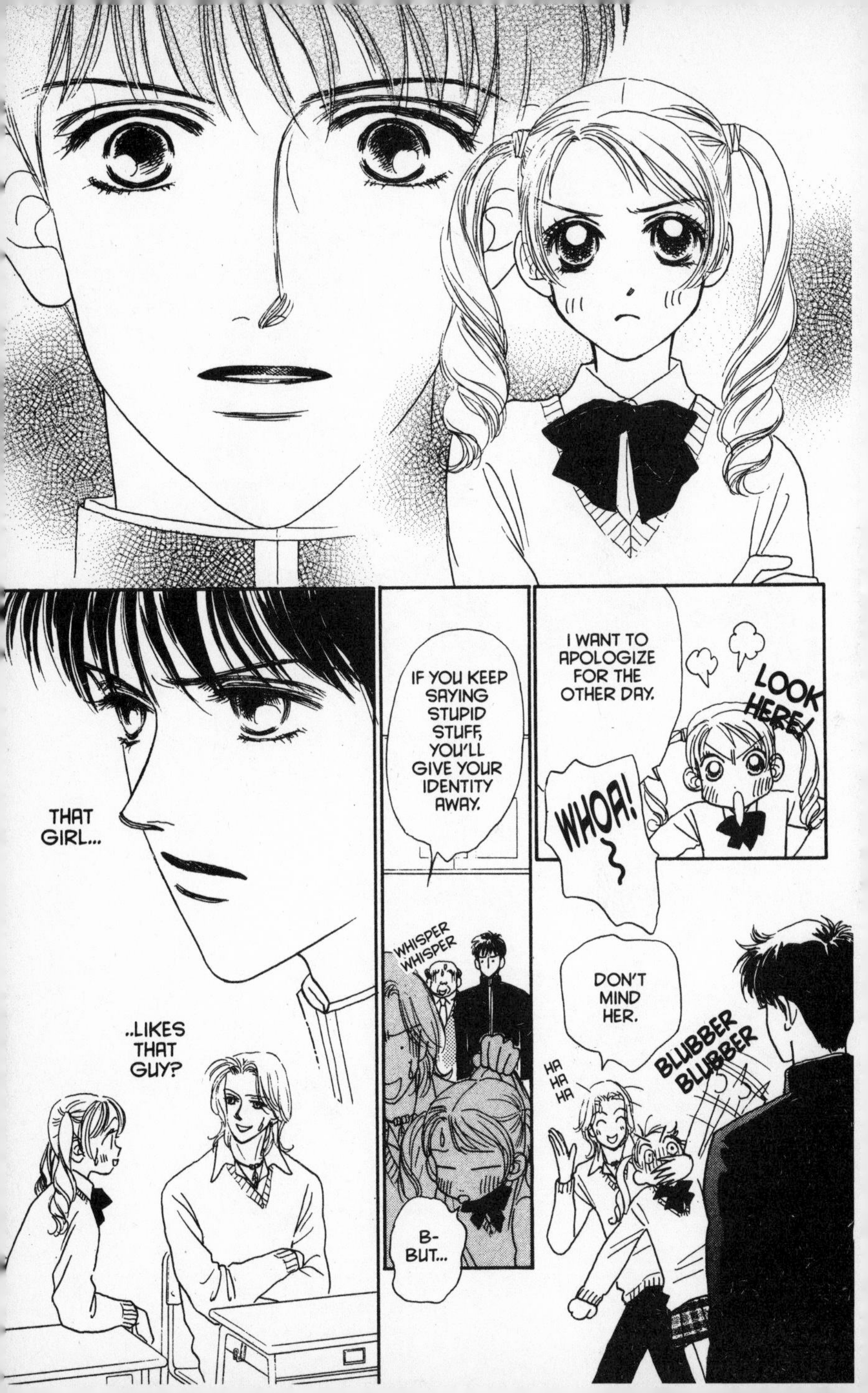
I WANT TO APOLOGIZE FOR THE OTHER DAY.
LOOK HERE!
WHOA!
IF YOU KEEP SAYING STUPID STUFF, YOU'LL GIVE YOUR IDENTITY AWAY.
DON'T MIND HER.
BLUBBER BLUBBER
HA HA HA
WHISPER WHISPER
B- BUT...
THAT GIRL...
..LIKES THAT GUY?

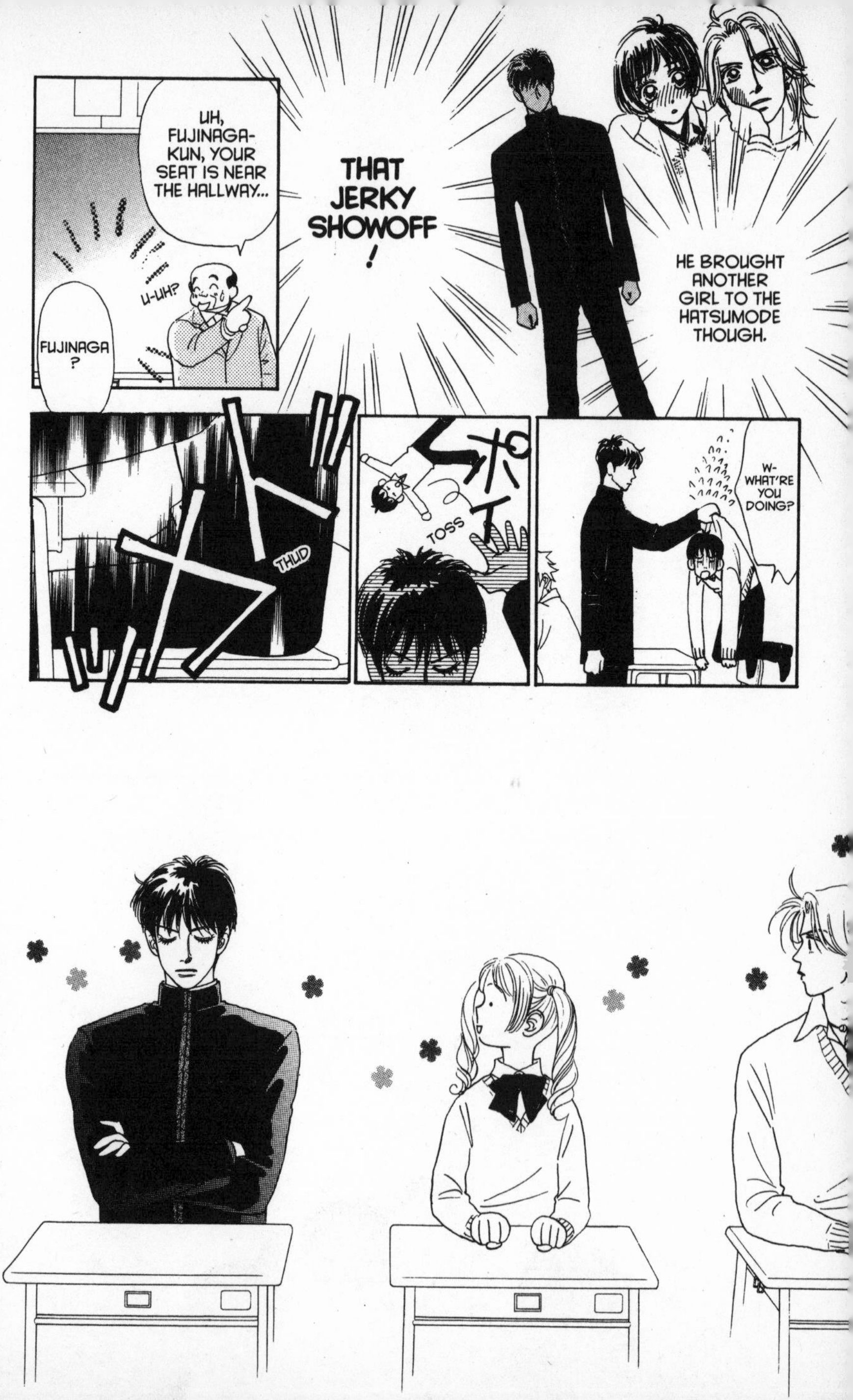
HE BROUGHT ANOTHER GIRL TO THE HATSUMODE THOUGH.
THAT JERKY SHOWOFF!
UH, FUJINAGA-KUN, YOUR SEAT IS NEAR THE HALLWAY...
U-UH?
FUJINAGA?
W-WHAT'RE YOU DOING?
TOSS
THUD

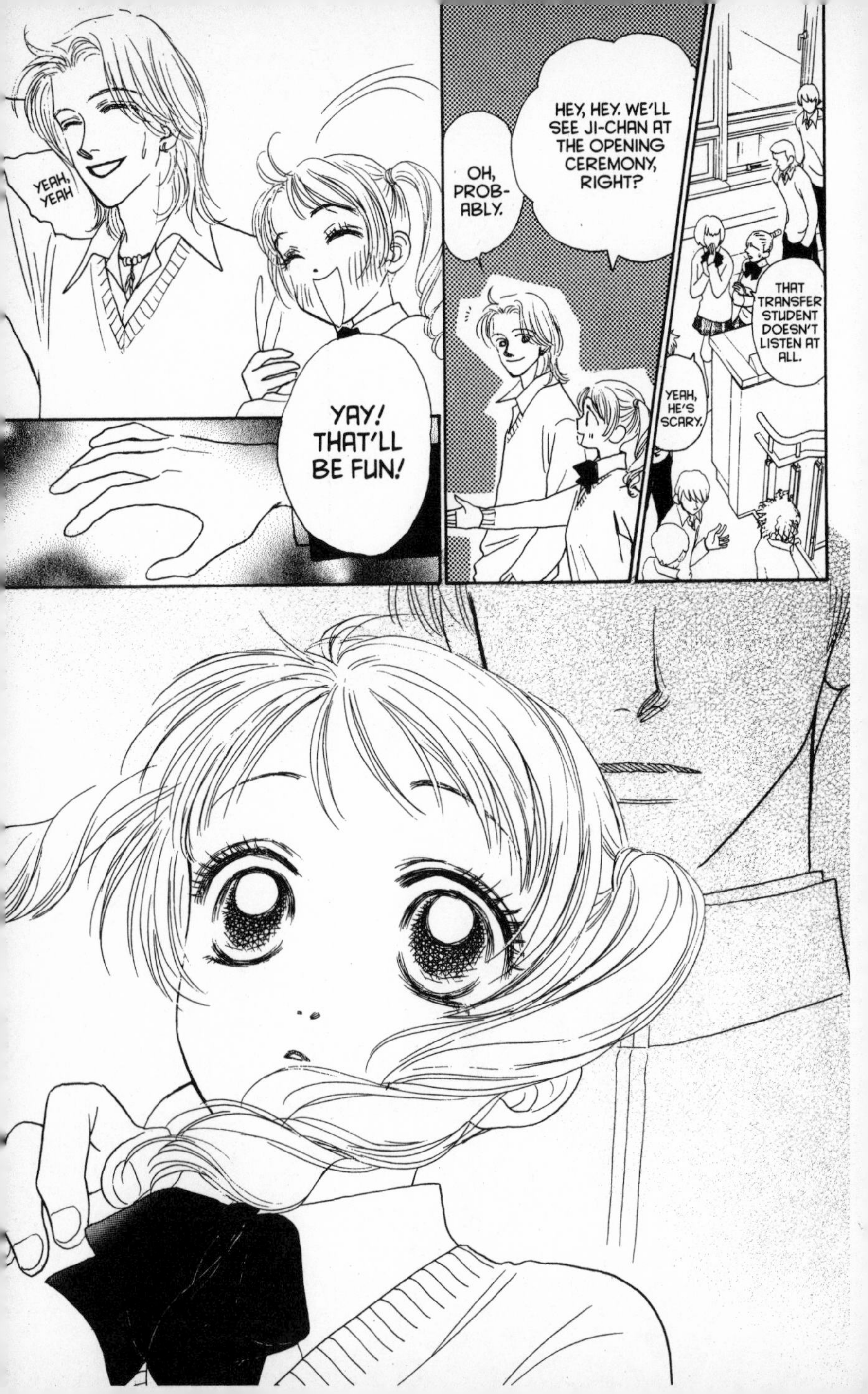
THAT TRANSFER STUDENT DOESN'T LISTEN AT ALL.
YEAH, HE'S SCARY.
HEY, HEY. WE'LL SEE JI-CHAN AT THE OPENING CEREMONY, RIGHT?
OH, PROBABLY.
YAY! THAT'LL BE FUN!
YEAH, YEAH

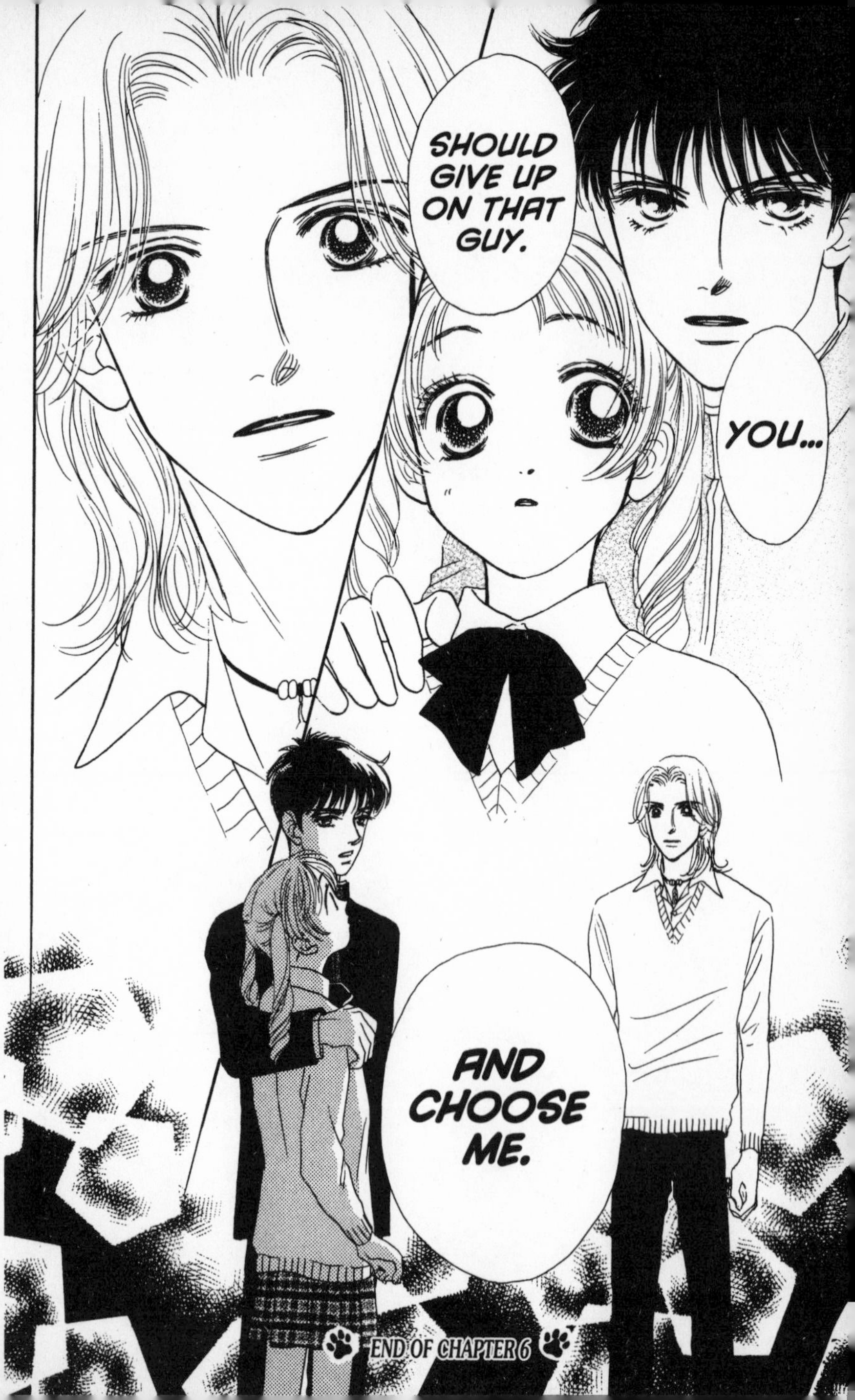
YOU...
SHOULD GIVE UP ON THAT GUY.
AND CHOOSE ME.
END OF CHAPTER 6

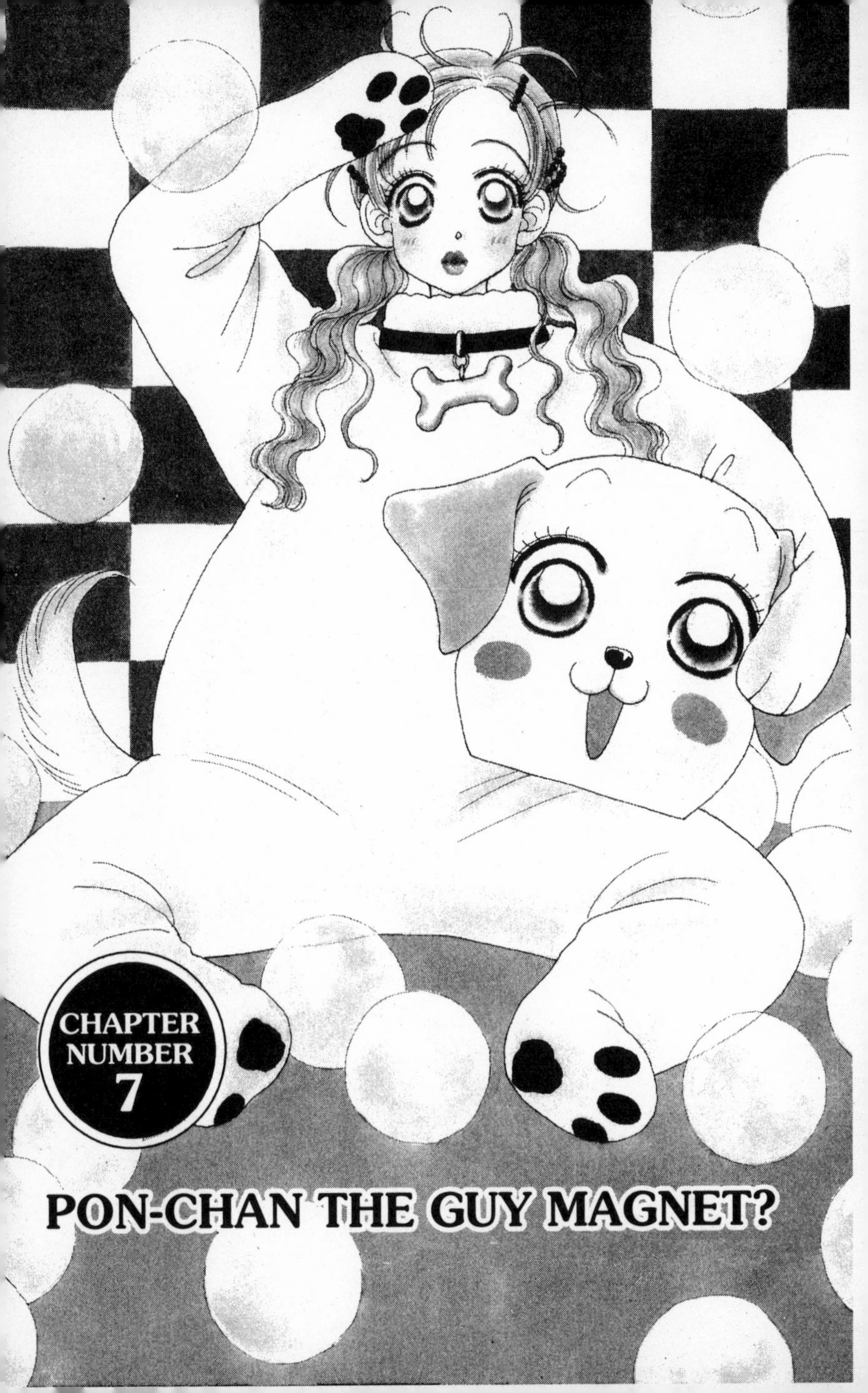
CHAPTER NUMBER 7
PON-CHAN THE GUY MAGNET?

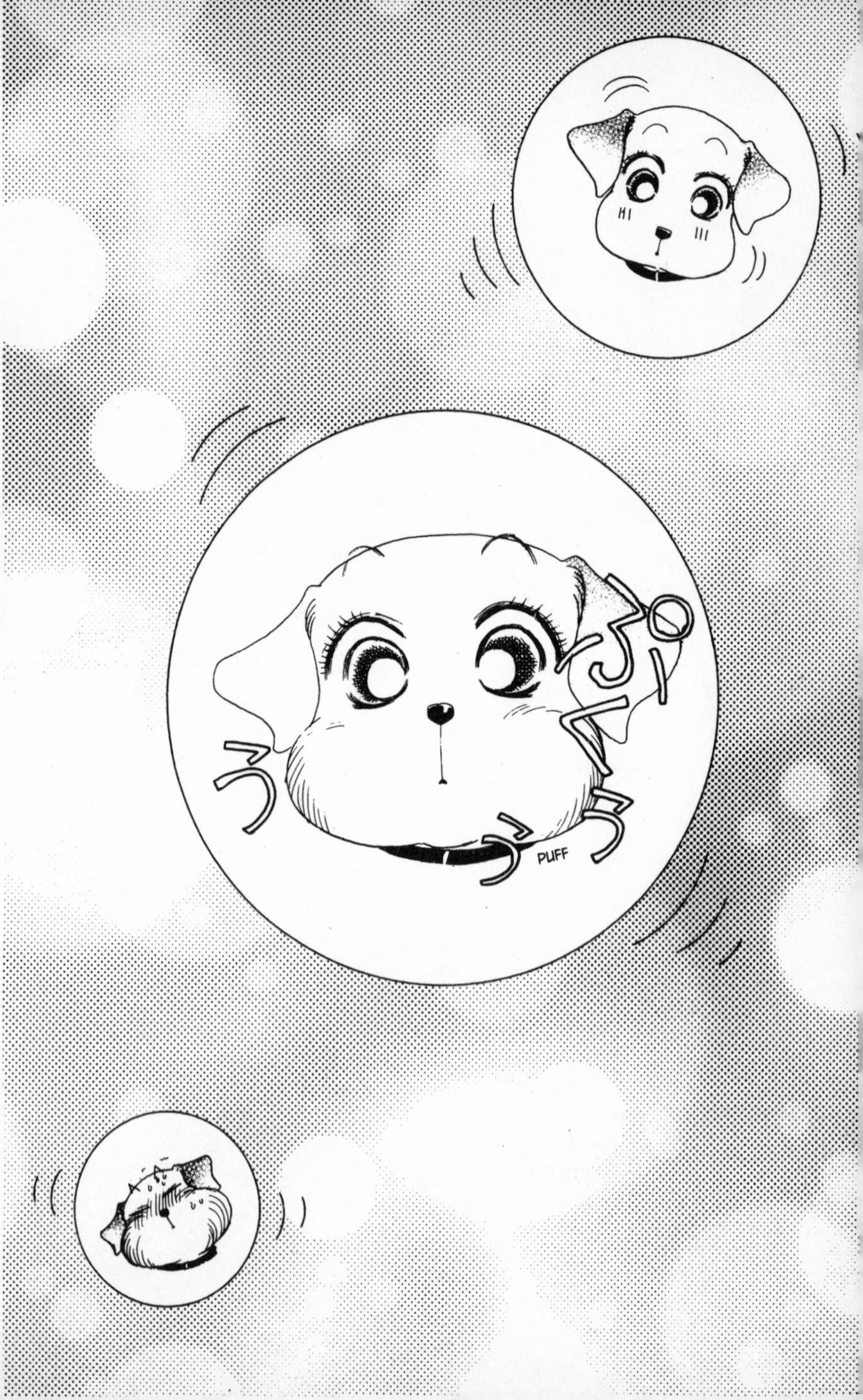
PUFF

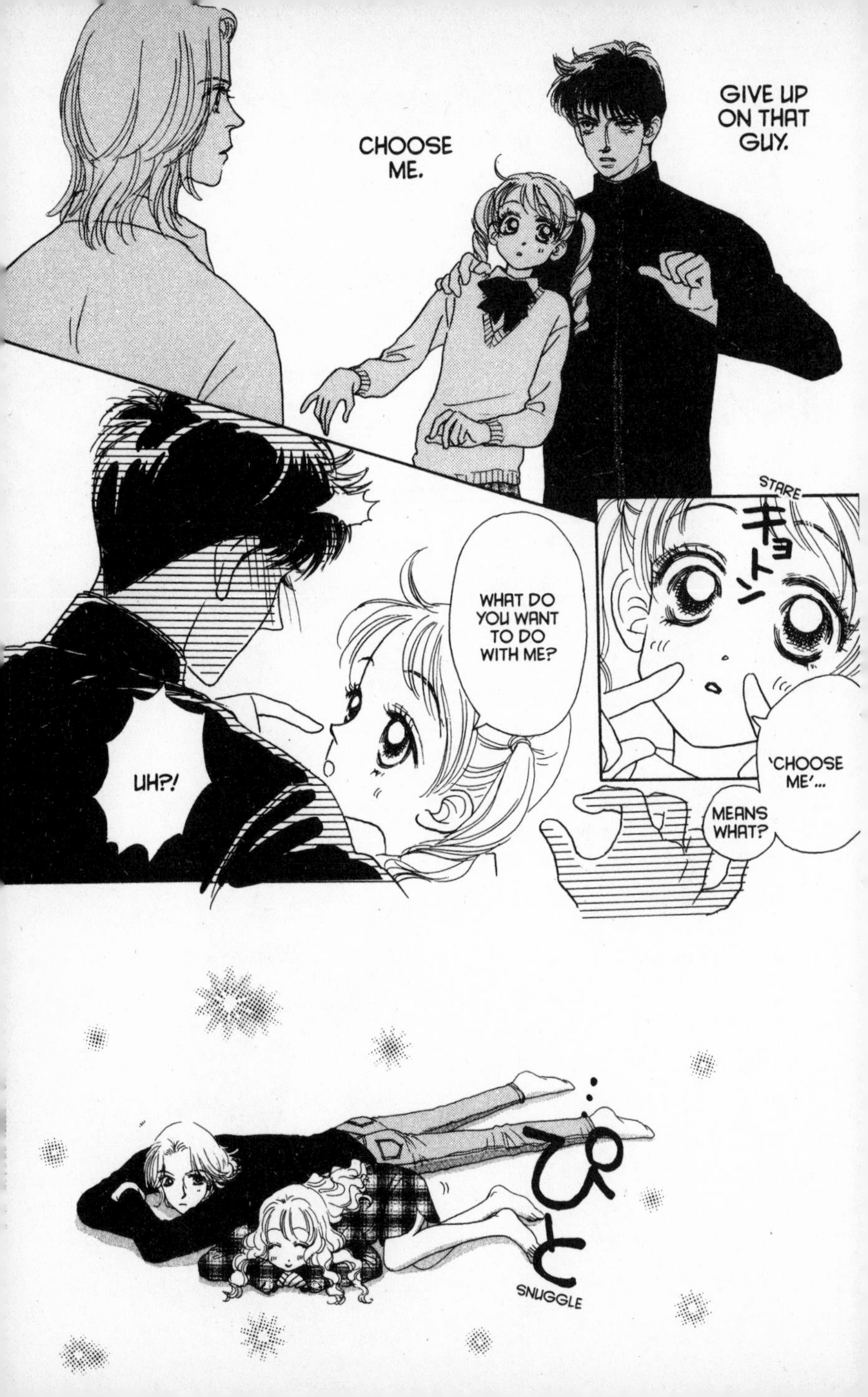
GIVE UP ON THAT GUY.
CHOOSE ME.
STARE
キョトン
'CHOOSE ME'...
MEANS WHAT?
WHAT DO YOU WANT TO DO WITH ME?
UH?!
ぴと
SNUGGLE

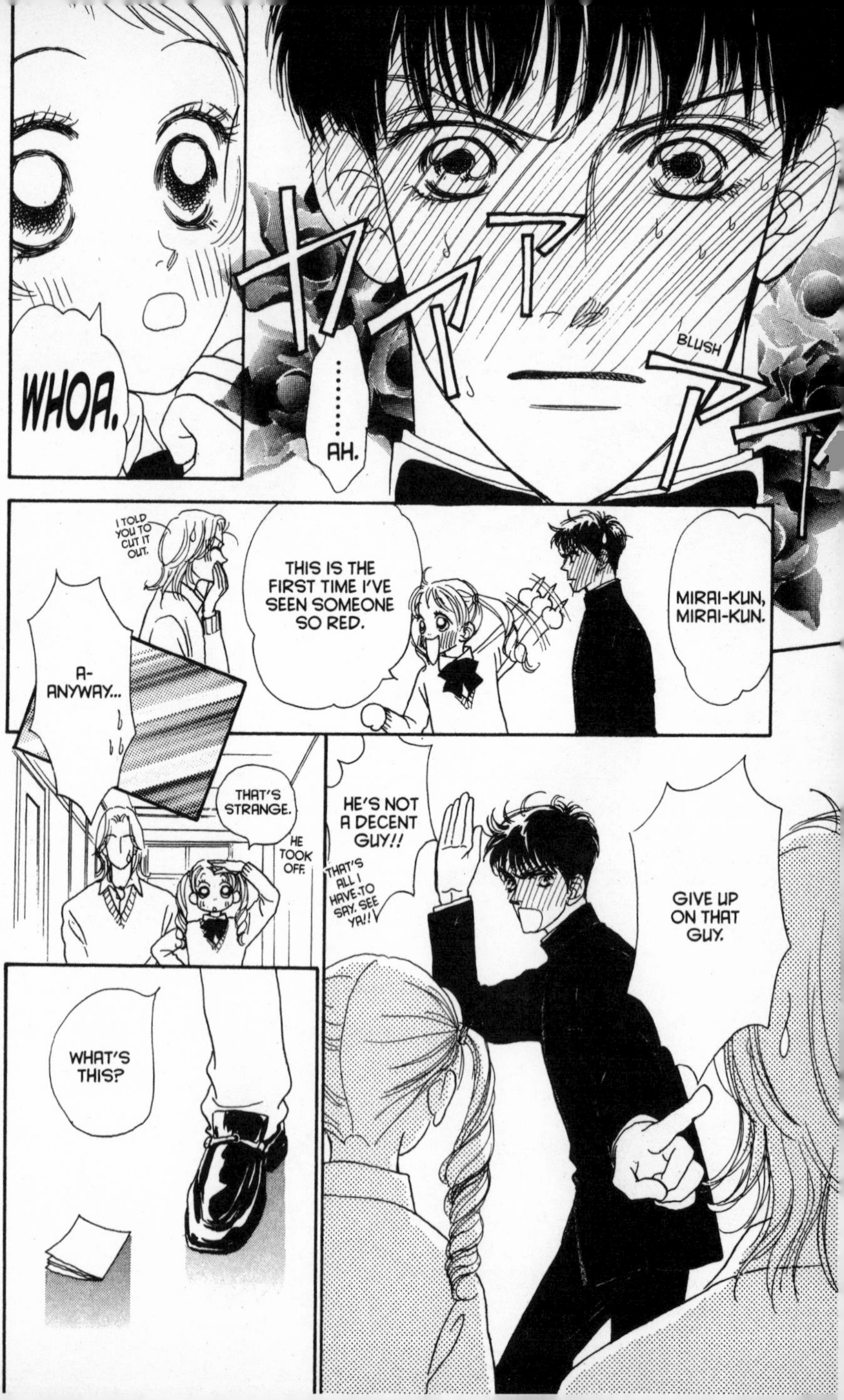
BLUSH
......AH.
WHOA.
MIRAI-KUN, MIRAI-KUN.
THIS IS THE FIRST TIME I'VE SEEN SOMEONE SO RED.
I TOLD YOU TO CUT IT OUT.
A- ANYWAY...
GIVE UP ON THAT GUY.
HE'S NOT A DECENT GUY!!
THAT'S ALL I HAVE TO SAY. SEE YA!!
HE TOOK OFF.
THAT'S STRANGE.
WHAT'S THIS?

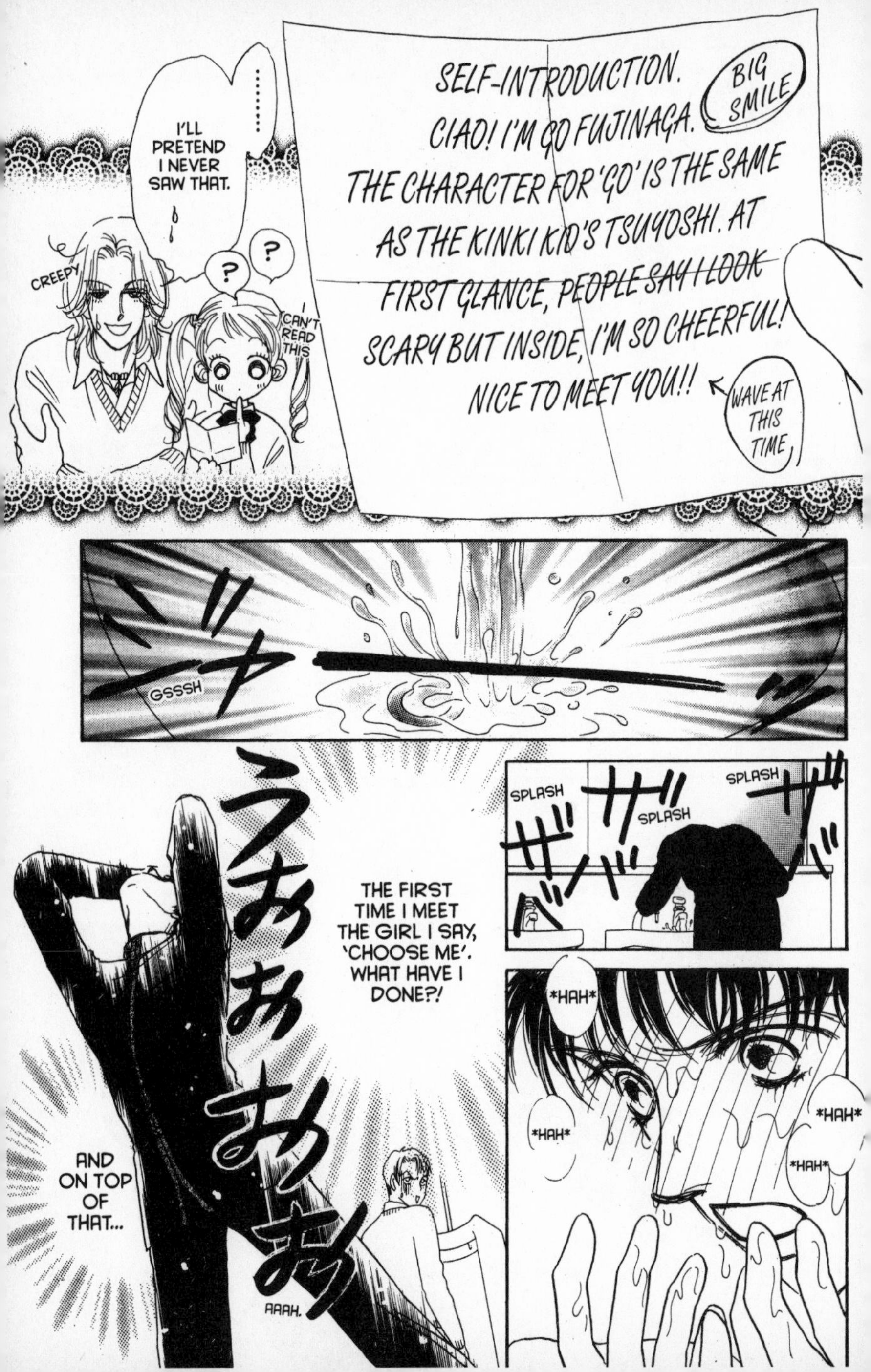
SELF-INTRODUCTION.
CIAO! I'M GO FUJINAGA.
BIG SMILE
THE CHARACTER FOR 'GO' IS THE SAME AS THE KINKI KID'S TSUYOSHI. AT FIRST GLANCE, PEOPLE SAY I LOOK SCARY BUT INSIDE, I'M SO CHEERFUL!
NICE TO MEET YOU!!
WAVE AT THIS TIME
I CAN'T READ THIS
?
?
......
I'LL PRETEND I NEVER SAW THAT.
CREEPY
GSSSH
SPLASH
SPLASH
SPLASH
HAH
HAH
HAH
HAH
THE FIRST TIME I MEET THE GIRL I SAY, 'CHOOSE ME'. WHAT HAVE I DONE?!
うあああ
AAAH.
AND ON TOP OF THAT...

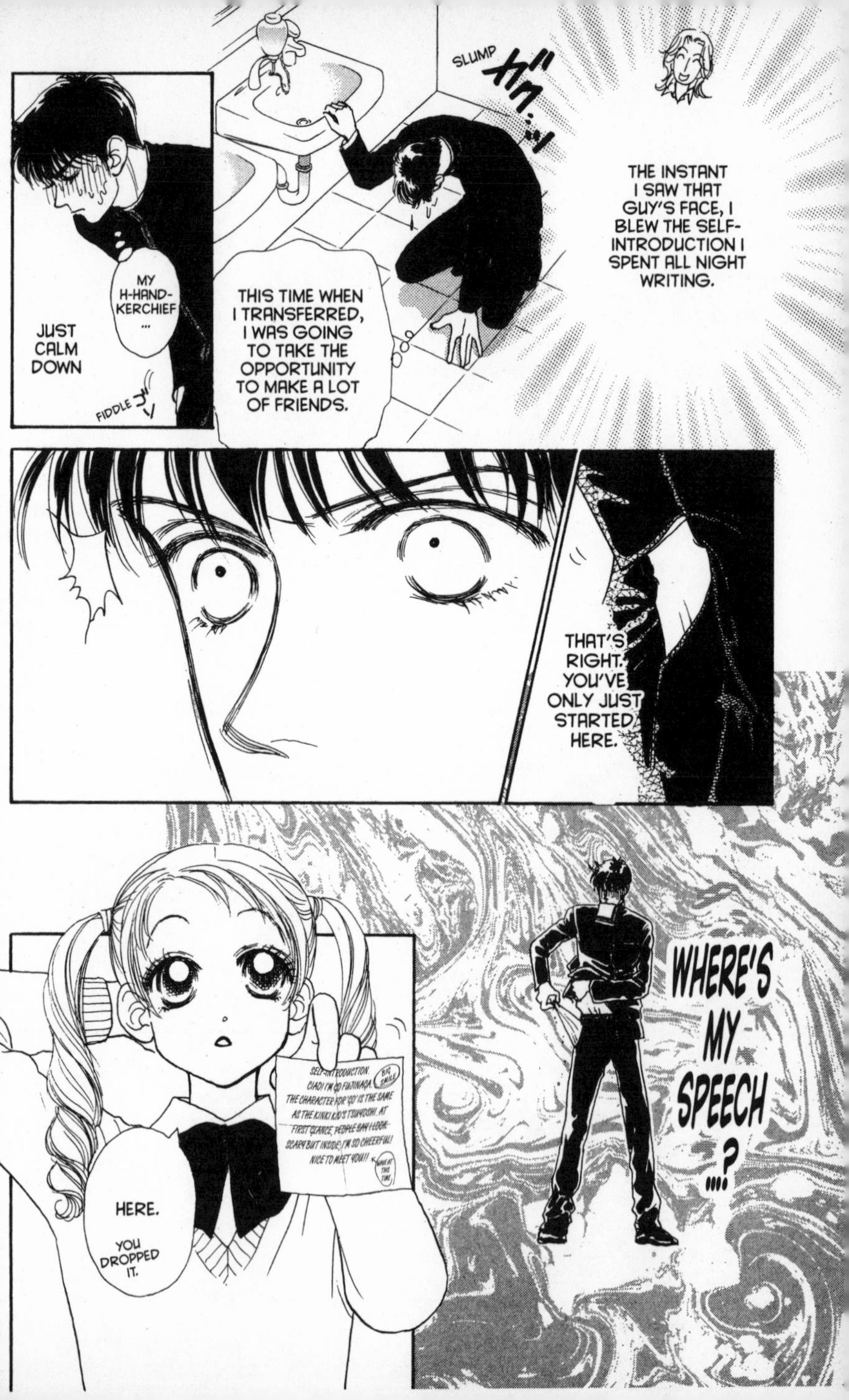
SLUMP
THE INSTANT I SAW THAT GUY'S FACE, I BLEW THE SELF-INTRODUCTION I SPENT ALL NIGHT WRITING.
THIS TIME WHEN I TRANSFERRED, I WAS GOING TO TAKE THE OPPORTUNITY TO MAKE A LOT OF FRIENDS.
MY H-HANDKERCHIEF ...
JUST CALM DOWN
FIDDLE
THAT'S RIGHT. YOU'VE ONLY JUST STARTED HERE.
WHERE'S MY SPEECH ...?
SELF-INTRODUCTION.
CIAO! I'M GO FUJINAGA.
BIG SMILE
THE CHARACTER FOR 'GO' IS THE SAME AS THE KINKI KID'S TSUYOSHI. AT FIRST GLANCE, PEOPLE SAY I LOOK SCARY BUT INSIDE, I'M SO CHEERFUL! NICE TO MEET YOU!!
WAVE AT THIS TIME
HERE.
YOU DROPPED IT.

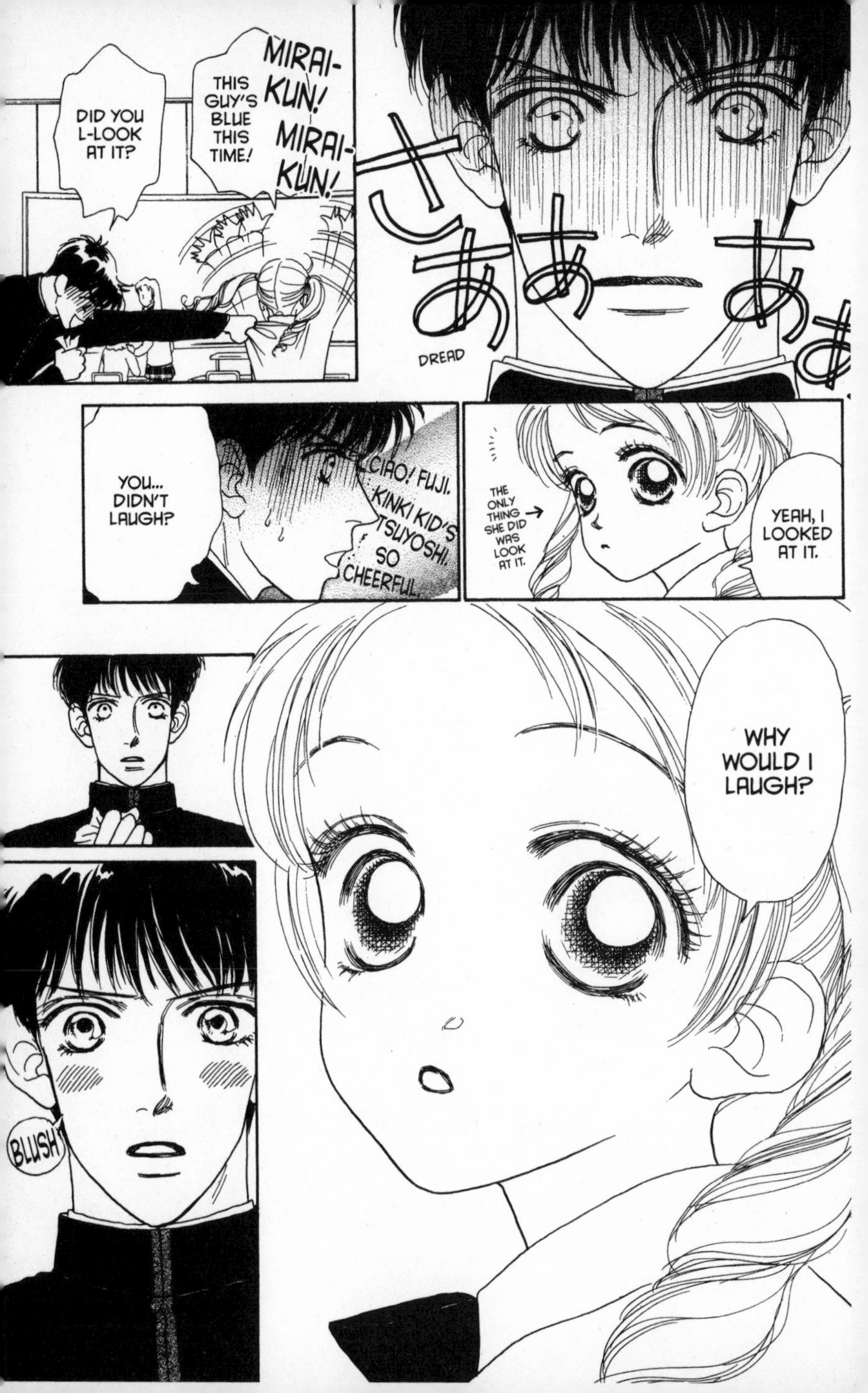
DREAD
MIRAI-KUN! MIRAI-KUN!
THIS GUY'S BLUE THIS TIME!
DID YOU L-LOOK AT IT?
YEAH, I LOOKED AT IT.
THE ONLY THING SHE DID WAS LOOK AT IT.
CIAO! FUJI. KINKI KID'S TSUYOSHI. SO CHEERFUL.
YOU... DIDN'T LAUGH?
WHY WOULD I LAUGH?
BLUSH

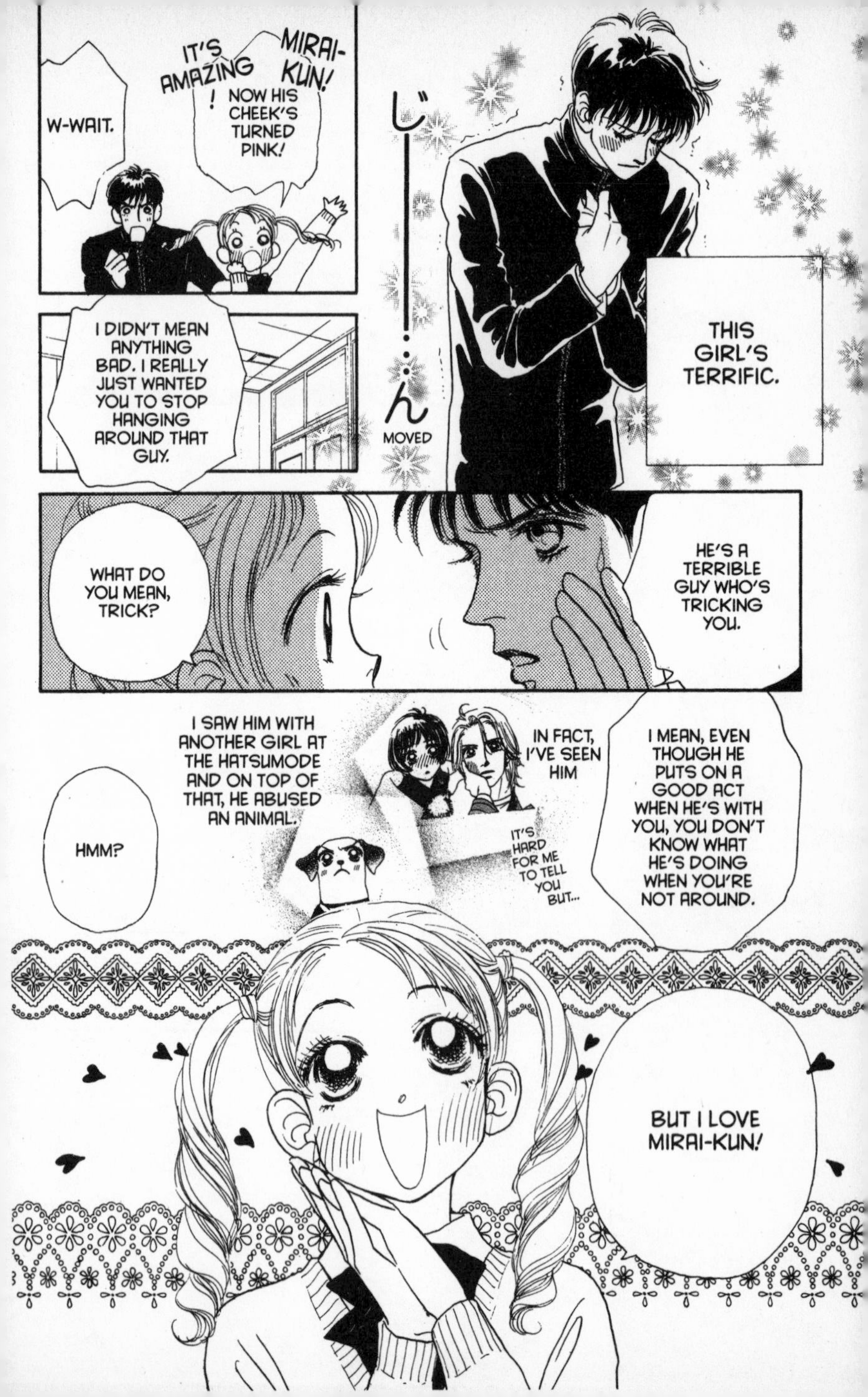

じーん……ん
MOVED
THIS GIRL'S TERRIFIC.
IT'S AMAZING! MIRAI-KUN!
NOW HIS CHEEK'S TURNED PINK!
W-WAIT.
I DIDN'T MEAN ANYTHING BAD. I REALLY JUST WANTED YOU TO STOP HANGING AROUND THAT GUY.
HE'S A TERRIBLE GUY WHO'S TRICKING YOU.
WHAT DO YOU MEAN, TRICK?
I MEAN, EVEN THOUGH HE PUTS ON A GOOD ACT WHEN HE'S WITH YOU, YOU DON'T KNOW WHAT HE'S DOING WHEN YOU'RE NOT AROUND.
IT'S HARD FOR ME TO TELL YOU BUT...
IN FACT, I'VE SEEN HIM
I SAW HIM WITH ANOTHER GIRL AT THE HATSUMODE AND ON TOP OF THAT, HE ABUSED AN ANIMAL.
HMM?
BUT I LOVE MIRAI-KUN!

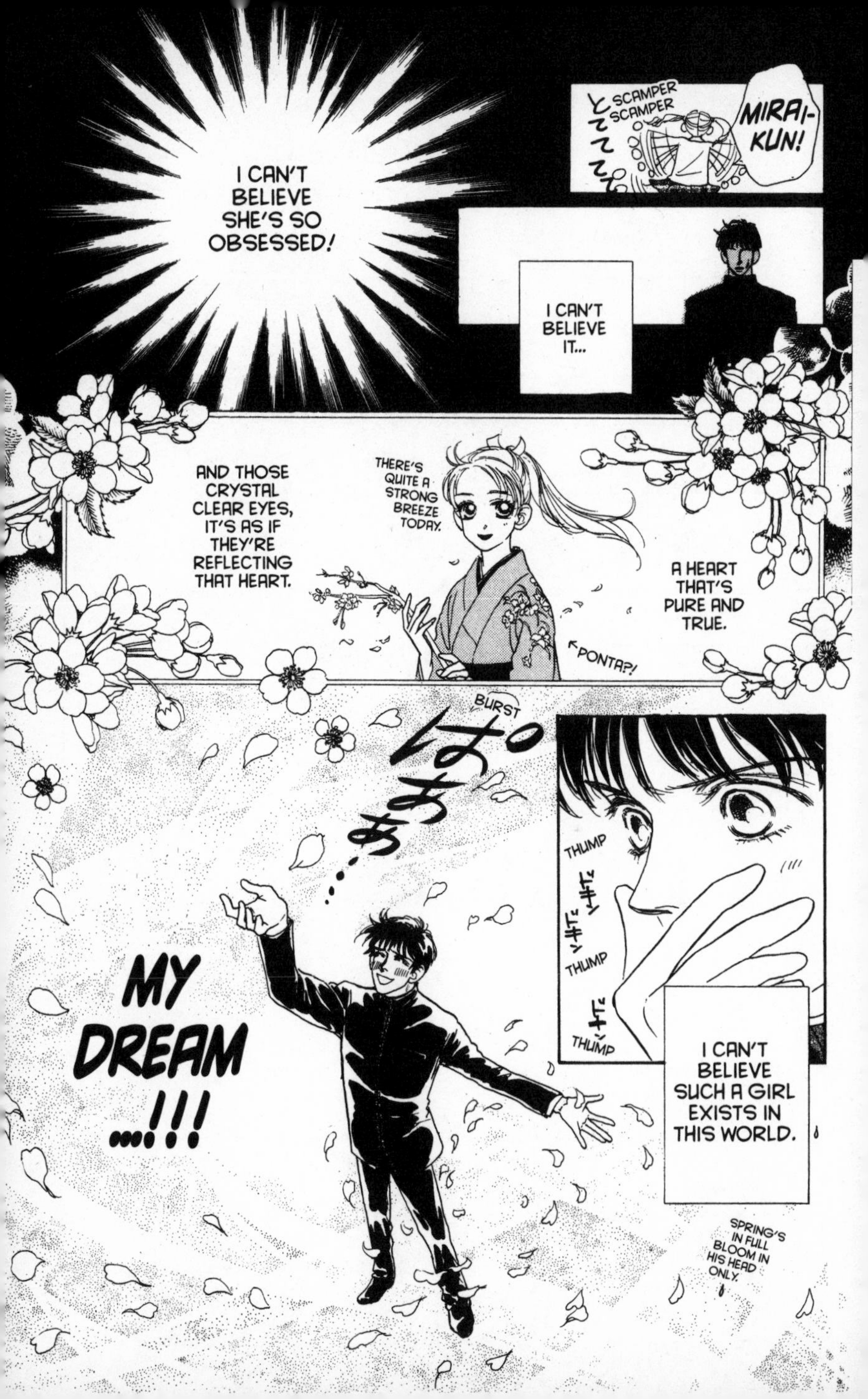

MIRAI-KUN!
SCAMPER SCAMPER
I CAN'T BELIEVE SHE'S SO OBSESSED!
I CAN'T BELIEVE IT...
A HEART THAT'S PURE AND TRUE.
THERE'S QUITE A STRONG BREEZE TODAY.
←PONTA?!
AND THOSE CRYSTAL CLEAR EYES, IT'S AS IF THEY'RE REFLECTING THAT HEART.
THUMP
THUMP
THUMP
I CAN'T BELIEVE SUCH A GIRL EXISTS IN THIS WORLD.
BURST
MY DREAM ...!!!
SPRING'S IN FULL BLOOM IN HIS HEAD ONLY.

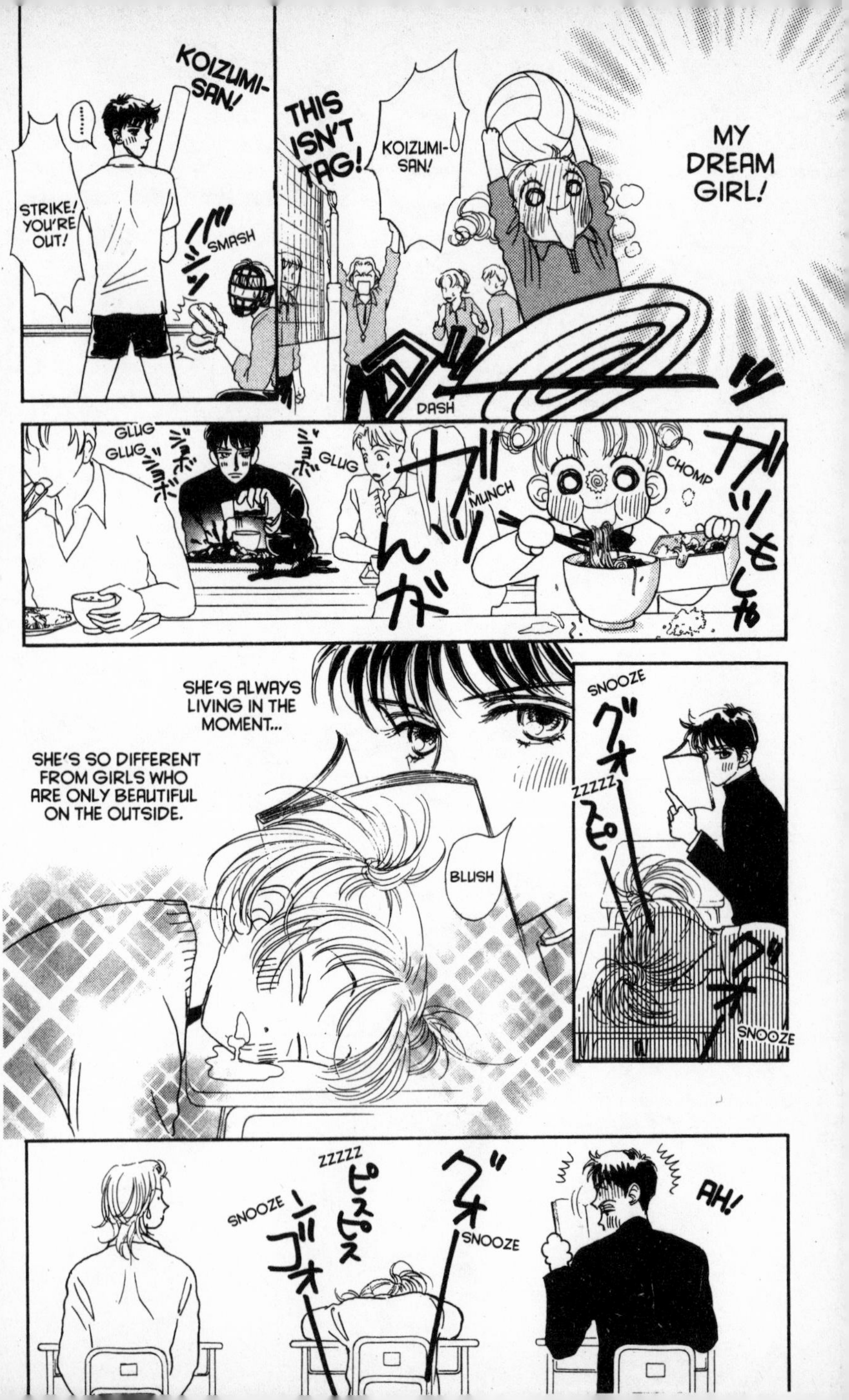

KOIZUMI-SAN!
......
STRIKE! YOU'RE OUT!
SMASH
THIS ISN'T TAG!
KOIZUMI-SAN!
MY DREAM GIRL!
DASH
GLUG GLUG
GLUG
MUNCH
CHOMP
SHE'S ALWAYS LIVING IN THE MOMENT...
SHE'S SO DIFFERENT FROM GIRLS WHO ARE ONLY BEAUTIFUL ON THE OUTSIDE.
BLUSH
SNOOZE
ZZZZZ
SNOOZE
ZZZZZ
SNOOZE
SNOOZE
AH!

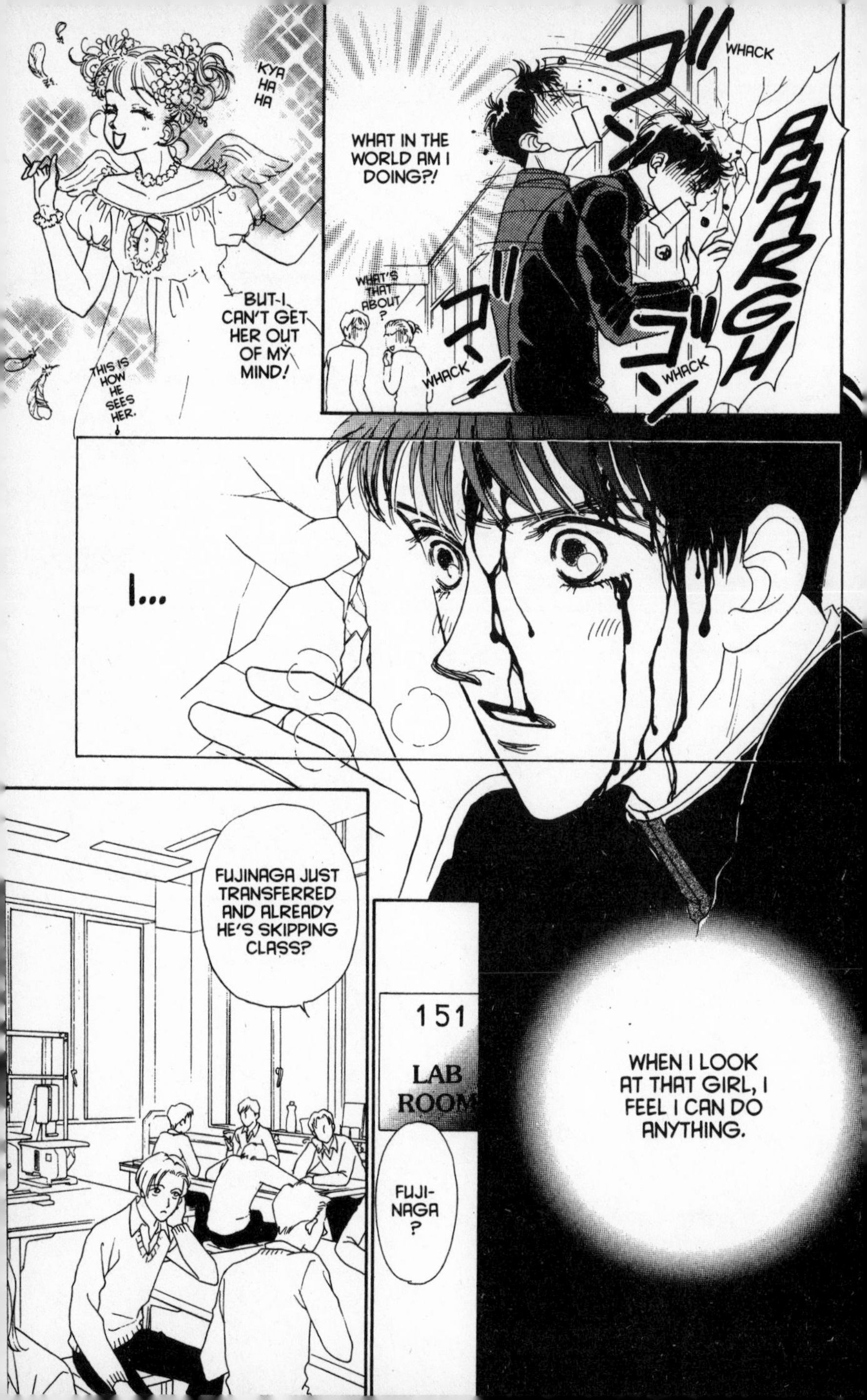
WHACK
AAARGH
WHAT IN THE WORLD AM I DOING?!
WHACK
WHACK
WHAT'S THAT ABOUT?
KYA HA HA
BUT I CAN'T GET HER OUT OF MY MIND!
THIS IS HOW HE SEES HER.
I...
WHEN I LOOK AT THAT GIRL, I FEEL I CAN DO ANYTHING.
151
LAB ROOM
FUJI-NAGA?
FUJINAGA JUST TRANSFERRED AND ALREADY HE'S SKIPPING CLASS?

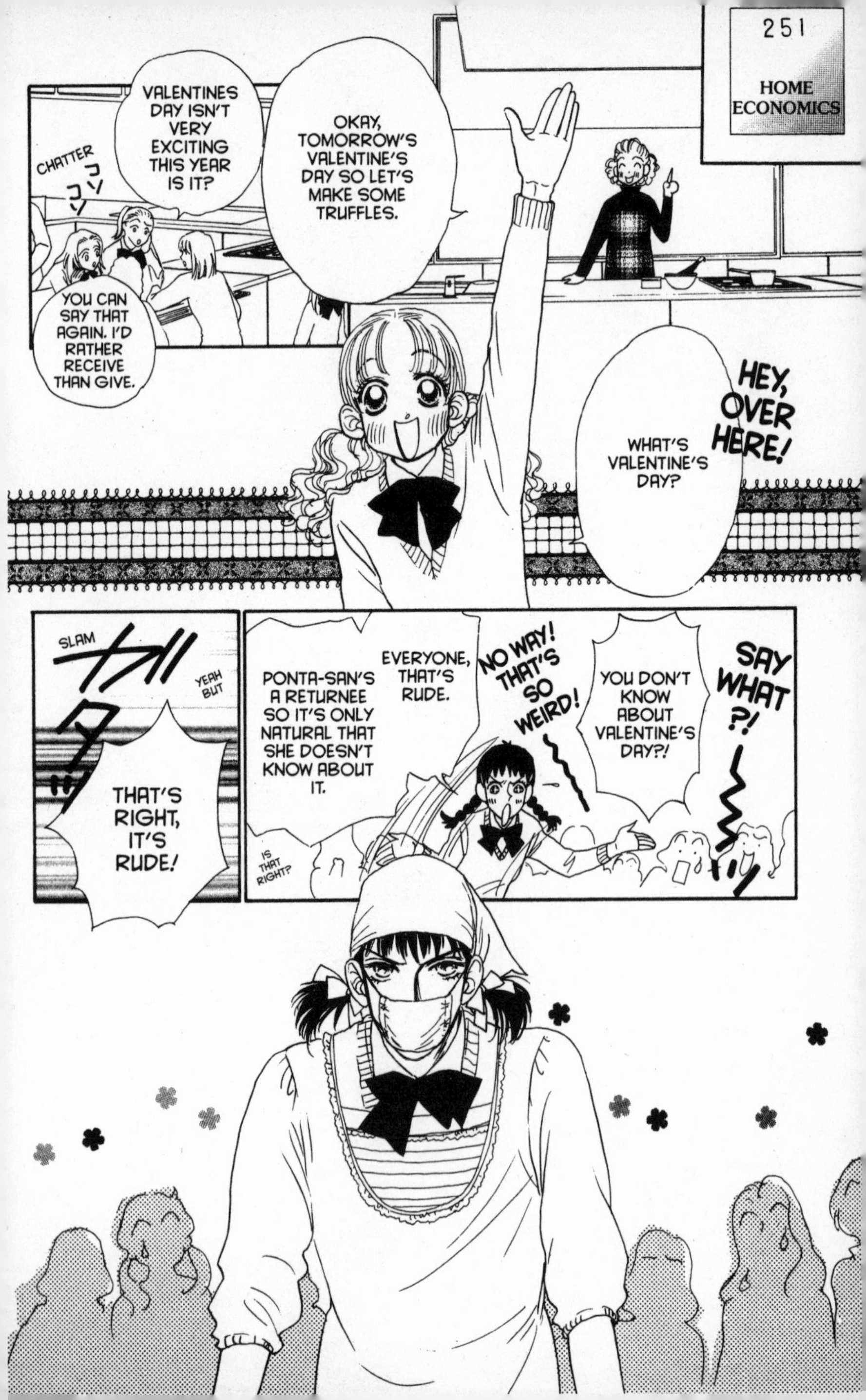
251
HOME ECONOMICS
OKAY, TOMORROW'S VALENTINE'S DAY SO LET'S MAKE SOME TRUFFLES.
VALENTINES DAY ISN'T VERY EXCITING THIS YEAR IS IT?
CHATTER
コソコソ
YOU CAN SAY THAT AGAIN. I'D RATHER RECEIVE THAN GIVE.
HEY, OVER HERE!
WHAT'S VALENTINE'S DAY?
SAY WHAT?!
YOU DON'T KNOW ABOUT VALENTINE'S DAY?!
NO WAY! THAT'S SO WEIRD!
EVERYONE, THAT'S RUDE.
PONTA-SAN'S A RETURNEE SO IT'S ONLY NATURAL THAT SHE DOESN'T KNOW ABOUT IT.
IS THAT RIGHT?
SLAM
YEAH BUT
THAT'S RIGHT, IT'S RUDE!

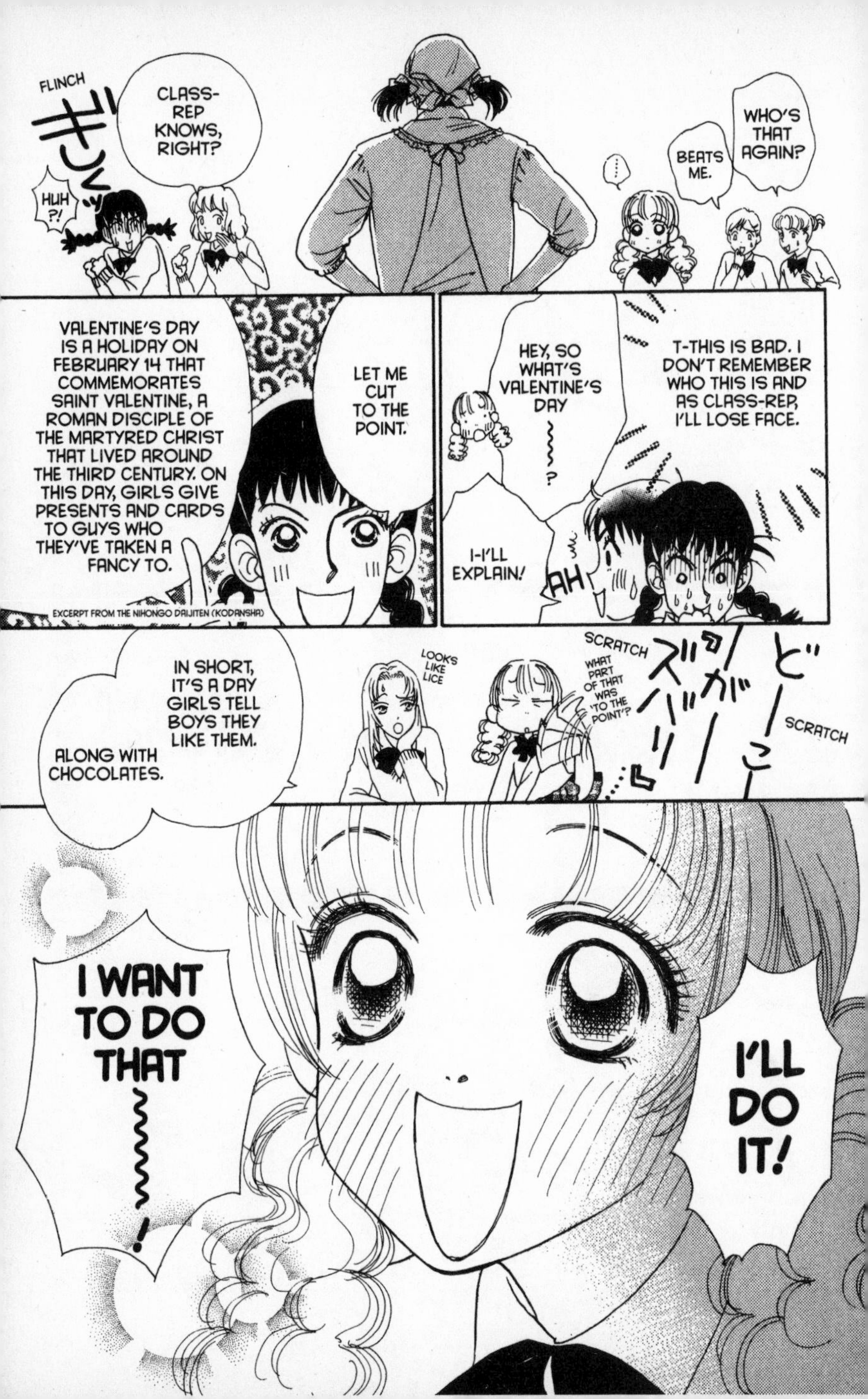
WHO'S THAT AGAIN?
BEATS ME.
...
CLASS-REP KNOWS, RIGHT?
FLINCH
HUH ?!
HEY, SO WHAT'S VALENTINE'S DAY ~~~?
T-THIS IS BAD. I DON'T REMEMBER WHO THIS IS AND AS CLASS-REP, I'LL LOSE FACE.
AH
I-I'LL EXPLAIN!
LET ME CUT TO THE POINT.
VALENTINE'S DAY IS A HOLIDAY ON FEBRUARY 14 THAT COMMEMORATES SAINT VALENTINE, A ROMAN DISCIPLE OF THE MARTYRED CHRIST THAT LIVED AROUND THE THIRD CENTURY. ON THIS DAY, GIRLS GIVE PRESENTS AND CARDS TO GUYS WHO THEY'VE TAKEN A FANCY TO.
EXCERPT FROM THE NIHONGO DAIJITEN (KODANSHA)
SCRATCH
SCRATCH
WHAT PART OF THAT WAS 'TO THE POINT'?
LOOKS LIKE LICE
IN SHORT, IT'S A DAY GIRLS TELL BOYS THEY LIKE THEM.
ALONG WITH CHOCOLATES.
I'LL DO IT!
I WANT TO DO THAT ~~~!

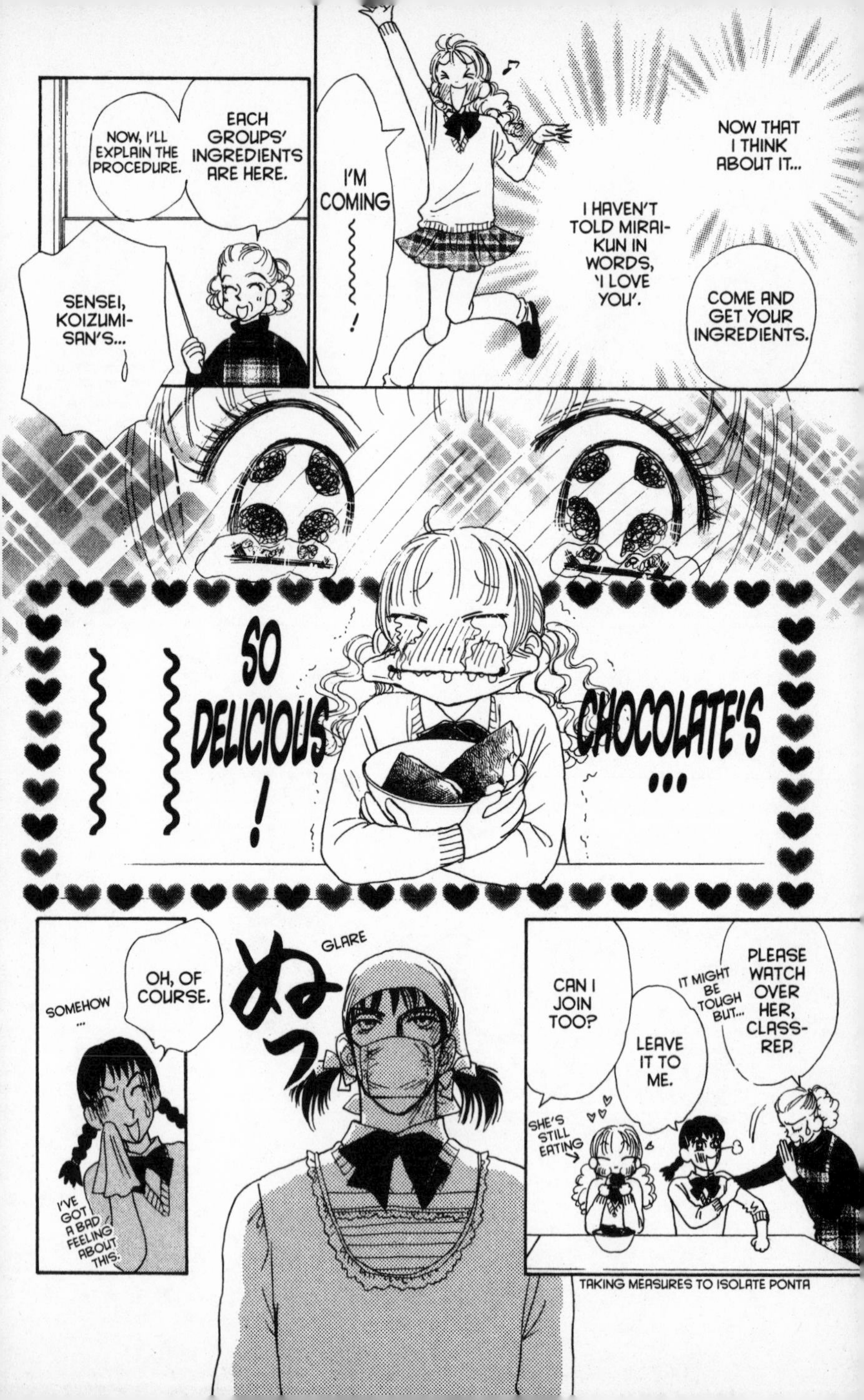
NOW THAT I THINK ABOUT IT...
I HAVEN'T TOLD MIRAI-KUN IN WORDS, 'I LOVE YOU'.
COME AND GET YOUR INGREDIENTS.
I'M COMING~~~!
EACH GROUPS' INGREDIENTS ARE HERE.
NOW, I'LL EXPLAIN THE PROCEDURE.
SENSEI, KOIZUMI-SAN'S...
CHOCOLATE'S...
SO DELICIOUS~~!
PLEASE WATCH OVER HER, CLASS-REP.
IT MIGHT BE TOUGH BUT...
LEAVE IT TO ME.
CAN I JOIN TOO?
SHE'S STILL EATING
TAKING MEASURES TO ISOLATE PONTA
ぬっ
GLARE
OH, OF COURSE.
SOMEHOW...
I'VE GOT A BAD FEELING ABOUT THIS.

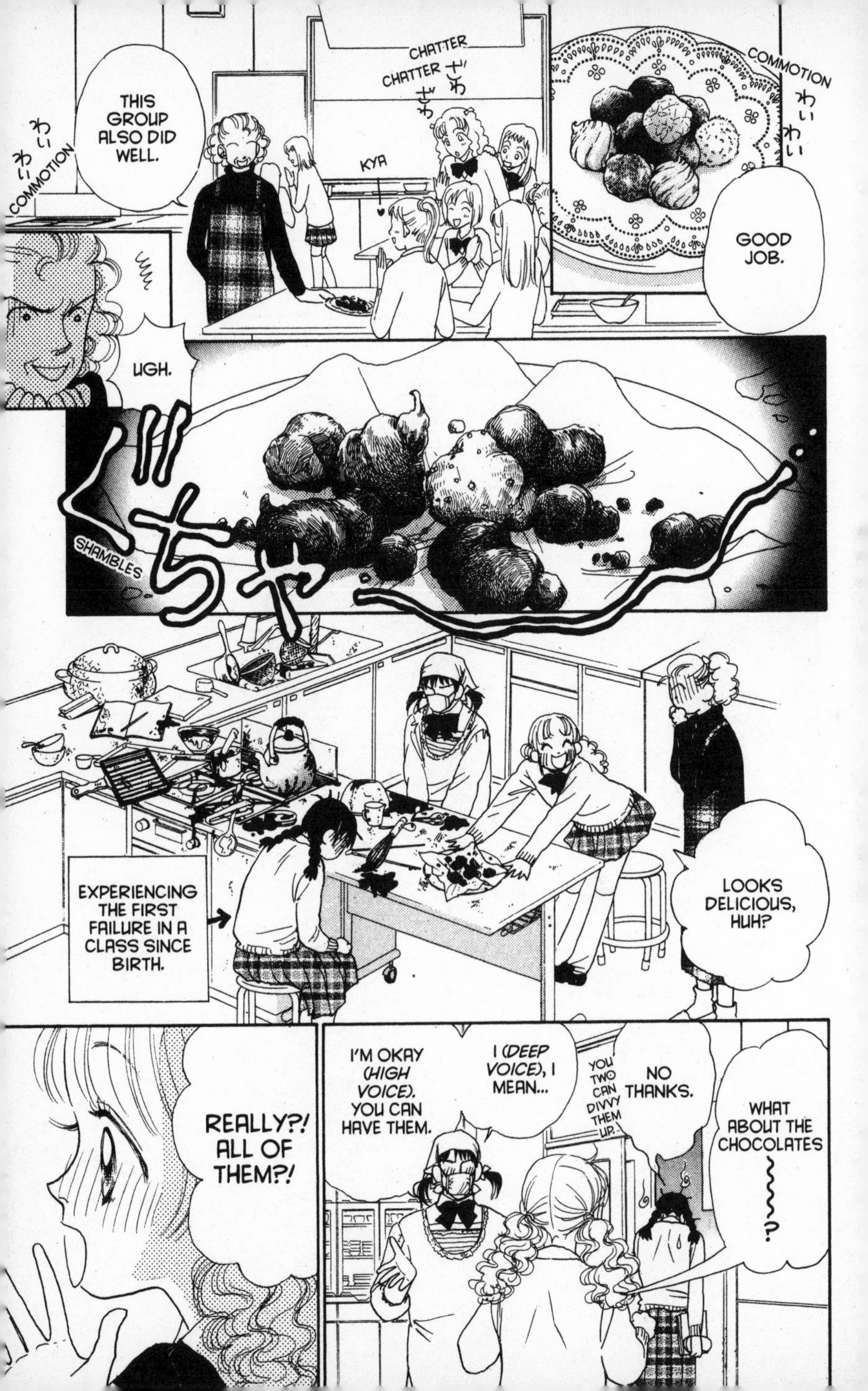

COMMOTION
わいわい
GOOD JOB.
CHATTER CHATTER
ざわざわ
KYA
COMMOTION
わいわい
THIS GROUP ALSO DID WELL.
UGH.
SHAMBLES
ぐちゃ
LOOKS DELICIOUS, HUH?
EXPERIENCING THE FIRST FAILURE IN A CLASS SINCE BIRTH.
WHAT ABOUT THE CHOCOLATES ~~~?
NO THANKS.
YOU TWO CAN DIVVY THEM UP.
I (DEEP VOICE), I MEAN...
I'M OKAY (HIGH VOICE). YOU CAN HAVE THEM.
REALLY?! ALL OF THEM?!

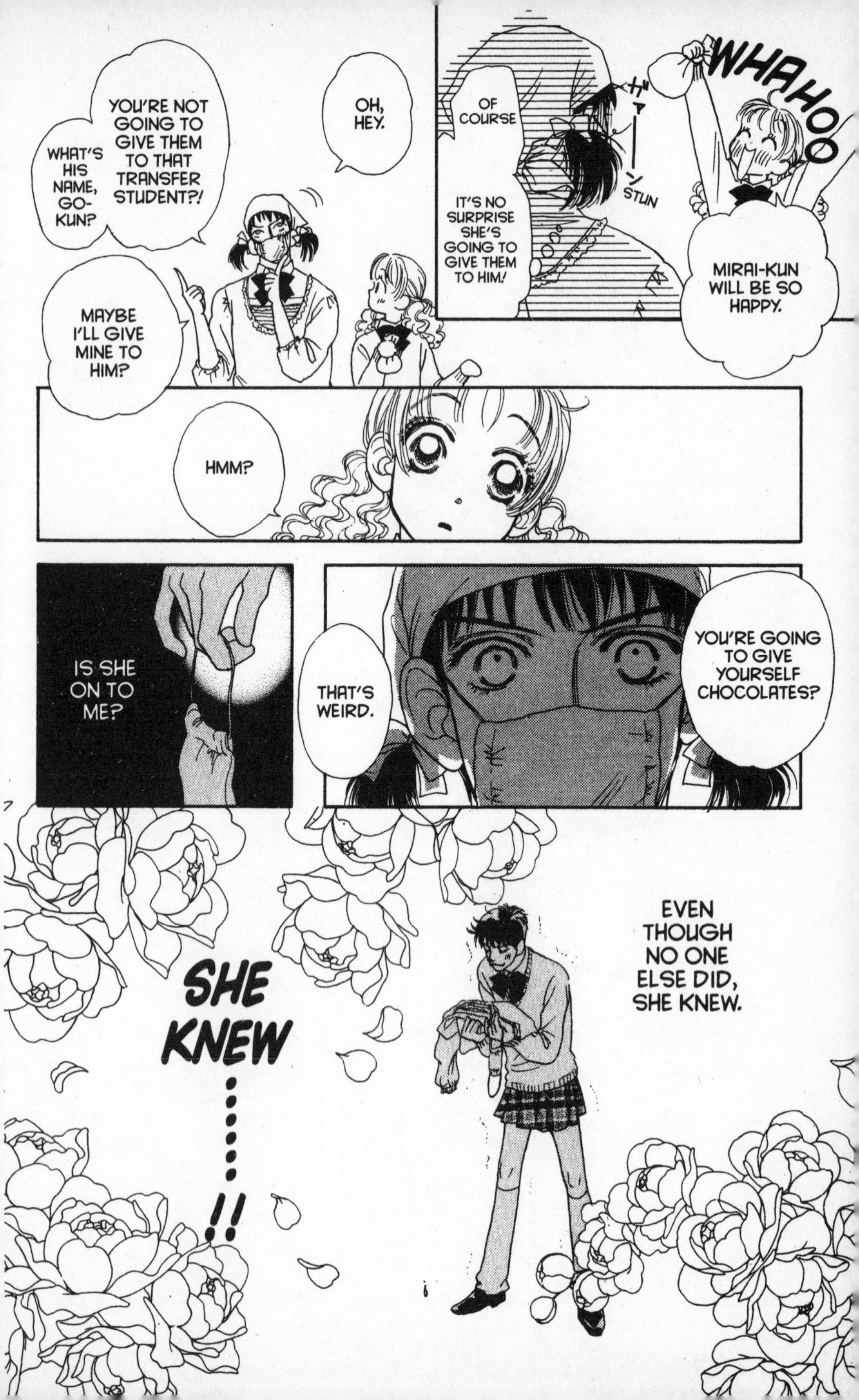
WHAHOO
MIRAI-KUN WILL BE SO HAPPY.
STUN
OF COURSE
IT'S NO SURPRISE SHE'S GOING TO GIVE THEM TO HIM!
OH, HEY.
YOU'RE NOT GOING TO GIVE THEM TO THAT TRANSFER STUDENT?!
WHAT'S HIS NAME, GO-KUN?
MAYBE I'LL GIVE MINE TO HIM?
HMM?
YOU'RE GOING TO GIVE YOURSELF CHOCOLATES?
THAT'S WEIRD.
IS SHE ON TO ME?
EVEN THOUGH NO ONE ELSE DID, SHE KNEW.
SHE KNEW......!!

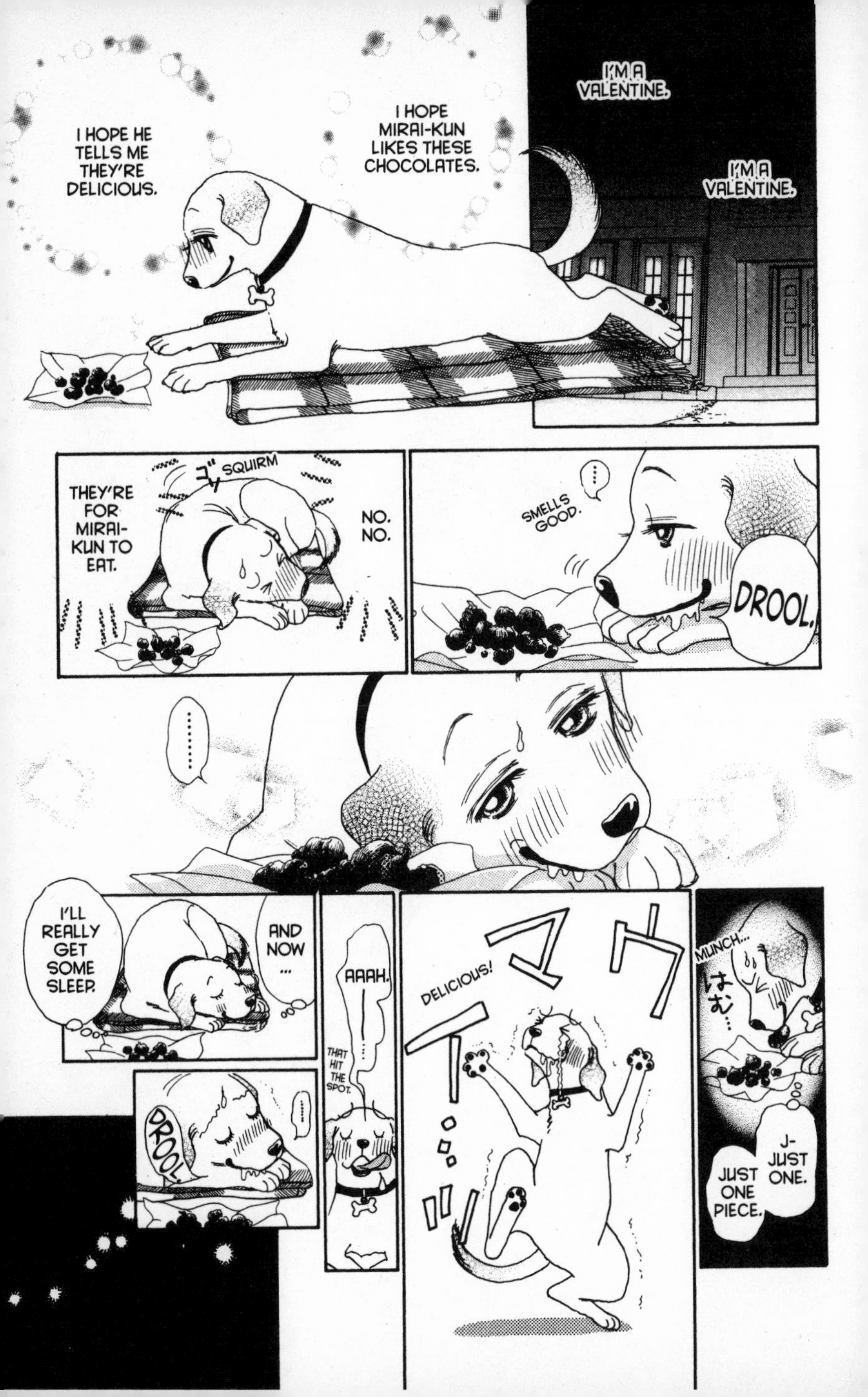

I'M A VALENTINE.
I'M A VALENTINE.
I HOPE MIRAI-KUN LIKES THESE CHOCOLATES.
I HOPE HE TELLS ME THEY'RE DELICIOUS.
...
SMELLS GOOD.
DROOL.
NO. NO.
SQUIRM
THEY'RE FOR MIRAI-KUN TO EAT.
......
MUNCH...
はむ...
J-JUST ONE.
JUST ONE PIECE.
ウマイ
DELICIOUS!
AAAH.
THAT HIT THE SPOT.
AND NOW...
I'LL REALLY GET SOME SLEEP.
DROOL.
......

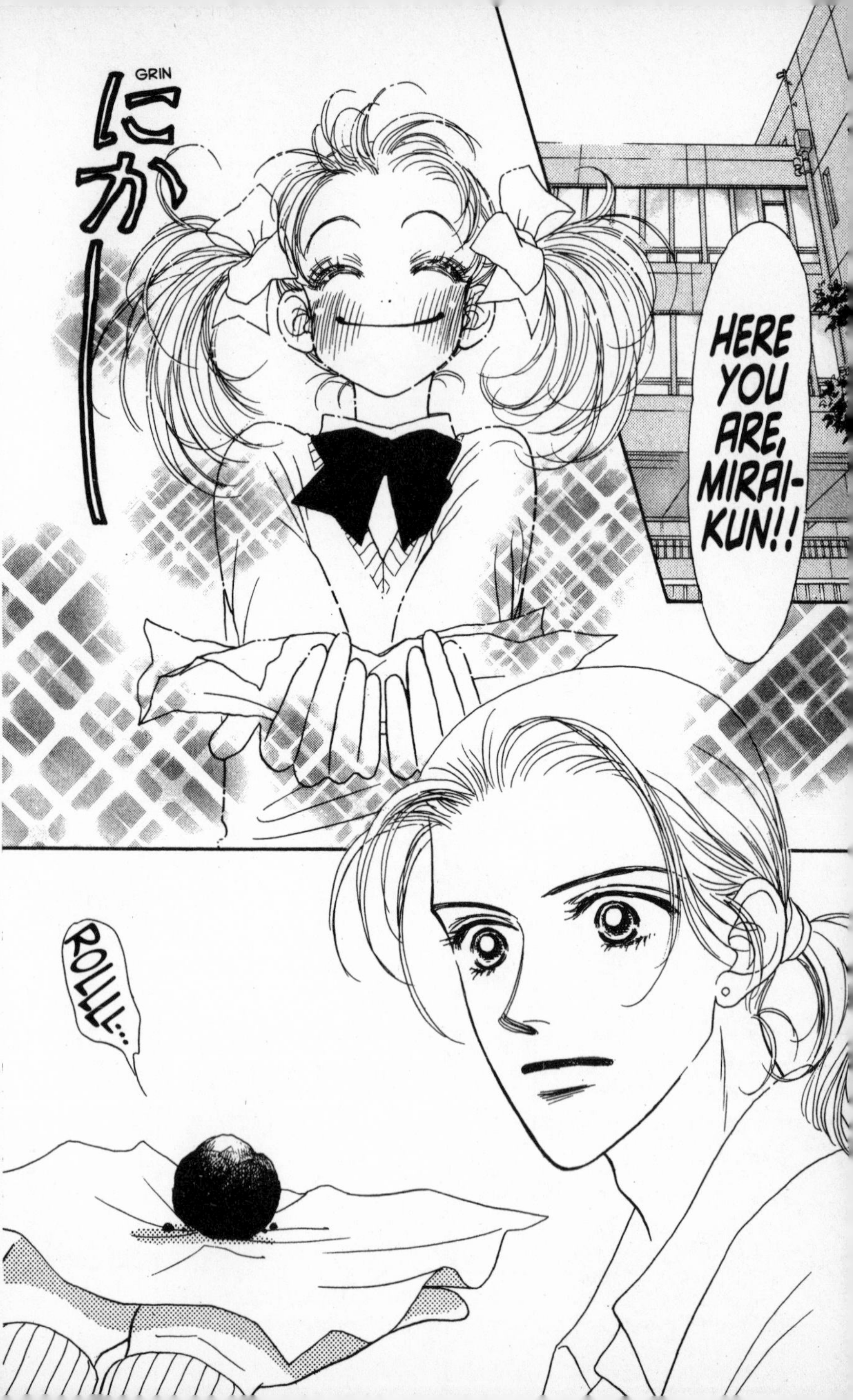
HERE YOU ARE, MIRAI-KUN!!
GRIN
にかー
ROLLLL...

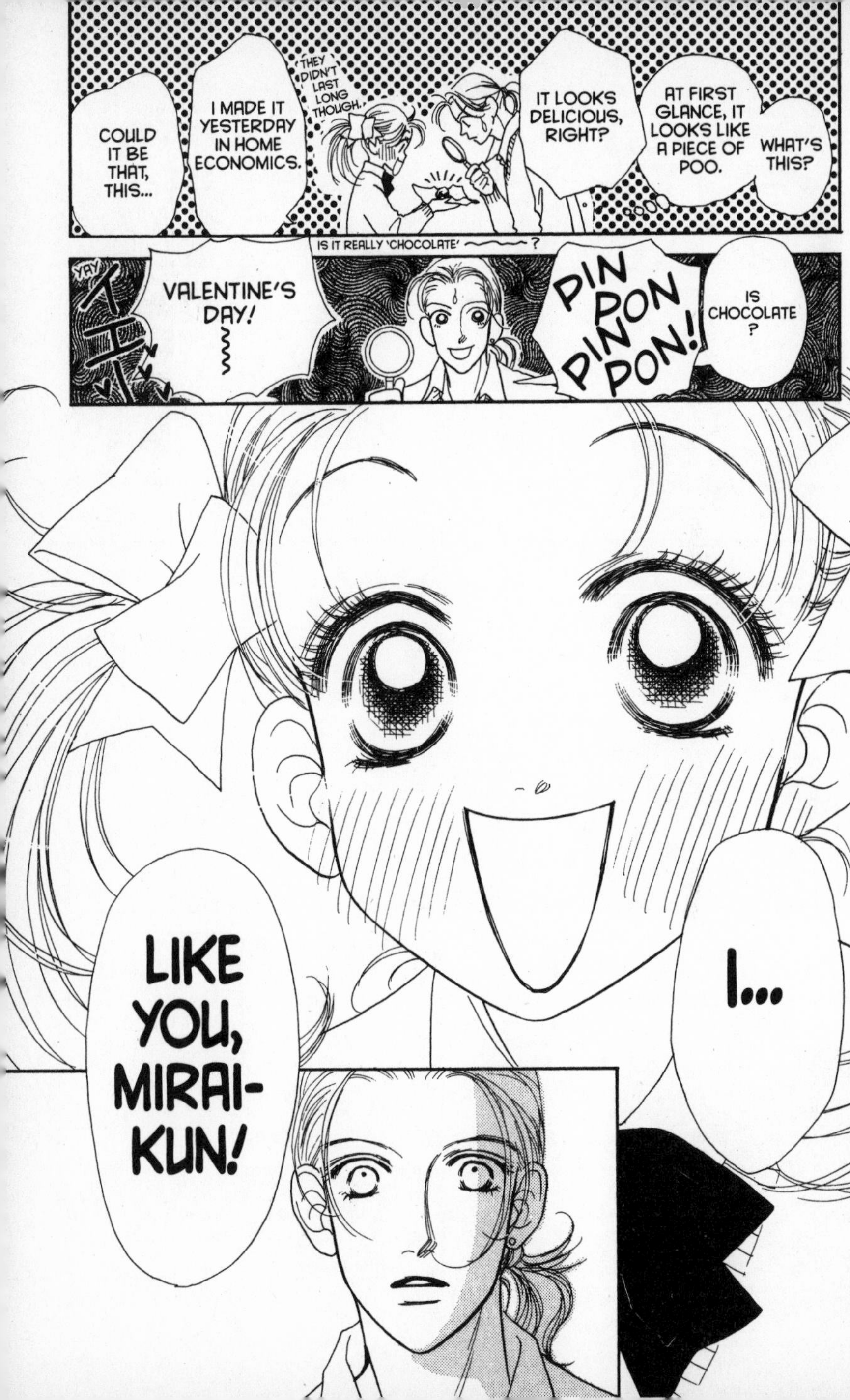

WHAT'S THIS?
AT FIRST GLANCE, IT LOOKS LIKE A PIECE OF POO.
IT LOOKS DELICIOUS, RIGHT?
THEY DIDN'T LAST LONG THOUGH.
I MADE IT YESTERDAY IN HOME ECONOMICS.
COULD IT BE THAT, THIS...
IS CHOCOLATE ?
PIN PON PIN PON!
IS IT REALLY 'CHOCOLATE' ~?
VALENTINE'S DAY!
YAY
I...
LIKE YOU, MIRAI-KUN!

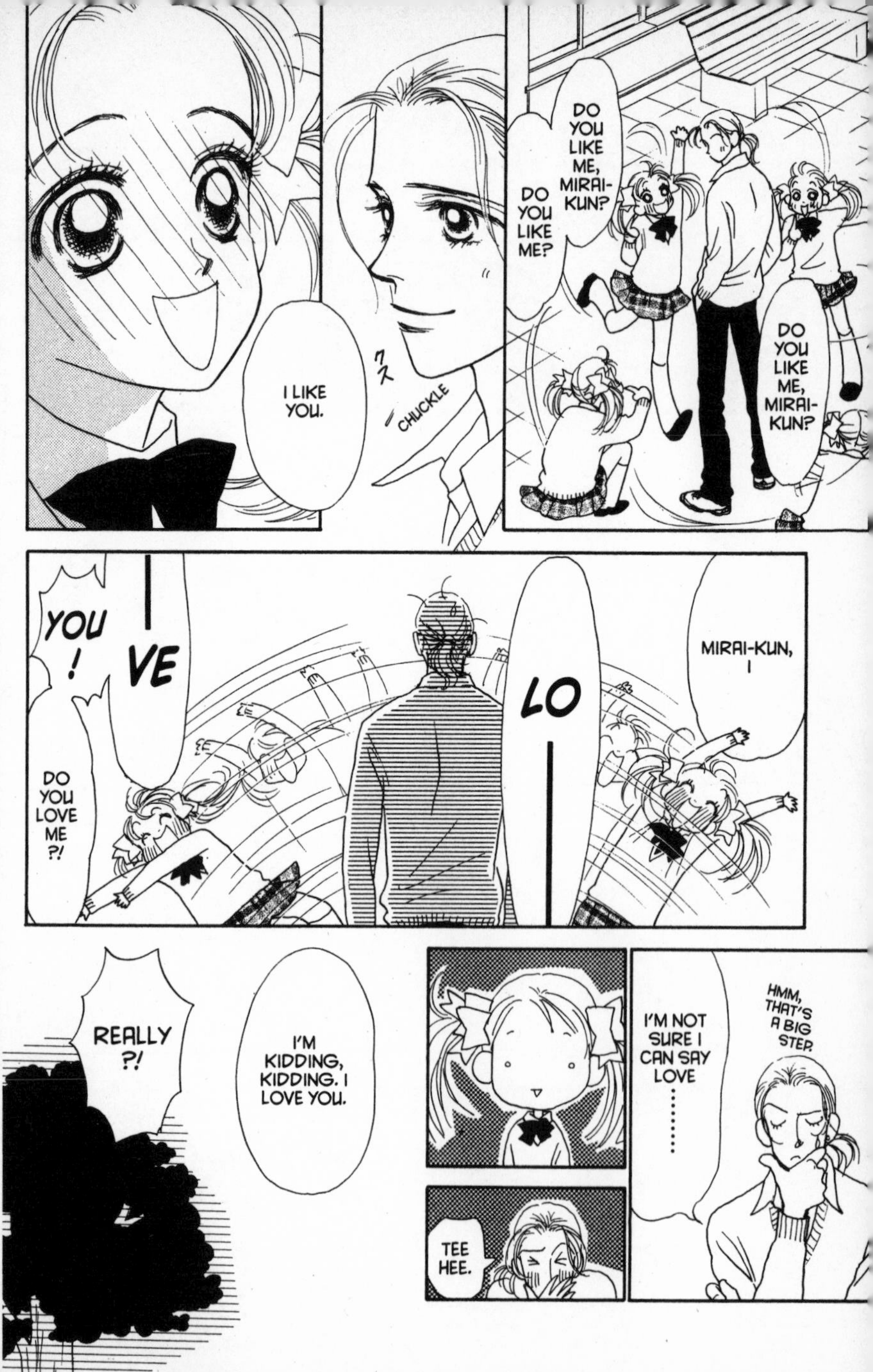
DO YOU LIKE ME, MIRAI-KUN?
DO YOU LIKE ME, MIRAI-KUN?
DO YOU LIKE ME?
クス
CHUCKLE
I LIKE YOU.
MIRAI-KUN, I
LO
VE
YOU!
DO YOU LOVE ME?!
HMM, THAT'S A BIG STEP.
I'M NOT SURE I CAN SAY LOVE ......
TEE HEE.
I'M KIDDING, KIDDING. I LOVE YOU.
REALLY?!

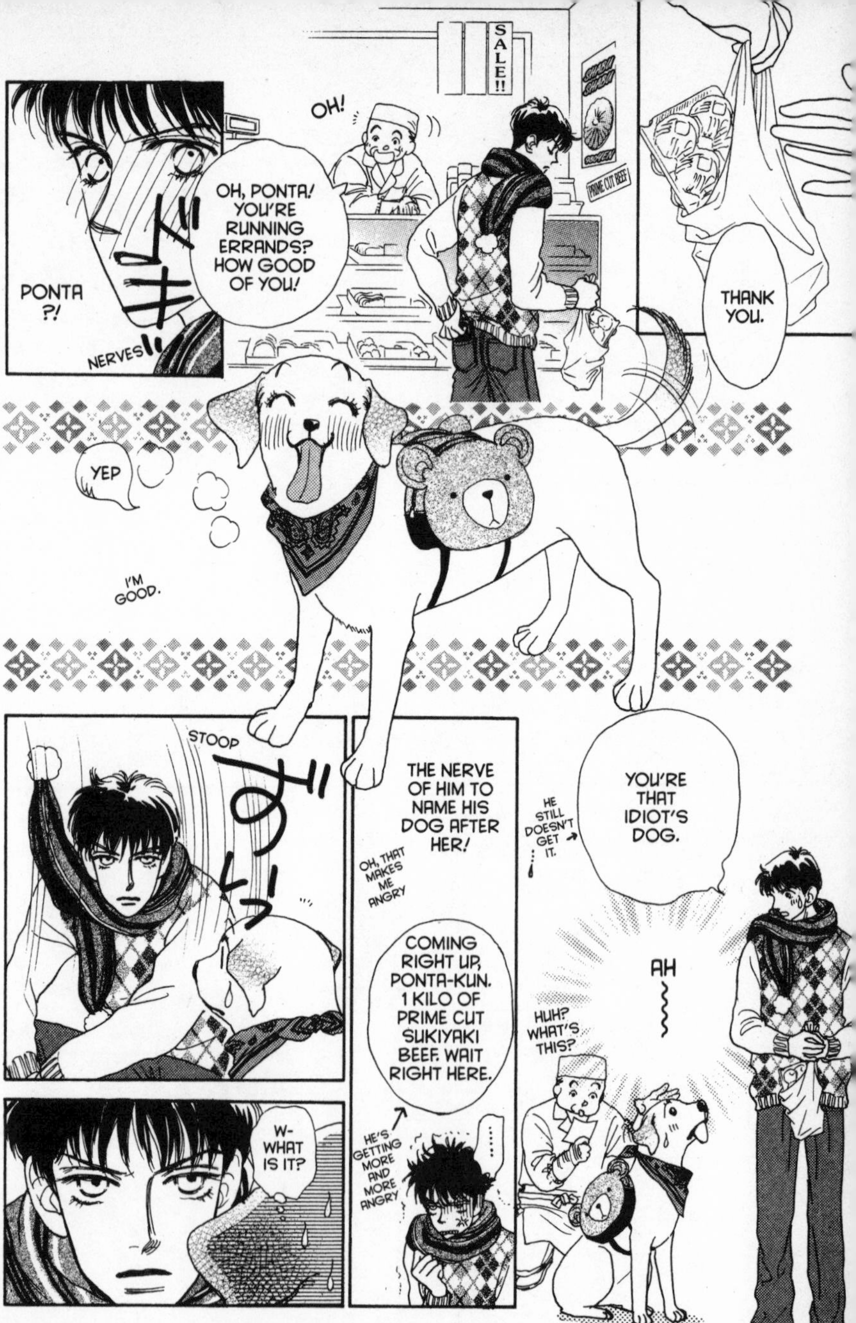
THANK YOU.
SALE!!
PRIME CUT BEEF
OH!
OH, PONTA! YOU'RE RUNNING ERRANDS? HOW GOOD OF YOU!
PONTA ?!
NERVES
YEP
I'M GOOD.
YOU'RE THAT IDIOT'S DOG.
HE STILL DOESN'T GET IT.
AH~
HUH? WHAT'S THIS?
COMING RIGHT UP, PONTA-KUN. 1 KILO OF PRIME CUT SUKIYAKI BEEF. WAIT RIGHT HERE.
HE'S GETTING MORE AND MORE ANGRY
......
THE NERVE OF HIM TO NAME HIS DOG AFTER HER!
OH, THAT MAKES ME ANGRY
STOOP
W-WHAT IS IT?

SMASH

ZOOM
ブオオッ

AH.

VROOM
ヴヴヴッ

THAT'S
OKAY.
I'M
FINE.

B-
BUT...

HERE'S
SOME
MONEY
FOR
THE
EGGS.

1000

DASHIMAKI
EGGS?

I WAS
PLANNING
ON MAKING
DASHIMAKI
EGGS
ANYWAY.

BREAK
THEM AND
BEAT
THEM.
YOU
SAVED
ME A LOT
OF WORK.

HE
DIDN'T
LAUGH.
HE
DIDN'T
WANT
MONEY.

WHAT A
STRANGE
GUY.

I'M
SORRY,
I'M
SORRY.

I JUST
STARTED
DRIVING.

EVER BEEN IN LOVE PONTA-KUN?

HAVE YOU

HE'S A SURPRISINGLY GOOD GUY.

IT'S QUITE A COINCIDENCE THAT WE'RE BOTH GOING HOME THE SAME WAY, HUH?

JUST LOITERING A LITTLE ALONG THE WAY.

SIGH

FIRST LOVE FOR ME, WHO DESPISES HUMANS...

SHE'S SO DIFFERENT FROM OTHER GIRLS. ANYWAY, I'M SURE IT'LL HAPPEN NATURALLY...

FIRST LOVE...

WHY...

THAT'S RIGHT.

SHE'S GOT CRYSTAL CLEAR EYES LIKE YOU.

PO...

THOSE EYES...

NOBODY LIKES TO BE HUGGED ALL OF A SUDDEN.

HUFF HUFF

WATER UNDER THE BRIDGE.

SORRY, SORRY.

I LOVE YOU!!

SPRING

PONTA-SAN!!

HE IS WEIRD.

HE'S NOT A BAD GUY BUT,

I'M SERIOUSLY ILL.

SIGH

I MADE THESE IN HOME ECONOMICS.

BUT IT DOES HAVE....

A GREAT SHAPE.

SHE CERTAINLY...

GAVE IT HER ALL MAKING IT.

CHUCKLE

IF SHE JUST DRESSED IT UP A LITTLE MORE...

SHUT UP! I CAN'T GET TO SLEEP!

IS THERE SOME MOUSE GOBLIN IN HERE?

TRAMP
TRAMP
TRAMP
TRAMP

TROMP
TROMP
TROMP
TROMP
TROMP

CLATTER
CLATTER

RUSTLE

SQUEAK SQUEAK

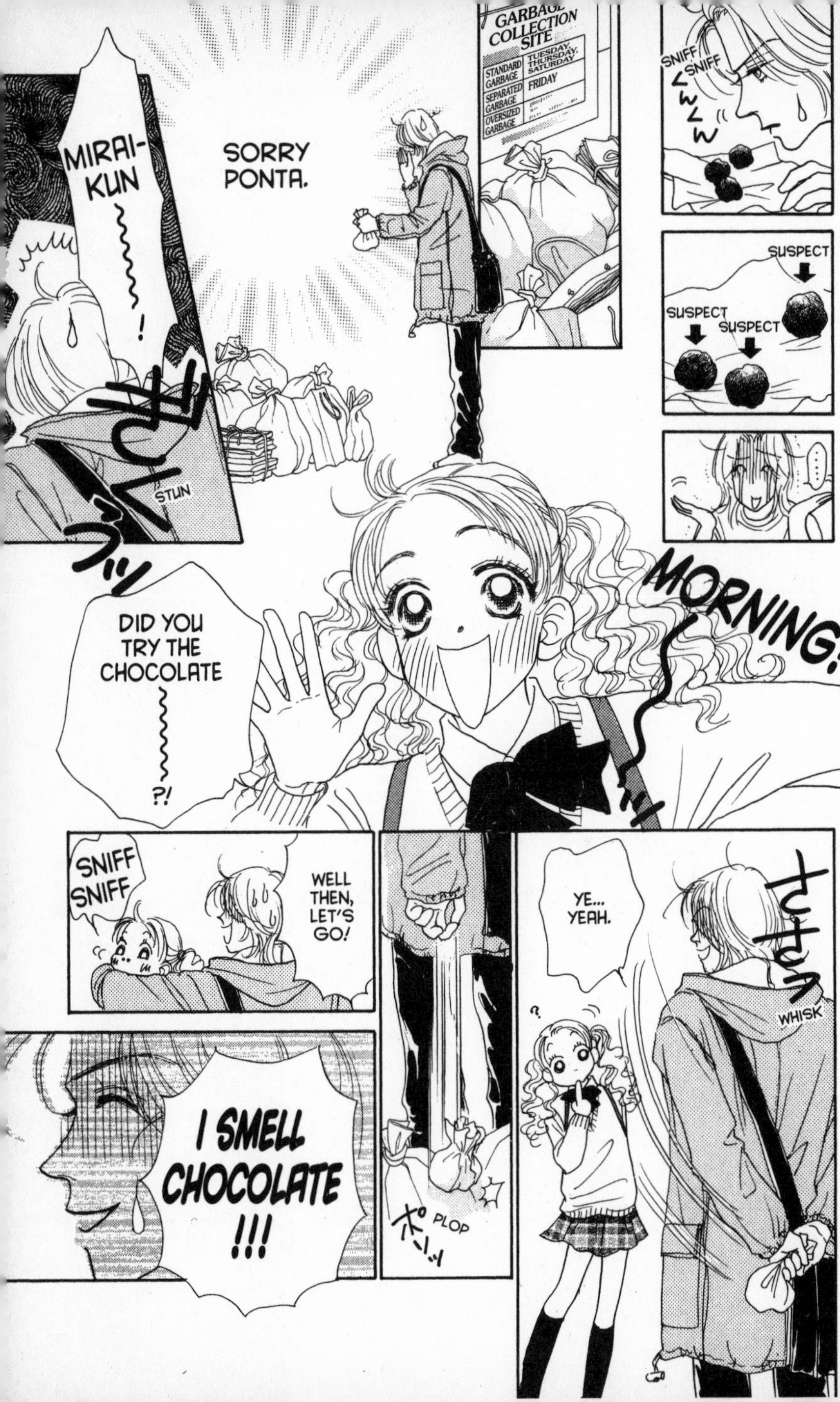
SNIFF SNIFF
SUSPECT
SUSPECT
SUSPECT
GARBAGE COLLECTION SITE
STANDARD GARBAGE TUESDAY, THURSDAY, SATURDAY
SEPARATED GARBAGE FRIDAY
OVERSIZED GARBAGE
SORRY PONTA.
MIRAI-KUN ~ !
STUN
MORNING!
DID YOU TRY THE CHOCOLATE ~ ?!
YE... YEAH.
WHISK
PLOP
WELL THEN, LET'S GO!
SNIFF SNIFF
I SMELL CHOCOLATE !!!

RUSTLE

RUSTLE

SORRY!!

WHAT'S THIS?!

I COULD'VE TOLD RIGHT AWAY IF I SMELLED THEM.

MOUSE POOP?!

しゅ～ん GLOOM

I COULDN'T TELL.

MY NOSE ISN'T AS GOOD AS YOURS.

I CAN'T TELL THEM APART NO MATTER HOW MUCH I TRY.

SHHHHH SHHHHH

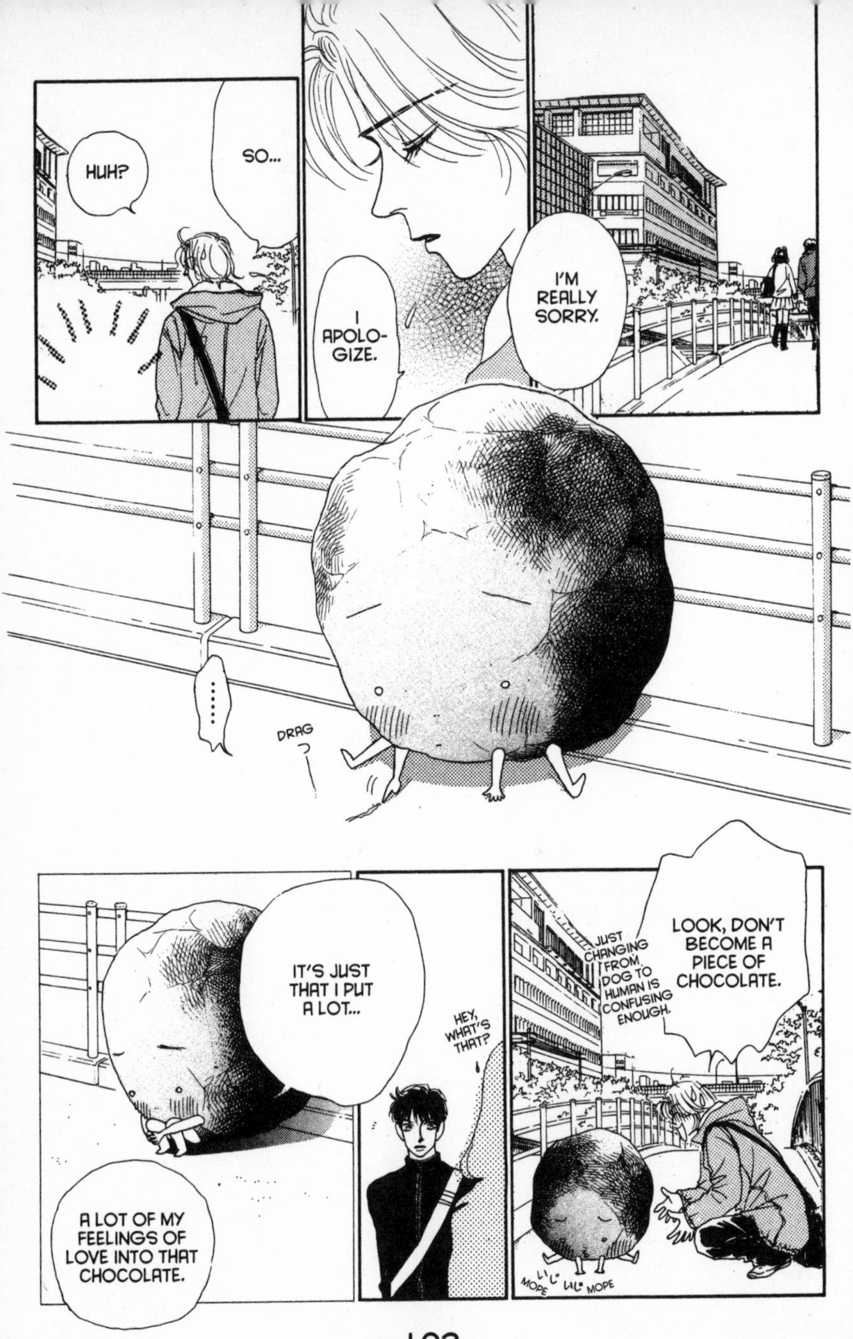
SO...
HUH?
I APOLOGIZE.
I'M REALLY SORRY.
......
DRAG
IT'S JUST THAT I PUT A LOT...
A LOT OF MY FEELINGS OF LOVE INTO THAT CHOCOLATE.
HEY, WHAT'S THAT?
LOOK, DON'T BECOME A PIECE OF CHOCOLATE.
JUST CHANGING FROM DOG TO HUMAN IS CONFUSING ENOUGH.
MOPE
MOPE

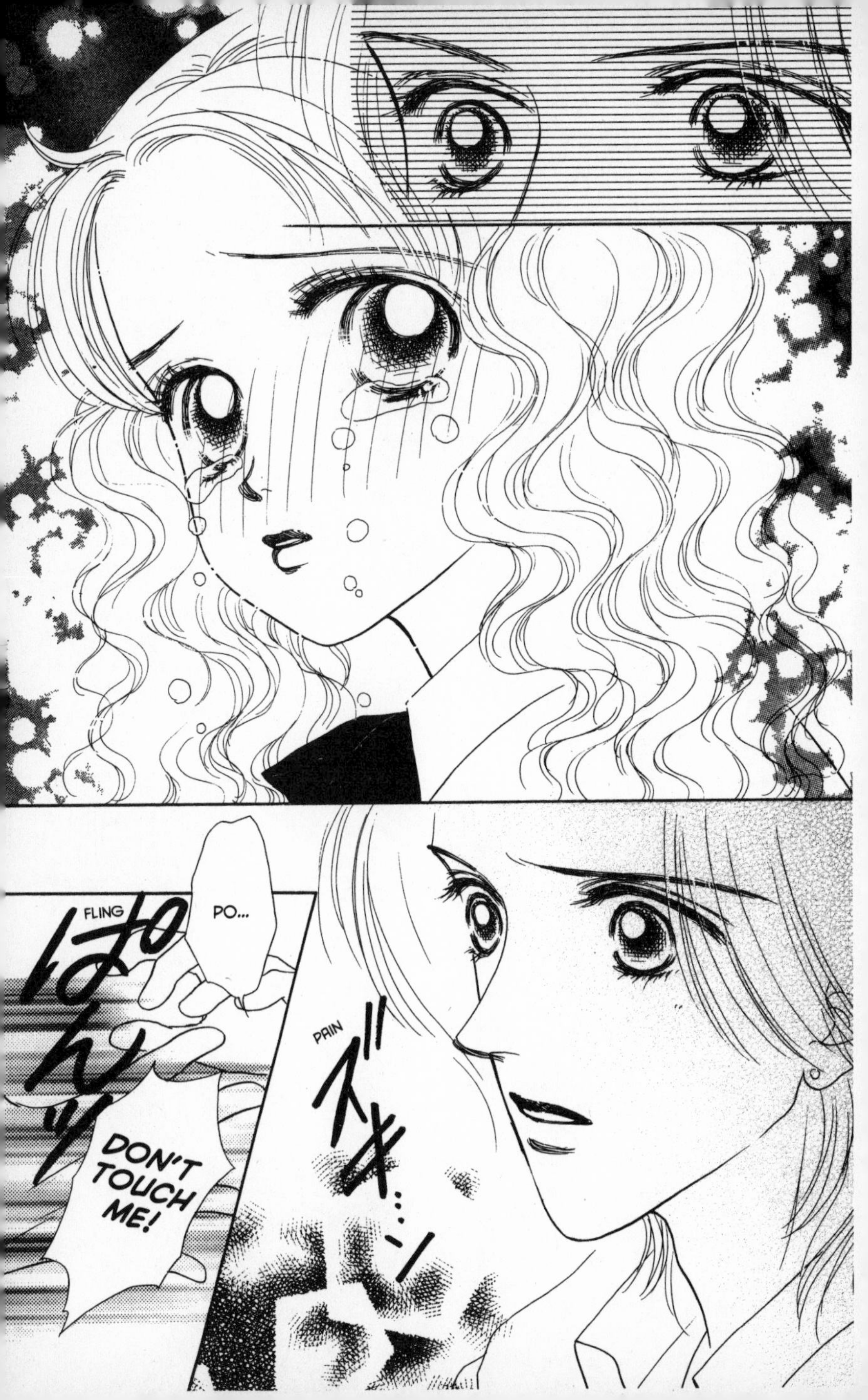

PO...
FLING
はんッ
DON'T TOUCH ME!
PAIN
ズキ…ン

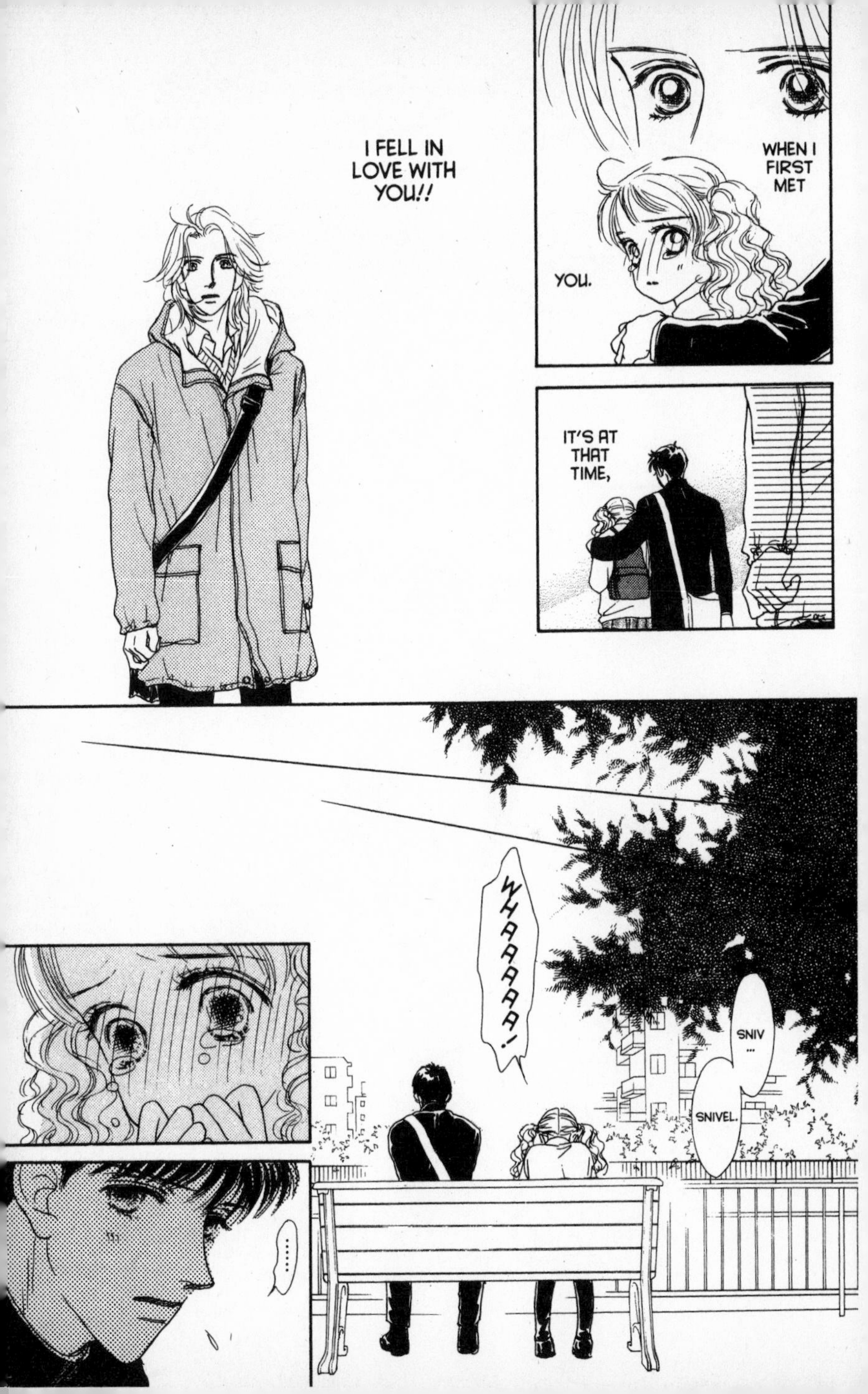
WHEN I FIRST MET
YOU.
I FELL IN LOVE WITH YOU!!
IT'S AT THAT TIME,
WHAAAAAA!
SNIV...
SNIVEL.
......

WHAAAA!

OH, RATS! THAT HAD THE OPPOSITE EFFECT!

NOT FOR THAT GUY.

THAT GUY... START

DON'T...

DON'T CRY ANYMORE.

IT'S ONLY BEEN A FEW DAYS SINCE I'VE MET HER BUT...

I'VE HAD MY EYE ON HER THE WHOLE TIME...

DURING THAT TIME,

ドキン
THUMP

ドキン
THUMP

IF IT WAS ME...

"CLENCH"

I WOULDN'T MAKE YOU CRY...

THERE'S NO WAY!

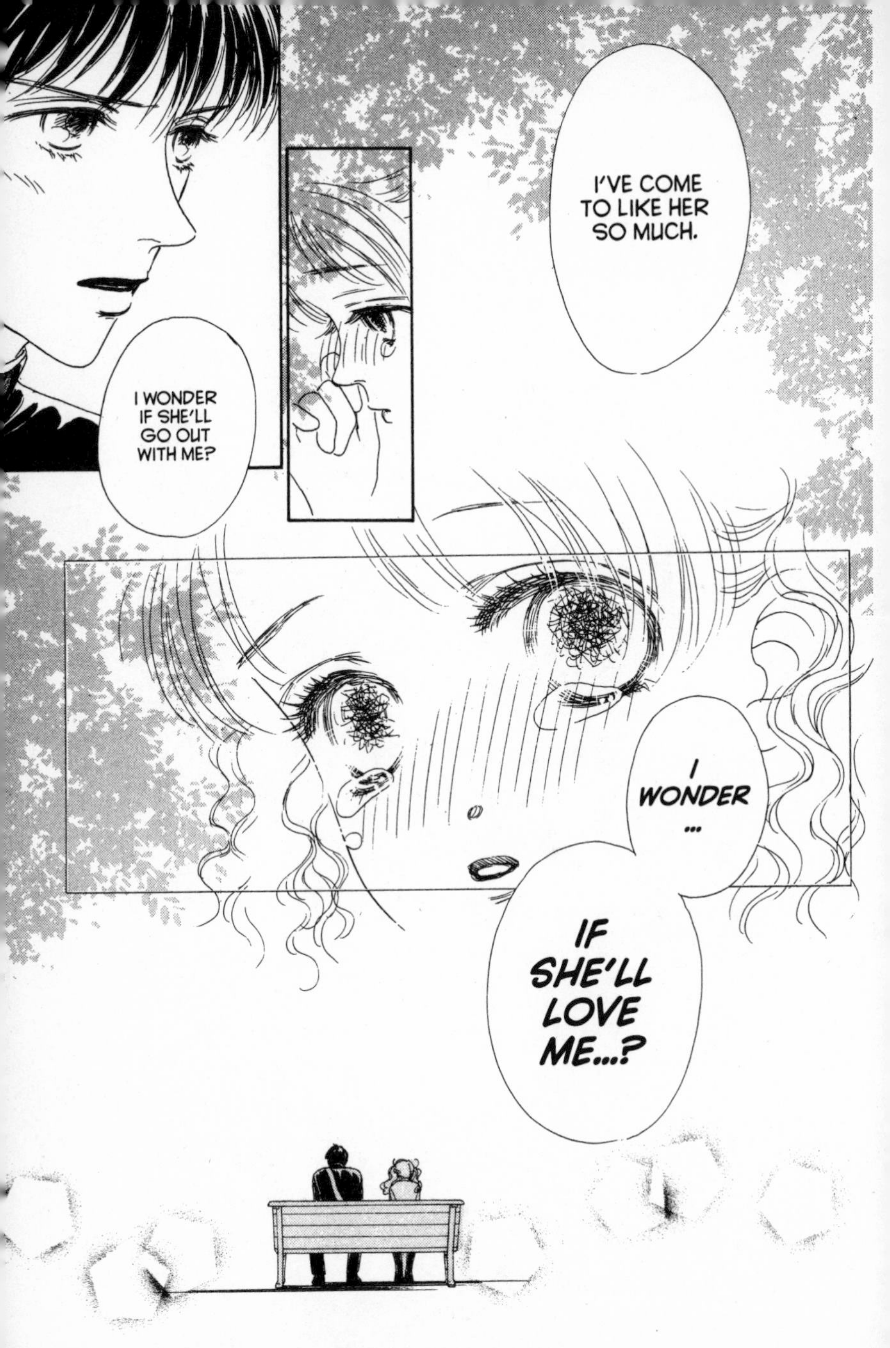
I'VE COME TO LIKE HER SO MUCH.
I WONDER IF SHE'LL GO OUT WITH ME?
I WONDER ...
IF SHE'LL LOVE ME...?

END OF CHAPTER 7

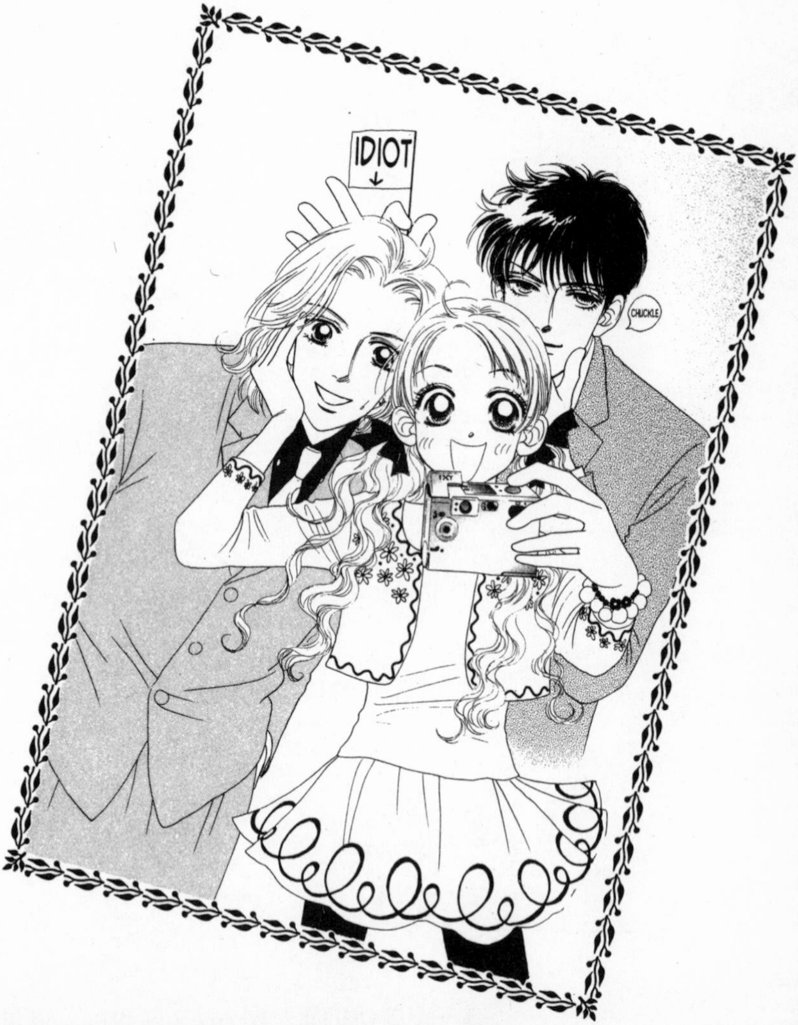
IDIOT
CHUCKLE

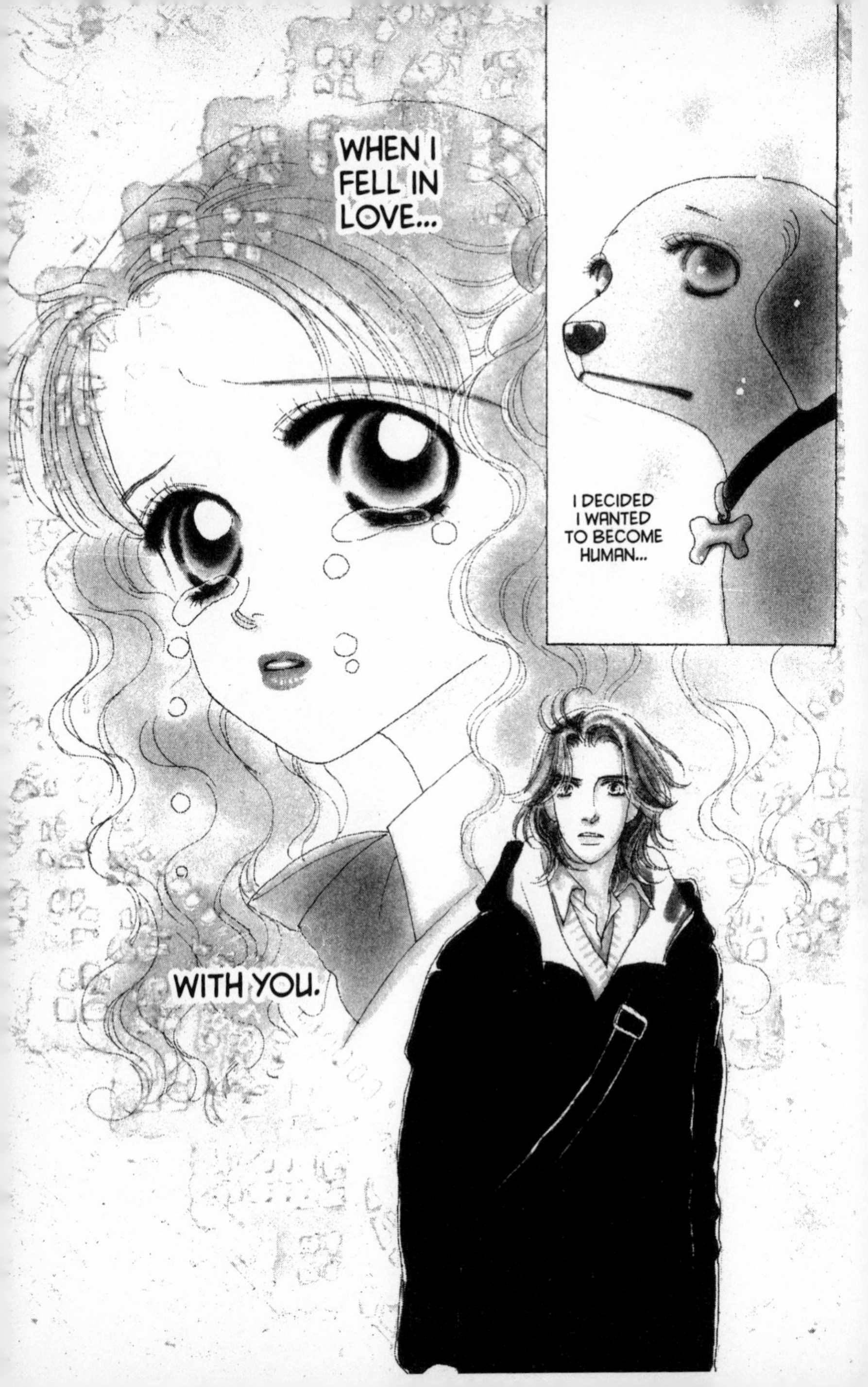
I DECIDED I WANTED TO BECOME HUMAN...
WHEN I FELL IN LOVE...
WITH YOU.

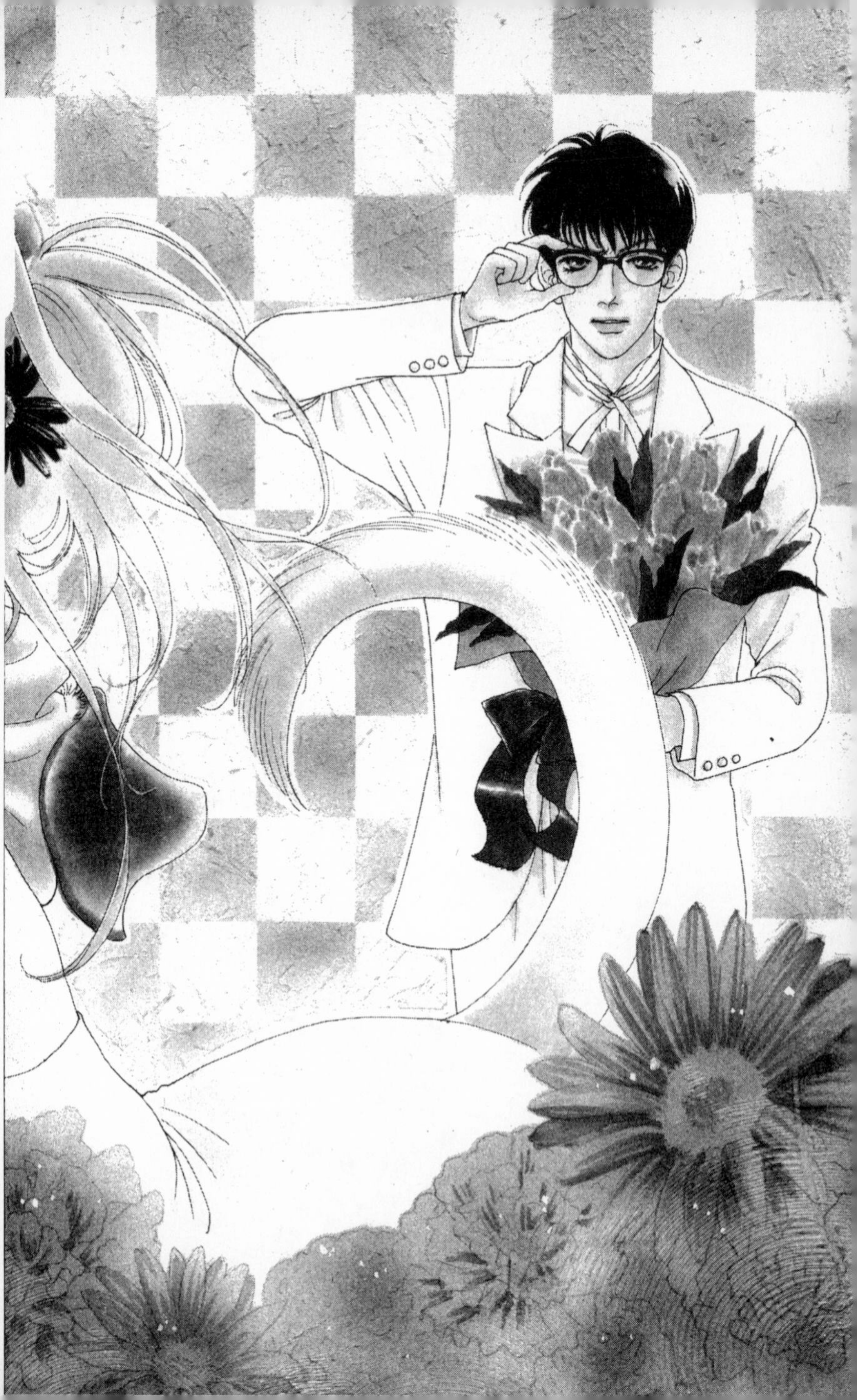

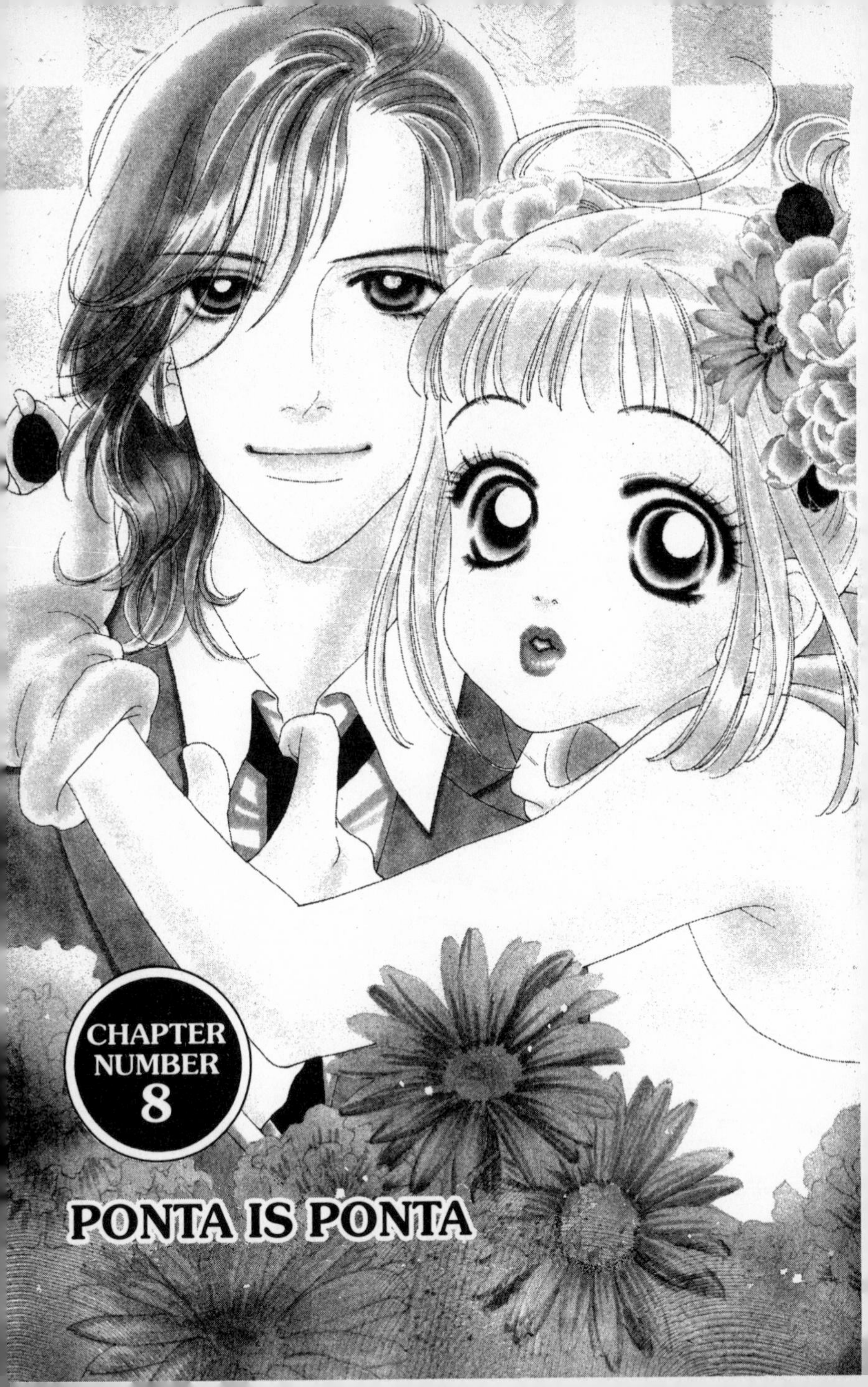
CHAPTER
NUMBER
8
PONTA IS PONTA

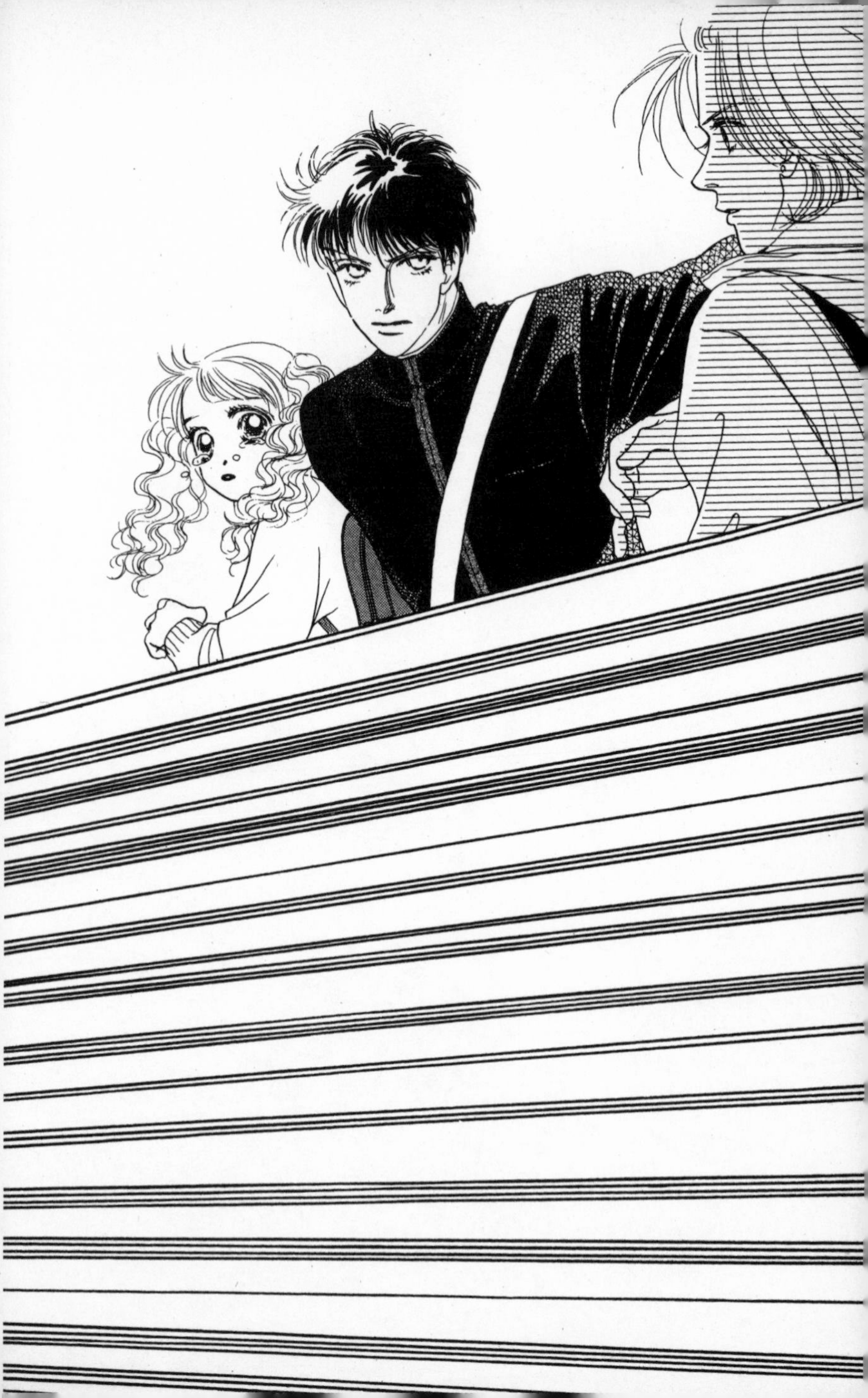

A HAT? BUT WHY?

TO HIDE YOUR BALD SPOT.

WELL... UH...

SO DON'T TAKE IT OFF, NO MATTER WHAT.

IT'S A CHARM TO HELP THINGS GO WELL WITH MIRAI-KUN.

WHOA!

WHY, YOU ASK? UM...

GOT IT! SEE YOU LATER!

SHE'S A DOG.

SCARY

I DON'T EXPECT HE KNOWS...

LIKES PONTA...?

I WONDER IF THAT GUY...

SOME-HOW...

I'VE...

CHEERFULLY, CHEERFULLY.

SKI-IP
すきーっ。ふ。

HOW CAN SHE BE SO CUTE!

SKI-IP
すきーっ。ふ。

GOT THE URGE TO SKIP TOO.

HOW...

HE'S GOT IT BAD

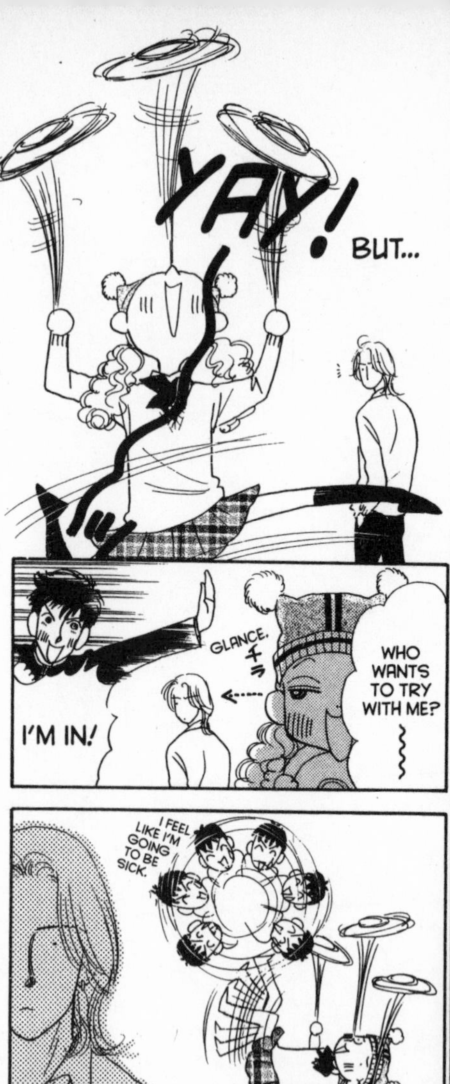
YAY!
BUT...
WHO WANTS TO TRY WITH ME?
GLANCE.
チラ
I'M IN!
I FEEL LIKE I'M GOING TO BE SICK.
OO AAH
オオ
SHE'S PRETTY CHEERFUL.

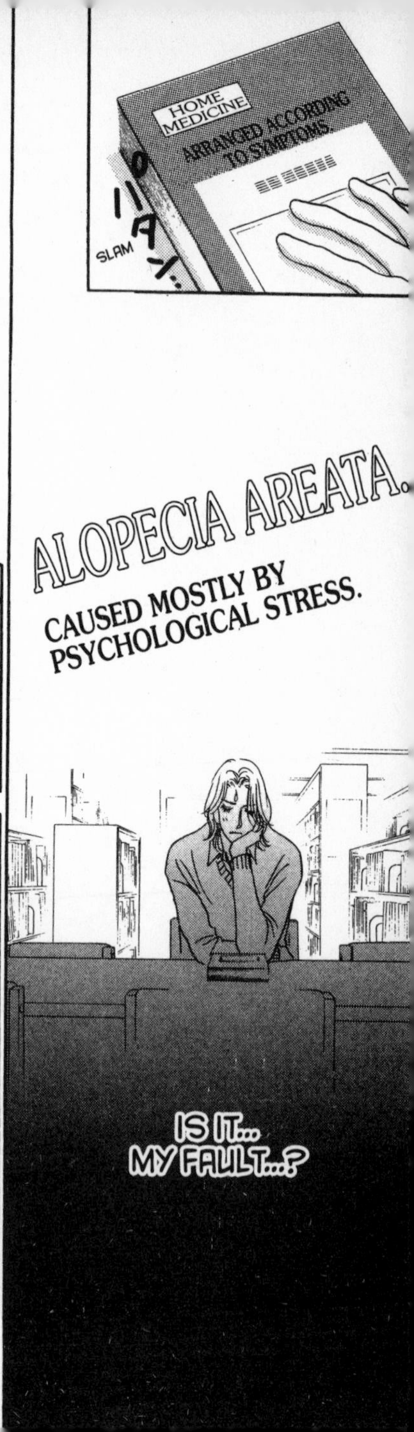
HOME MEDICINE
ARRANGED ACCORDING TO SYMPTOMS.
SLAM
ALOPECIA AREATA.
CAUSED MOSTLY BY PSYCHOLOGICAL STRESS.
IS IT... MY FAULT...?

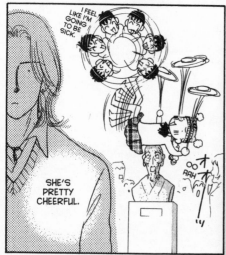

I'M JUST TOO CHEERFUL.

AM I A FOOL...

FOR WORRYING ...?

SHE'S CHEERFUL AS ALL GET OUT BUT...

PONTA-SAN.

...

SOMEHOW...

SOMEHOW IT SEEMS LIKE I'M

MORE DISTANT FROM MIRAI-KUN THAN BEFORE.

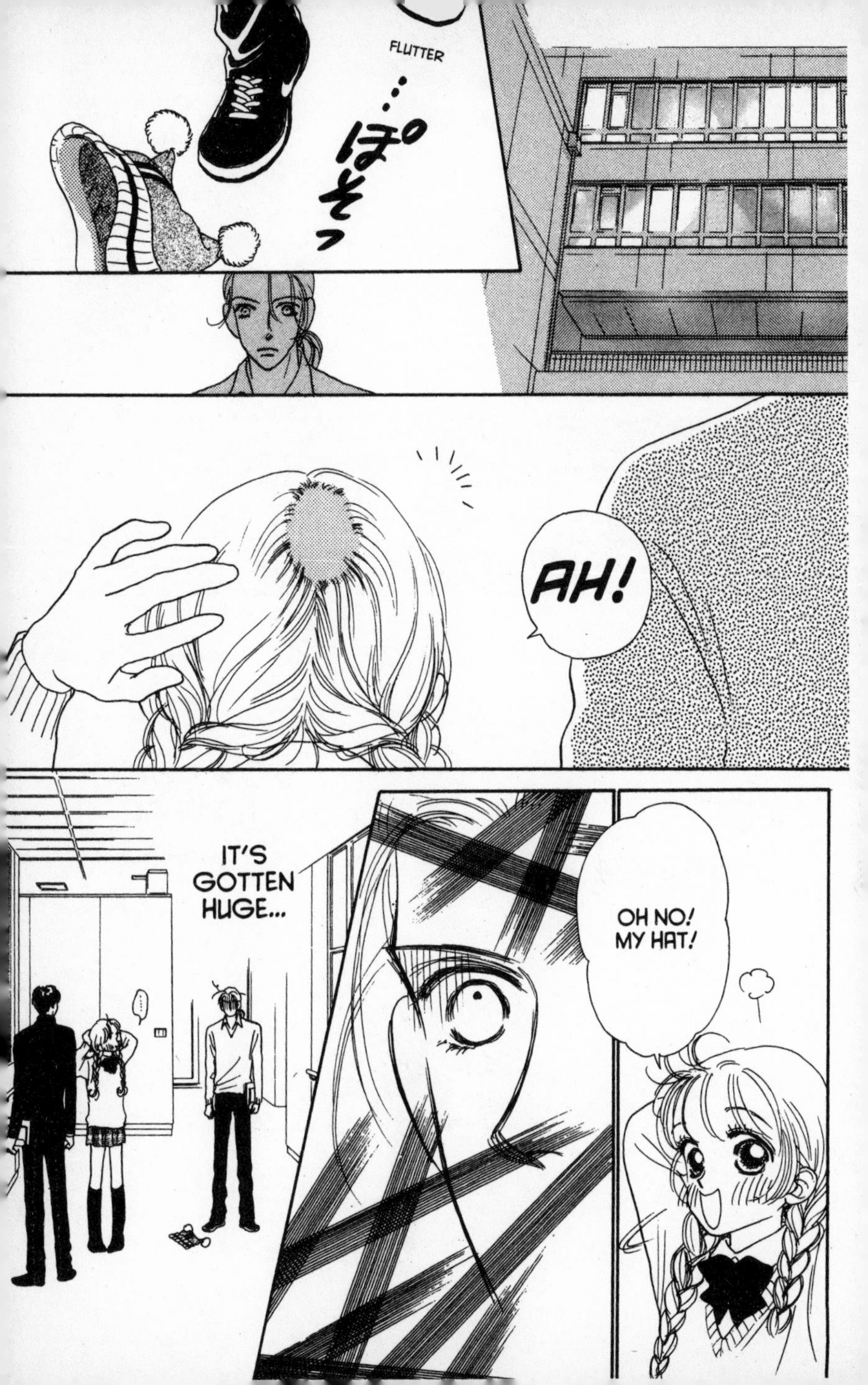
FLUTTER
…ぽそっ
AH!
OH NO! MY HAT!
IT'S GOTTEN HUGE...

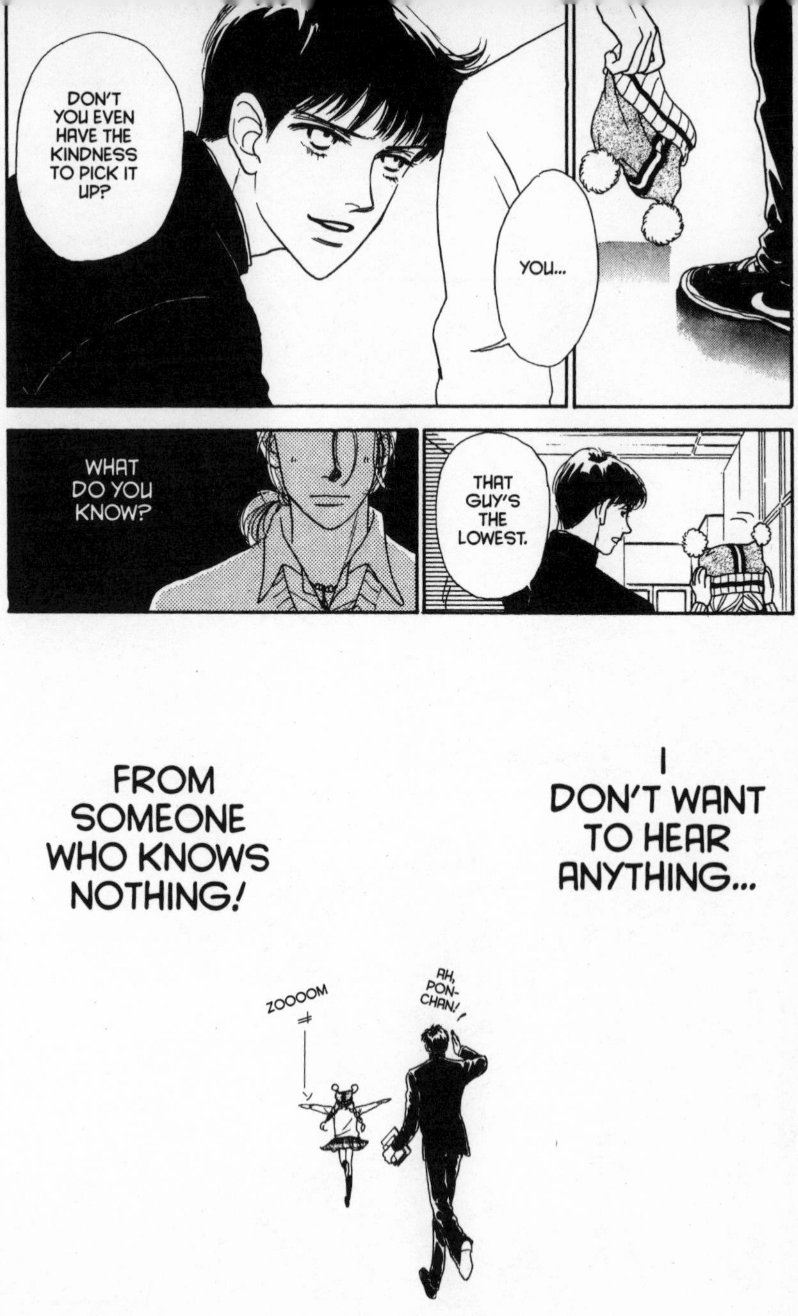

YOU...
DON'T YOU EVEN HAVE THE KINDNESS TO PICK IT UP?
THAT GUY'S THE LOWEST.
WHAT DO YOU KNOW?
I DON'T WANT TO HEAR ANYTHING...
FROM SOMEONE WHO KNOWS NOTHING!
AH, PON-CHAN!
ZOOOOM

IKEZAWA
MC

THANK YOU FOR READING VOLUME 2!
WELL THEN, HOW ARE EVERYBODY'S DOGS? BOTH OF MINE ARE WELL. THE OTHER DAY, SOMEONE SAID ONE WAS TOO FAT (40 KG) SO I PUT HIM ON A DIET. HE'S DOWN TO 37 KG NOW BUT THAT'S STILL HUGE (HA HA). RAISING THE TWO OF THEM AT THE SAME TIME HAS MADE ME REALIZE MORE AND MORE THAT DOGS HAVE THEIR OWN PERSONALITY AND CHARACTER. PONTA HAS A "FIRST SON" PERSONALITY AND HE HAS STRONG SELF-CONTROL AND A PRIZE TEMPERAMENT. HE LIKES TO PLAY WITH OTHER DOGS. HE GETS EXCITED WHEN HE SEES A CAT AND DASHES OFF. HE LOOKS LIKE A BIG IDIOT WHEN HE SLEEPS AND WHEN I ENTER THE ROOM, HE BARKS AS IF TO SAY, 'WHO GOES THERE?' IT'S A LITTLE AGGRAVATING. ← SCAREDY CAT. ON THE OTHER HAND, GUTS IS LIKE THE SECOND SON AND HAS THE TEMPERAMENT OF THE BABY OF THE FAMILY. LIKE A SPOILED CHILD HE'LL IMMEDIATELY WHINE LIKE, 'LET ME OUT!' OR 'FEED ME!'. HIS 'PET ME!' ATTACK IS ALSO FIERCE. HE LIKES PLAYING WITH OTHER OWNERS MORE THAN OTHER DOGS. HE'S GOT A LOT OF MOXY SO HE DOESN'T GET PARTICULARLY WORKED UP WHEN HE COMES ACROSS OTHER DOGS OR CATS. HE DOESN'T SNORE BUT, ON TOP OF MAKING LOUD NOISES WHEN HE BREATHES, THAT BREATH STINKS (PEE YOO!)

I ALMOST FORGOT, BUT HIS SNORING IS SOMETHING TO BEHOLD!

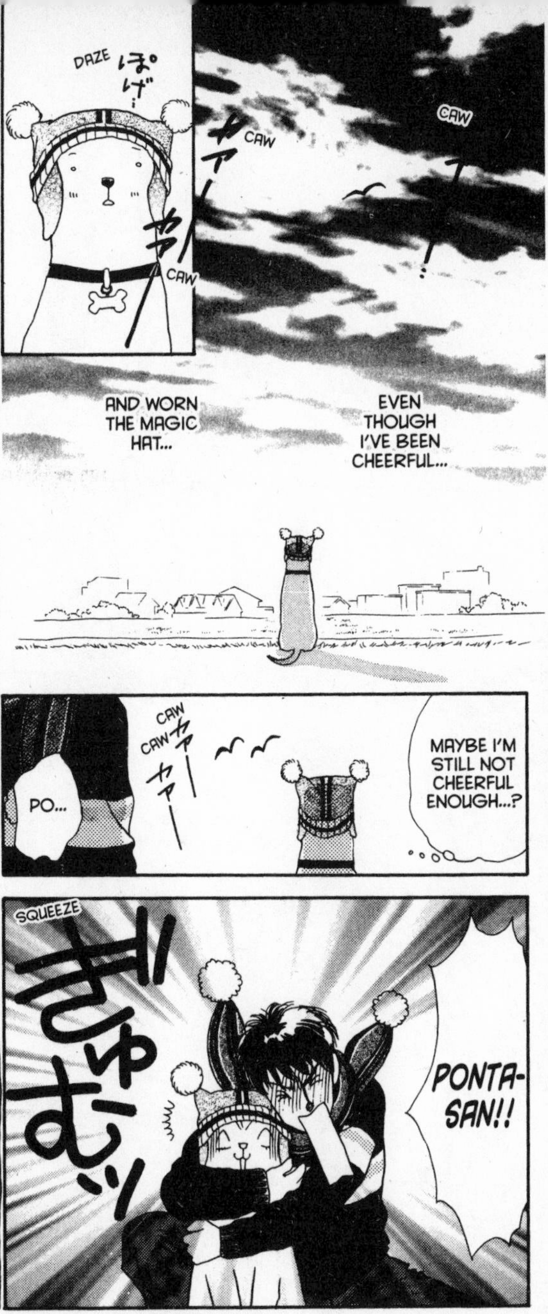
CAW
CAW
DAZE
CAW
EVEN THOUGH I'VE BEEN CHEERFUL...
AND WORN THE MAGIC HAT...
MAYBE I'M STILL NOT CHEERFUL ENOUGH...?
CAW
CAW
PO...
PONTA-SAN!!
SQUEEZE

LET ME KNOW WHAT YOUR DOG'S PERSONALITY IS LIKE, EVERYONE! SEE YOU!!

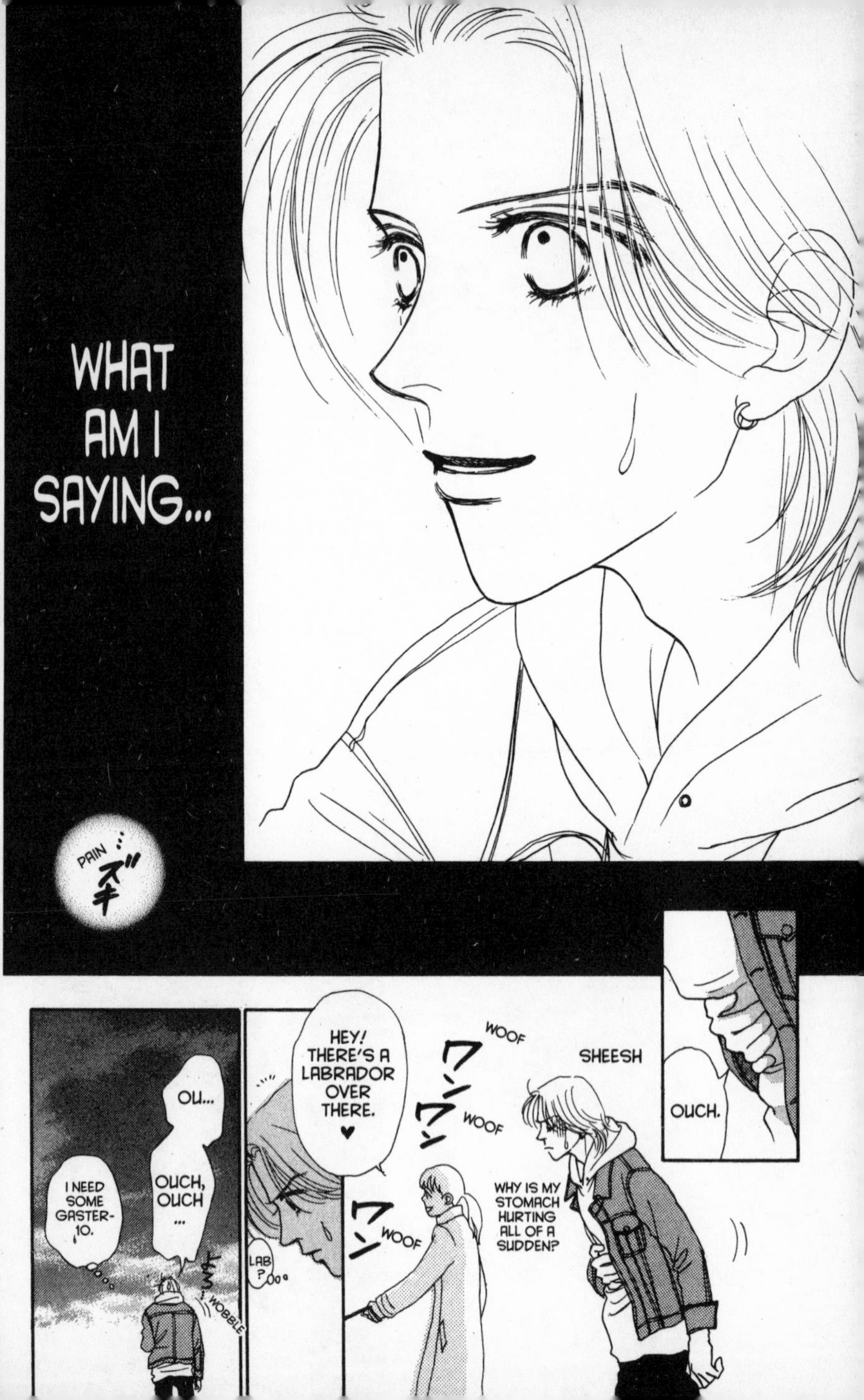

WHAT AM I SAYING...
PAIN
ズキ
OUCH.
SHEESH
WHY IS MY STOMACH HURTING ALL OF A SUDDEN?
WOOF
ワン
WOOF
ワン
WOOF
ワン
HEY! THERE'S A LABRADOR OVER THERE. ♥
LAB?
OU...
OUCH, OUCH ...
I NEED SOME GASTER-10.
WOBBLE

UH, NO, THAT WOULD BE BLOWING IT OUT OF PROPORTION.

I THOUGHT IT'D BE NICE TO TAKE A SIDE TRIP ON THE WAY HOME OCCASIONALLY.

DATE ?

...

OKAY, THEN IT'S DECIDED !

NOTHING IN PARTICULAR.

GLANCE

IF YOU DIDN'T HAVE OTHER PLANS...

...MIRAI-KUN...

THAT'S MIRAI-KUN'S SCENT!!

PONTA-SAN, LET'S GET ONE!

TWITCH TWITCH

HEY! THERE'S A SWEET SMELL IN THE AIR!!

CREPES

CREPES

AND THERE IT IS, A CREPE STAND!!

SNIFF SNIFF

WHIRL

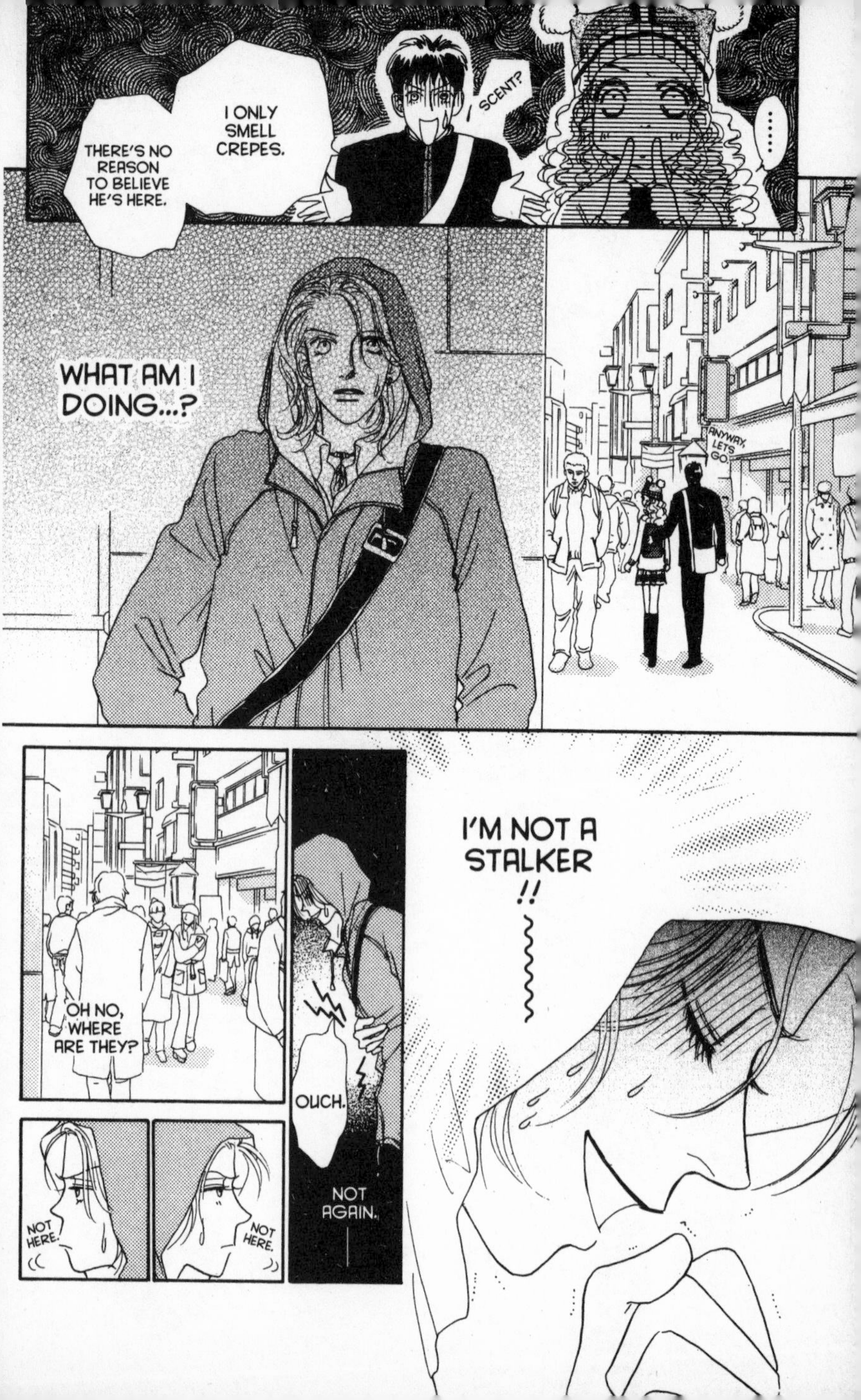
......
SCENT?
I ONLY SMELL CREPES.
THERE'S NO REASON TO BELIEVE HE'S HERE.
ANYWAY, LETS GO.
WHAT AM I DOING...?
I'M NOT A STALKER !!
OUCH.
NOT AGAIN.
OH NO, WHERE ARE THEY?
NOT HERE.
NOT HERE.

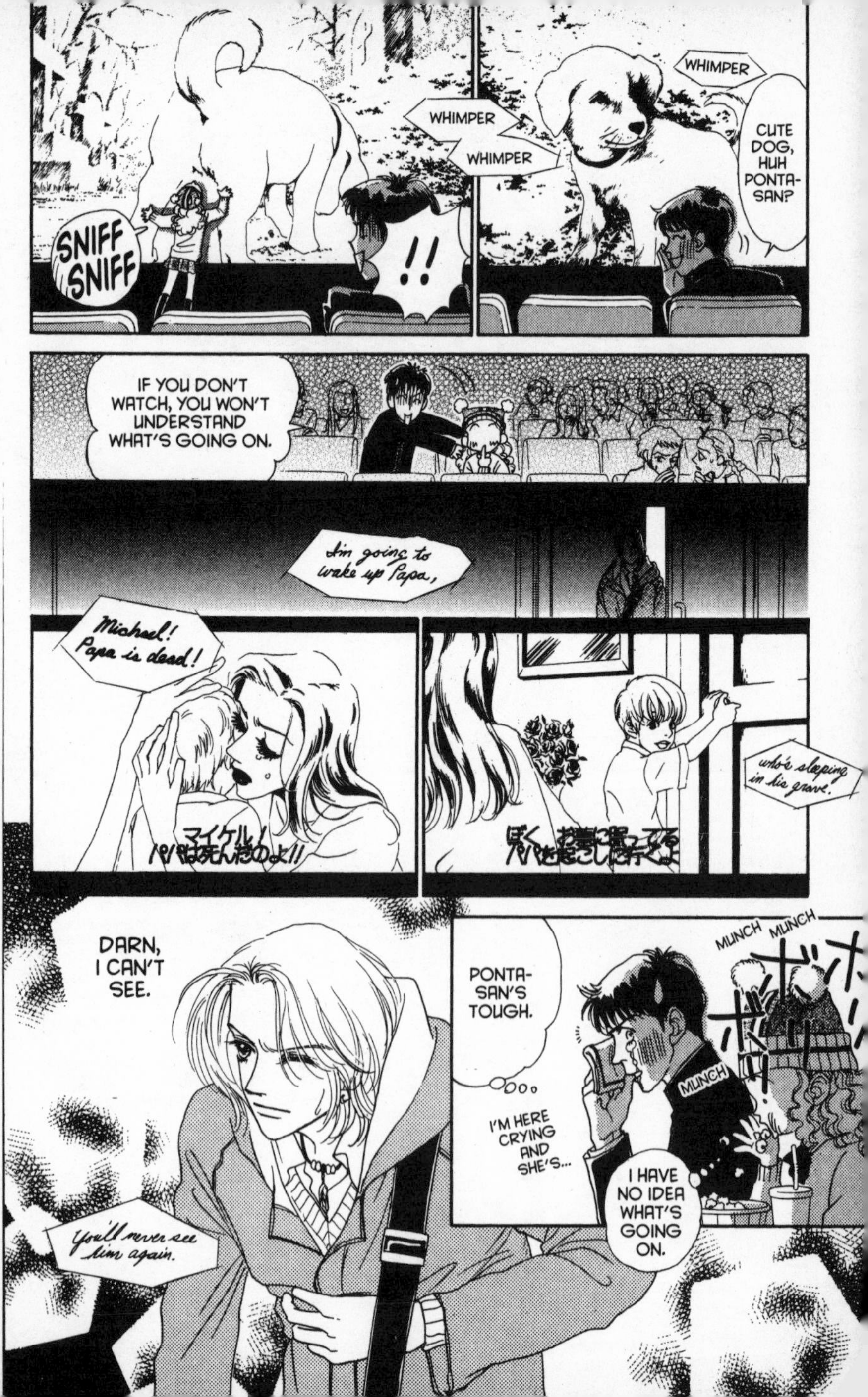

SNIFF SNIFF
WHIMPER
WHIMPER
!!
WHIMPER
CUTE DOG, HUH PONTA-SAN?
IF YOU DON'T WATCH, YOU WON'T UNDERSTAND WHAT'S GOING ON.
I'm going to wake up Papa,
Michael! Papa is dead!
マイケル！パパは死んだのよ!!
who's sleeping in his grave.
DARN, I CAN'T SEE.
You'll never see him again.
PONTA-SAN'S TOUGH.
I'M HERE CRYING AND SHE'S...
MUNCH MUNCH
MUNCH
I HAVE NO IDEA WHAT'S GOING ON.

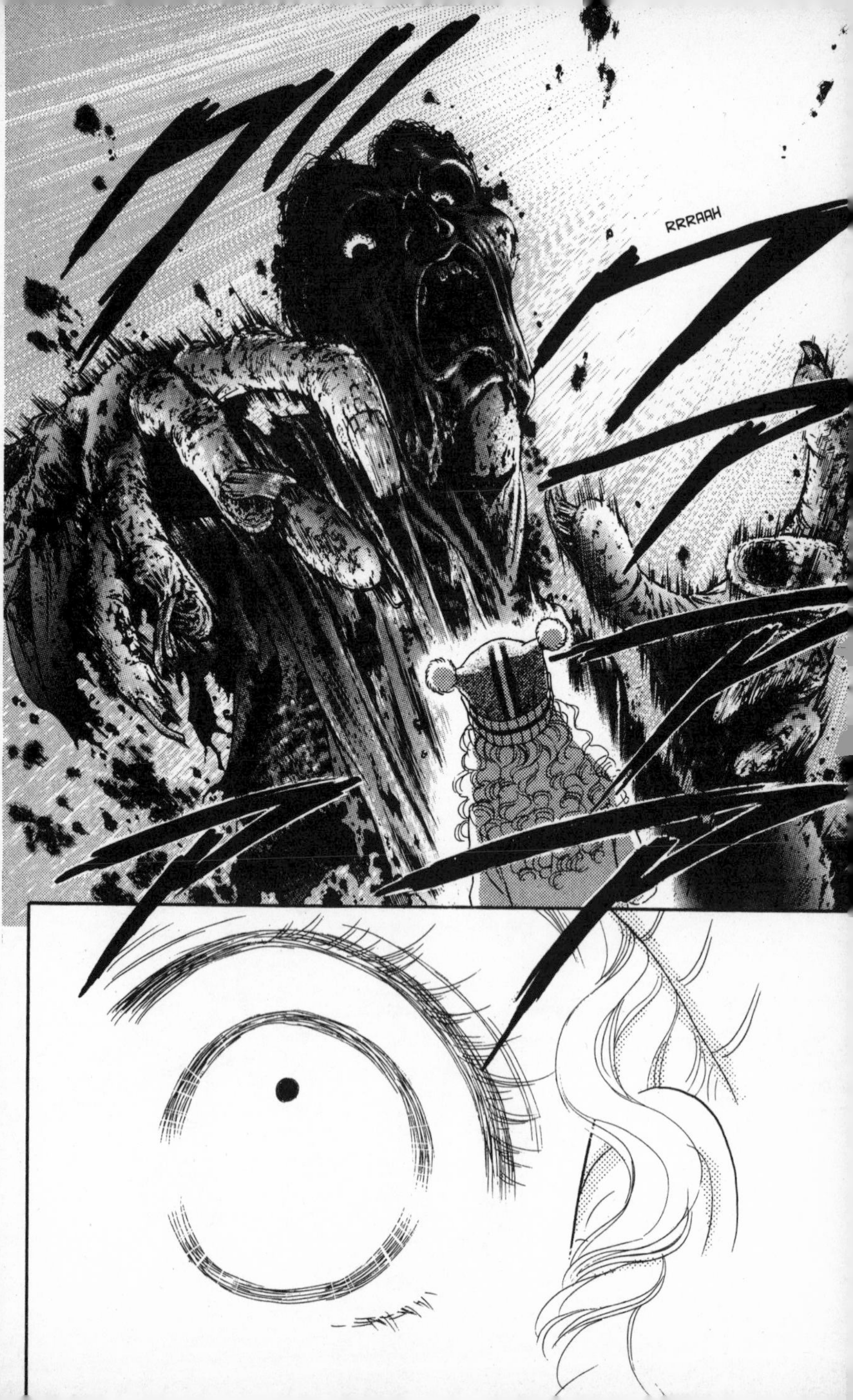
RRRAAH

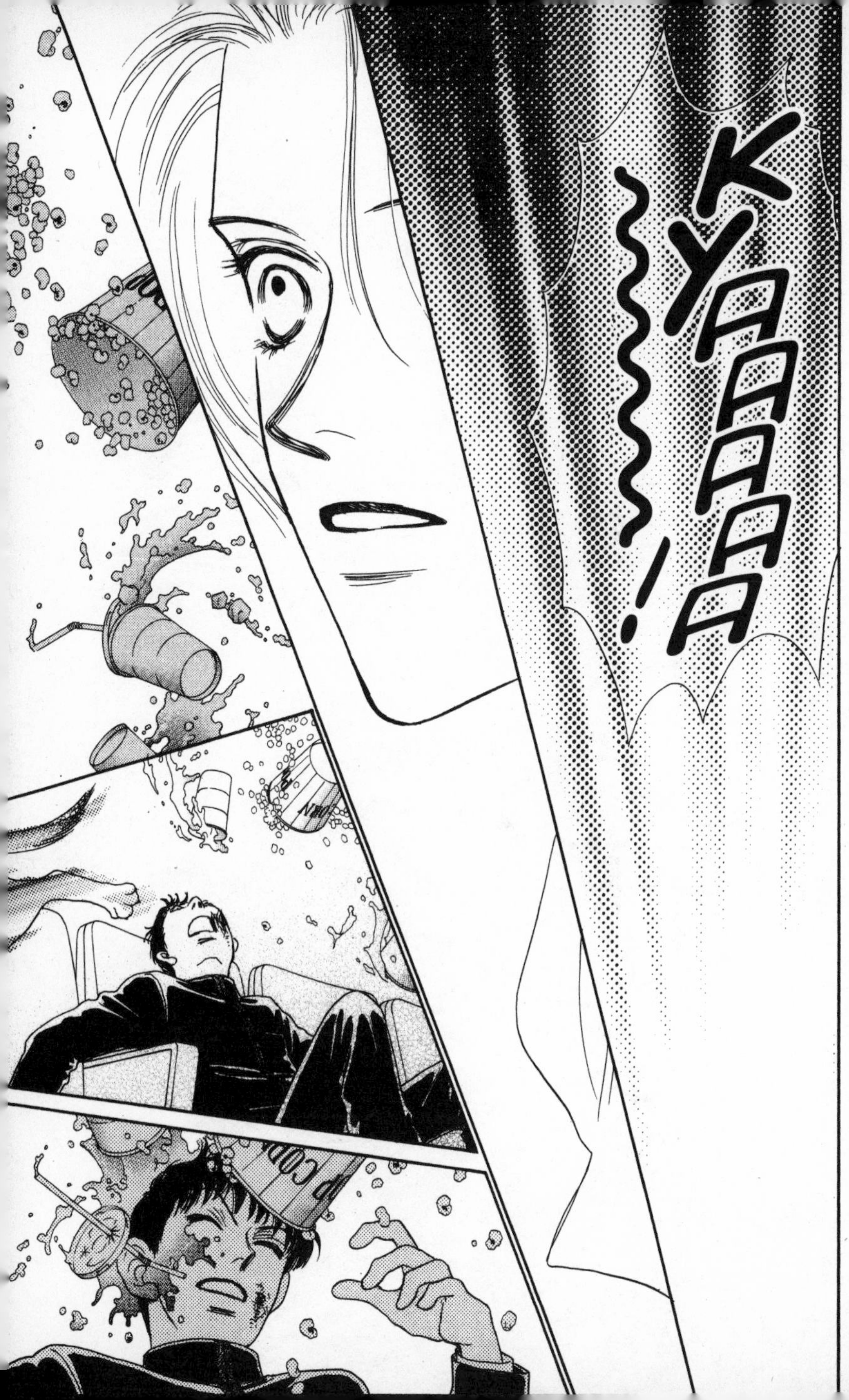
KYAAAAAA~~~!!

SOMEONE STEPPED ON MY FOOT.

OUCH!

WHAH

WHAT WAS THAT?

KYA

PO-

PONTA-SAN?!

KYAA!

WHSSSH

ZOMBIES ARE FINE BUT NOT DOGS!

KYA

HELP!

WHRAH

RUN!

A D...

DOG...

A DOG! THERE'S A DOG IN HERE!

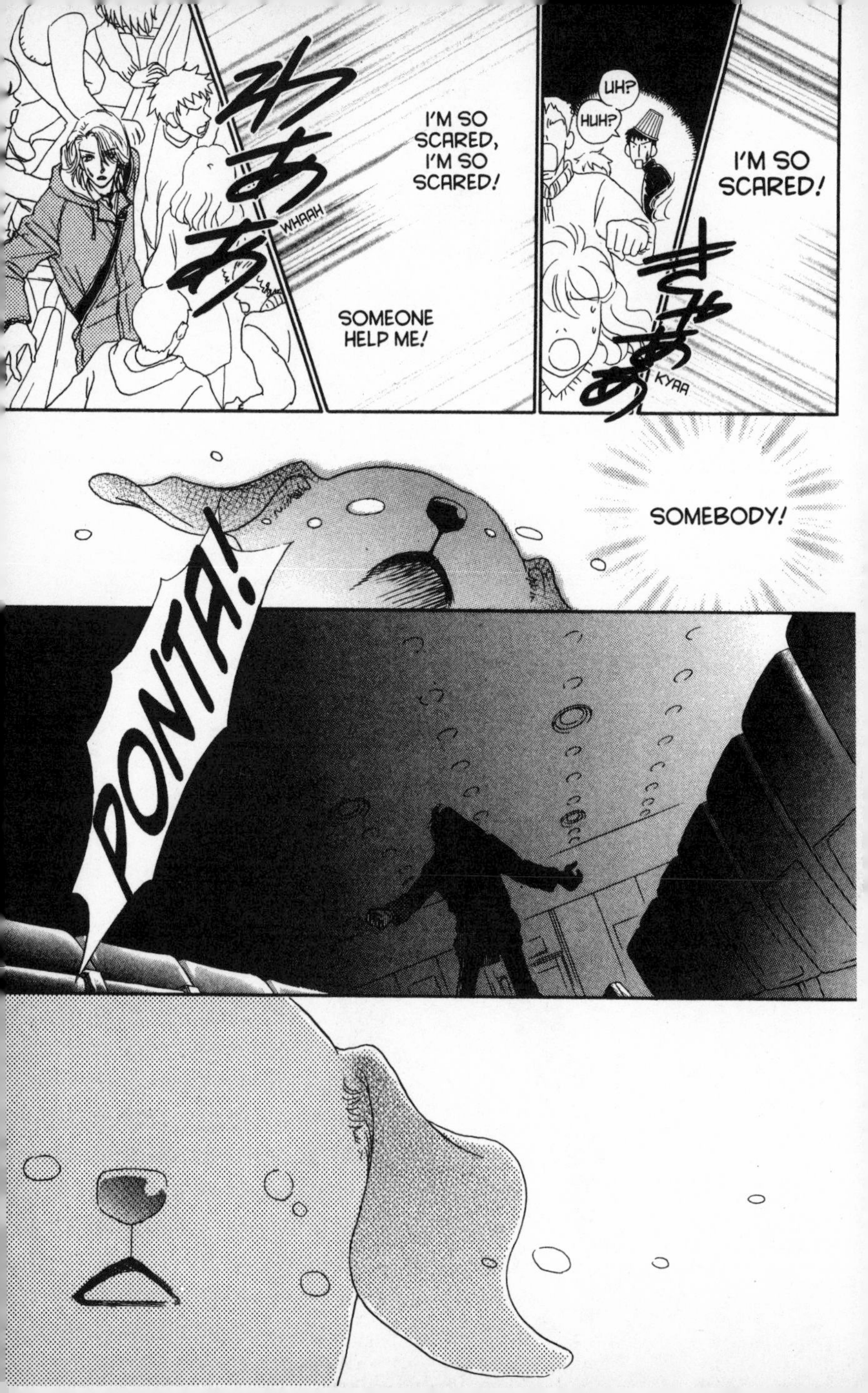

UH?
HUH?
I'M SO SCARED!
きゃああ
KYAA
I'M SO SCARED, I'M SO SCARED!
わああ
WHAAH
SOMEONE HELP ME!
SOMEBODY!
PONTA!

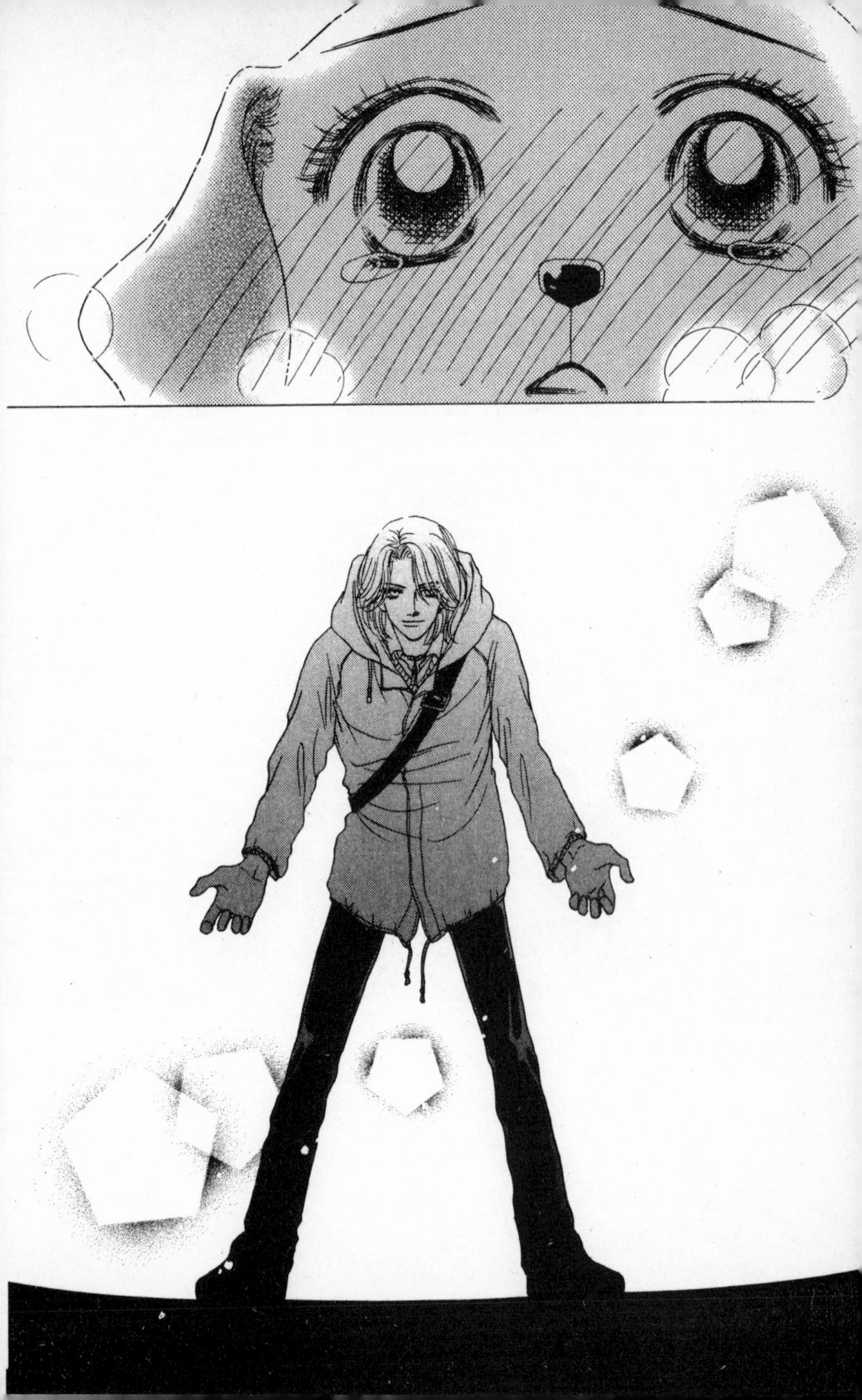

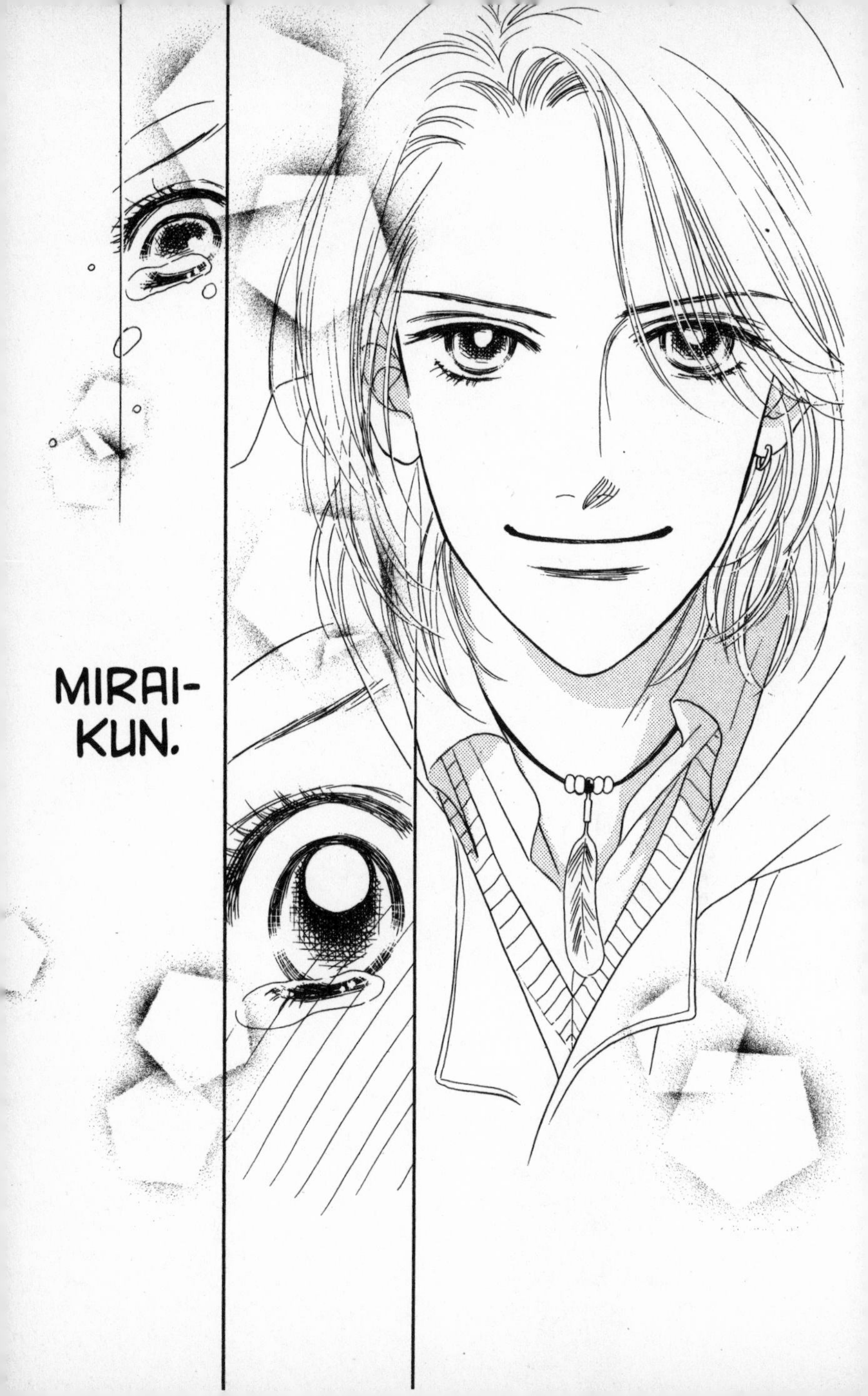
MIRAI-
KUN.

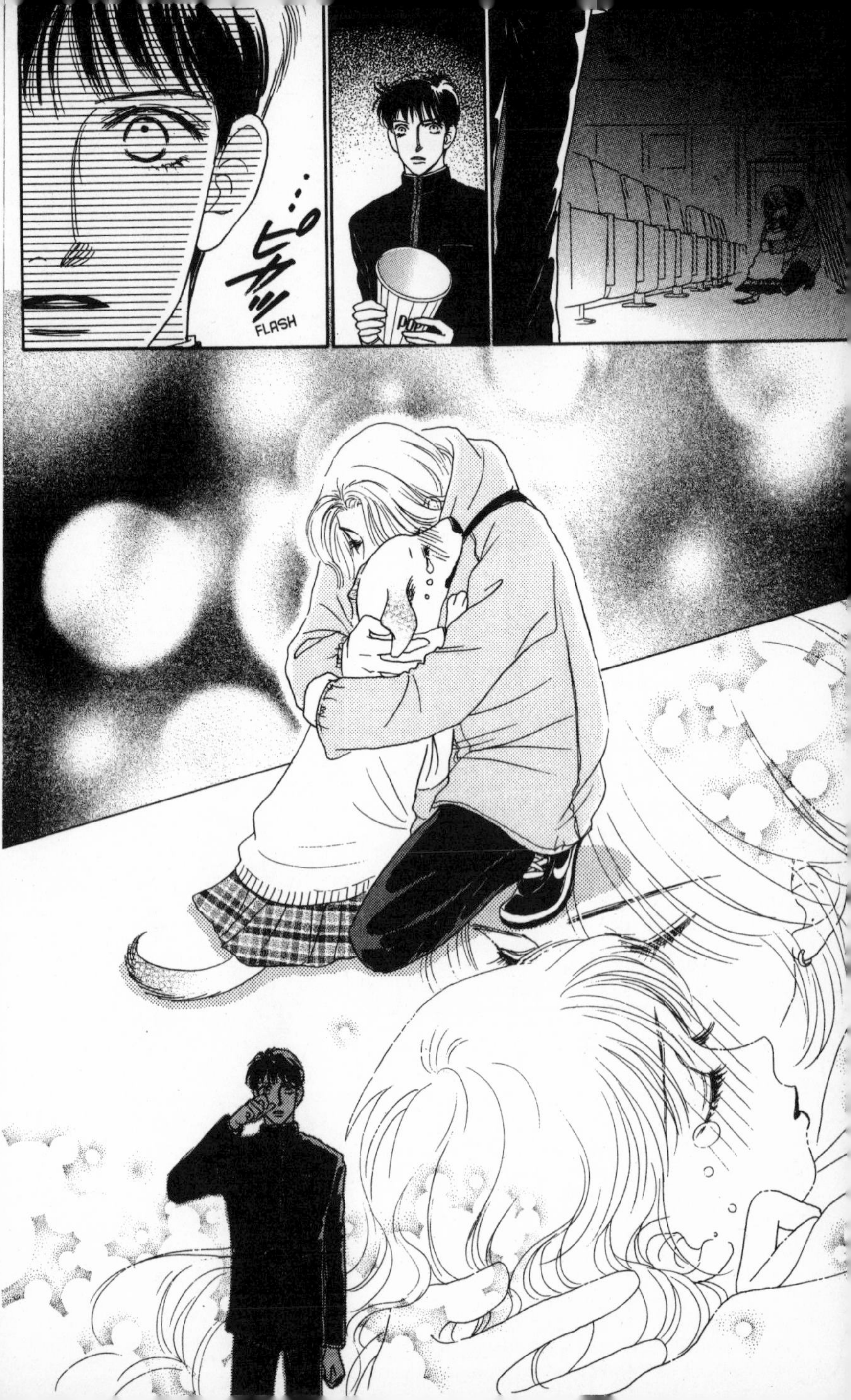
…ピカッ
FLASH

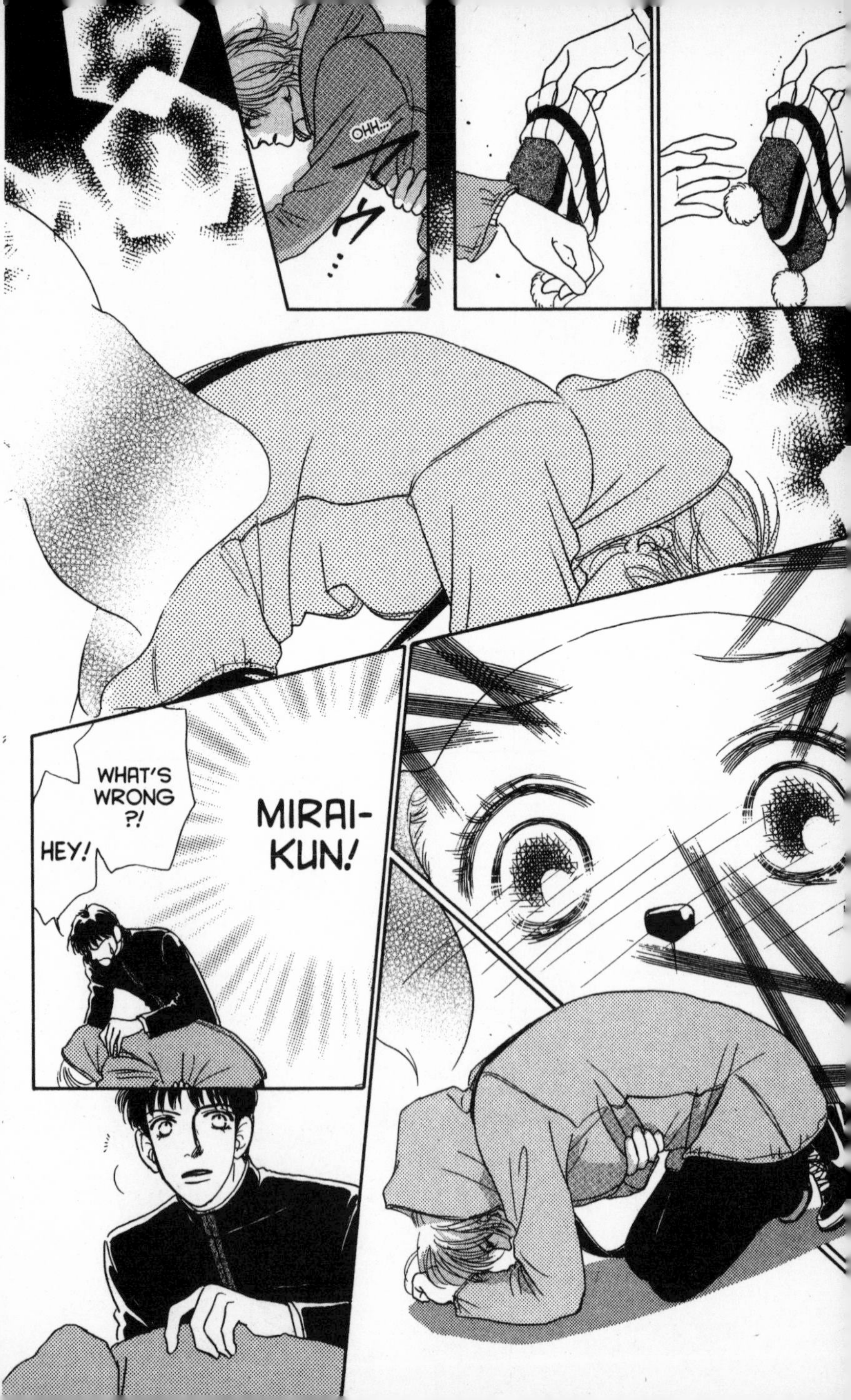
OHH...
MIRAI-KUN!
WHAT'S WRONG ?!
HEY!

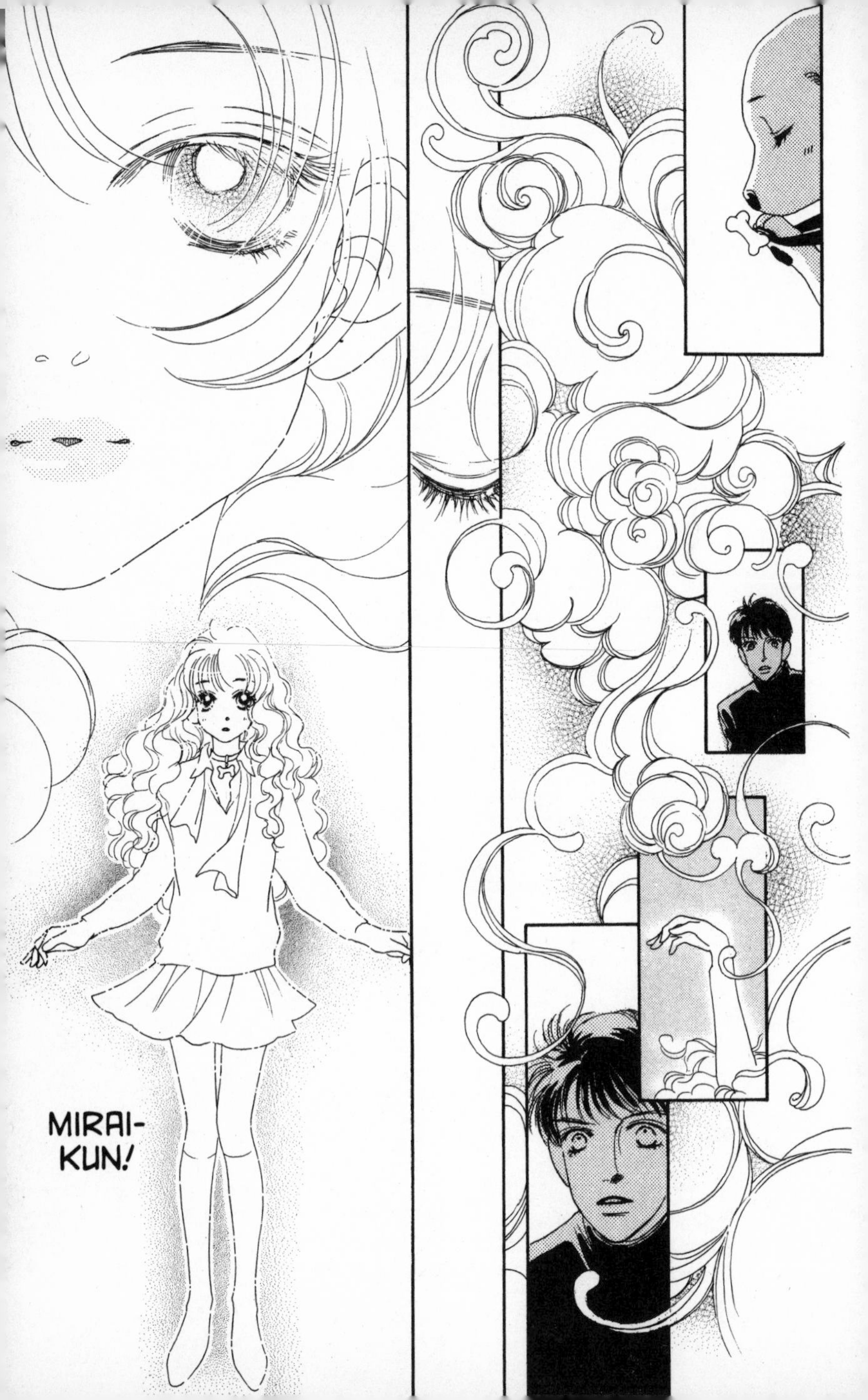
MIRAI-KUN!

NOTHING BUT A TRICK!

THAT WAS ALL A TRICK! YEAH! A TRICK!

THAT'S IT! I'M EASILY TRICKED!

HAVE YOU FORGOT HOW YOU'RE ALWAYS BEING TRICKED AND LAUGHED AT?!

GET A HOLD OF YOURSELF, GO!

THIS CAN'T BE HAPPENING!

THUD
ゴン
THUD
ゴン
WHRAAH
THUD
ゴンッ

うわああああ

WHAT'S THAT?

NEUROTIC GASTRITIS?

WHAT A PITY...

AT LEAST MY BALDNESS DOESN'T HURT.

HOW PITIFUL...

IT'S THE SAME THING THAT CAUSED YOUR BALDNESS.

OUCH, IT STILL HURTS.

HMM...

BUT YOU CRIED.

POOR MIRAI-KUN.

しょぼん...

BUMMED

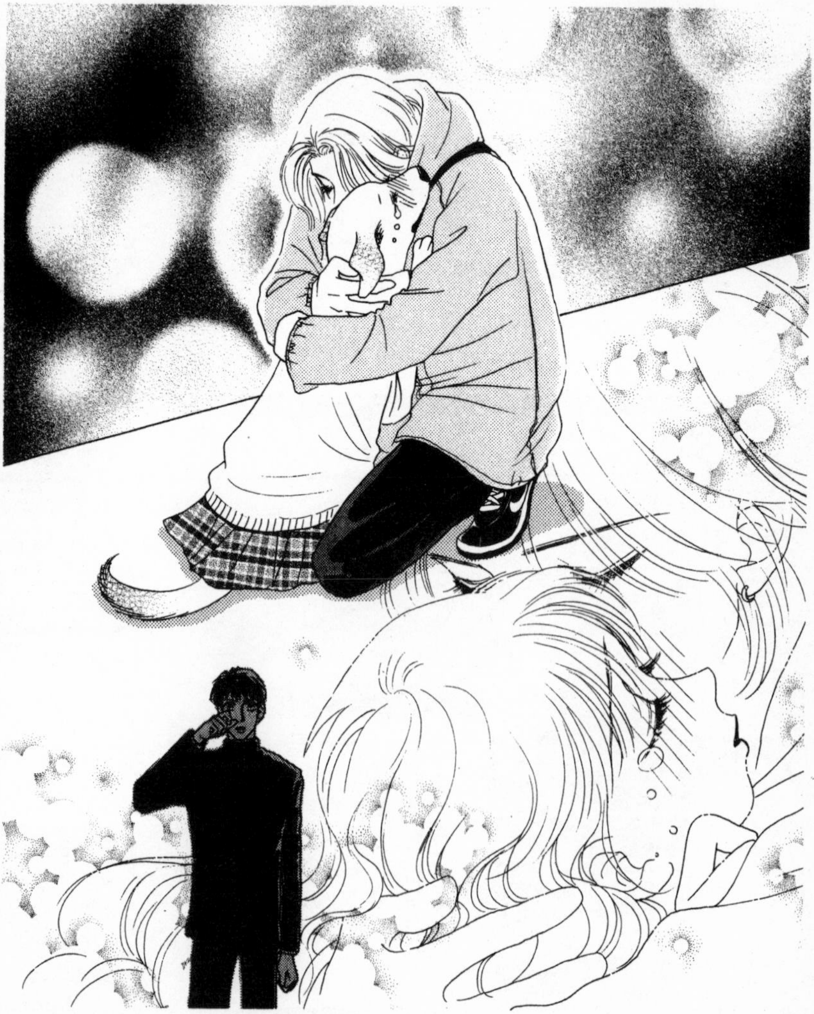

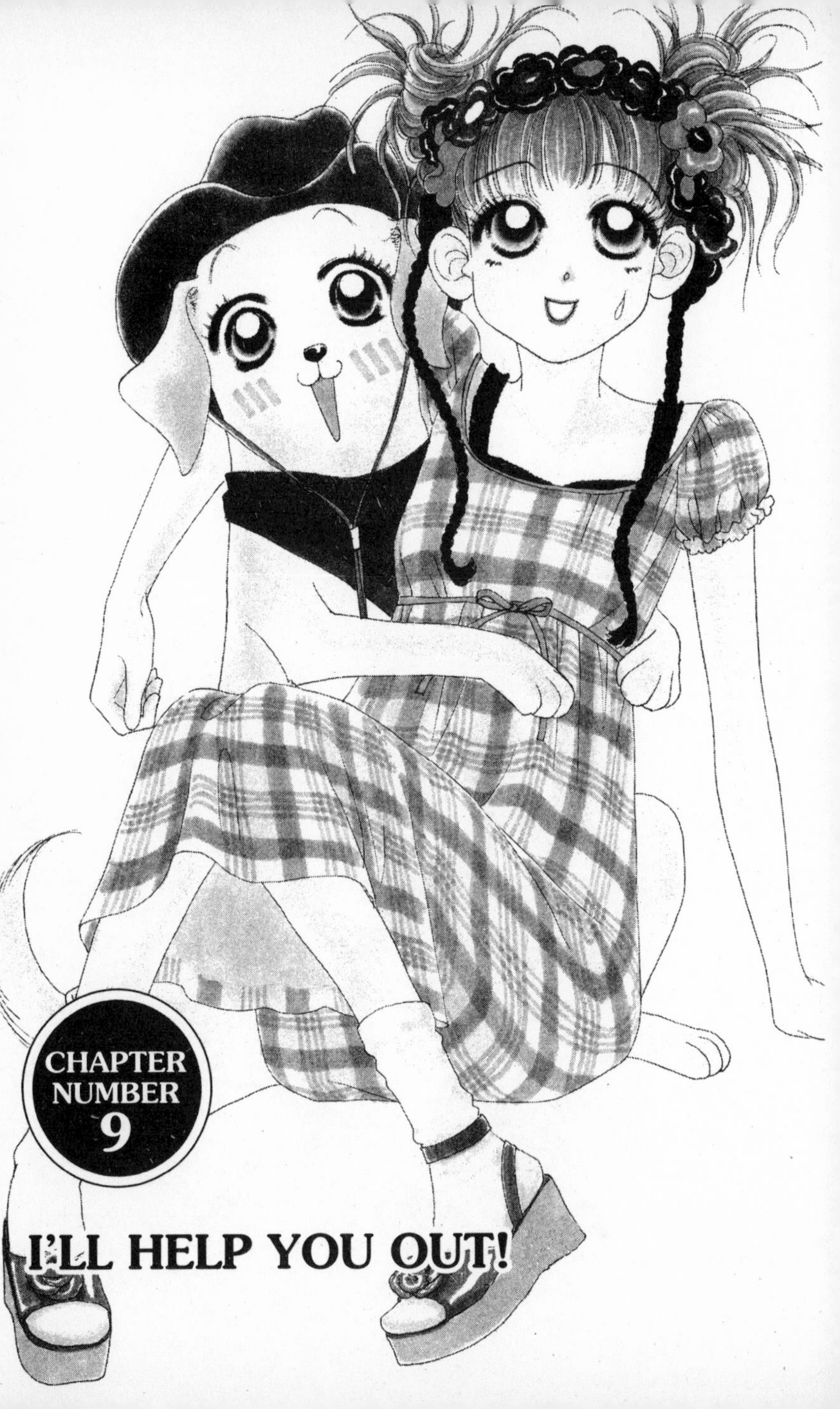
CHAPTER NUMBER 9
I'LL HELP YOU OUT!

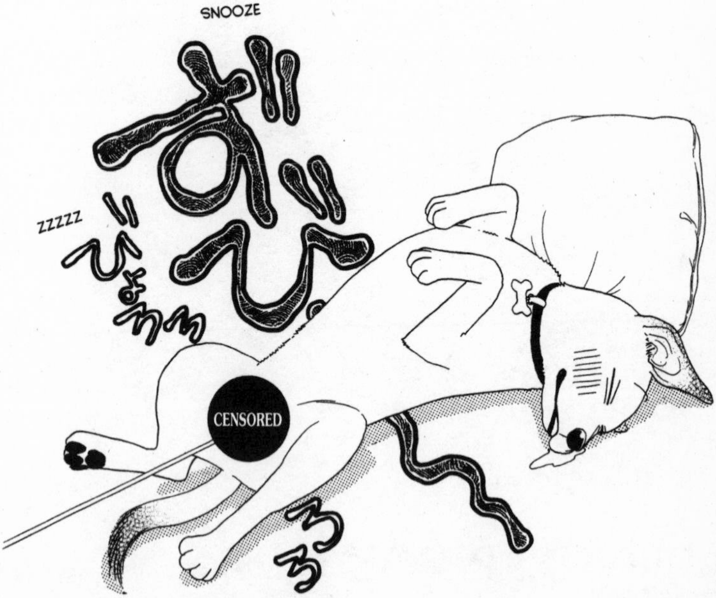
SNOOZE
ZZZZZ
CENSORED

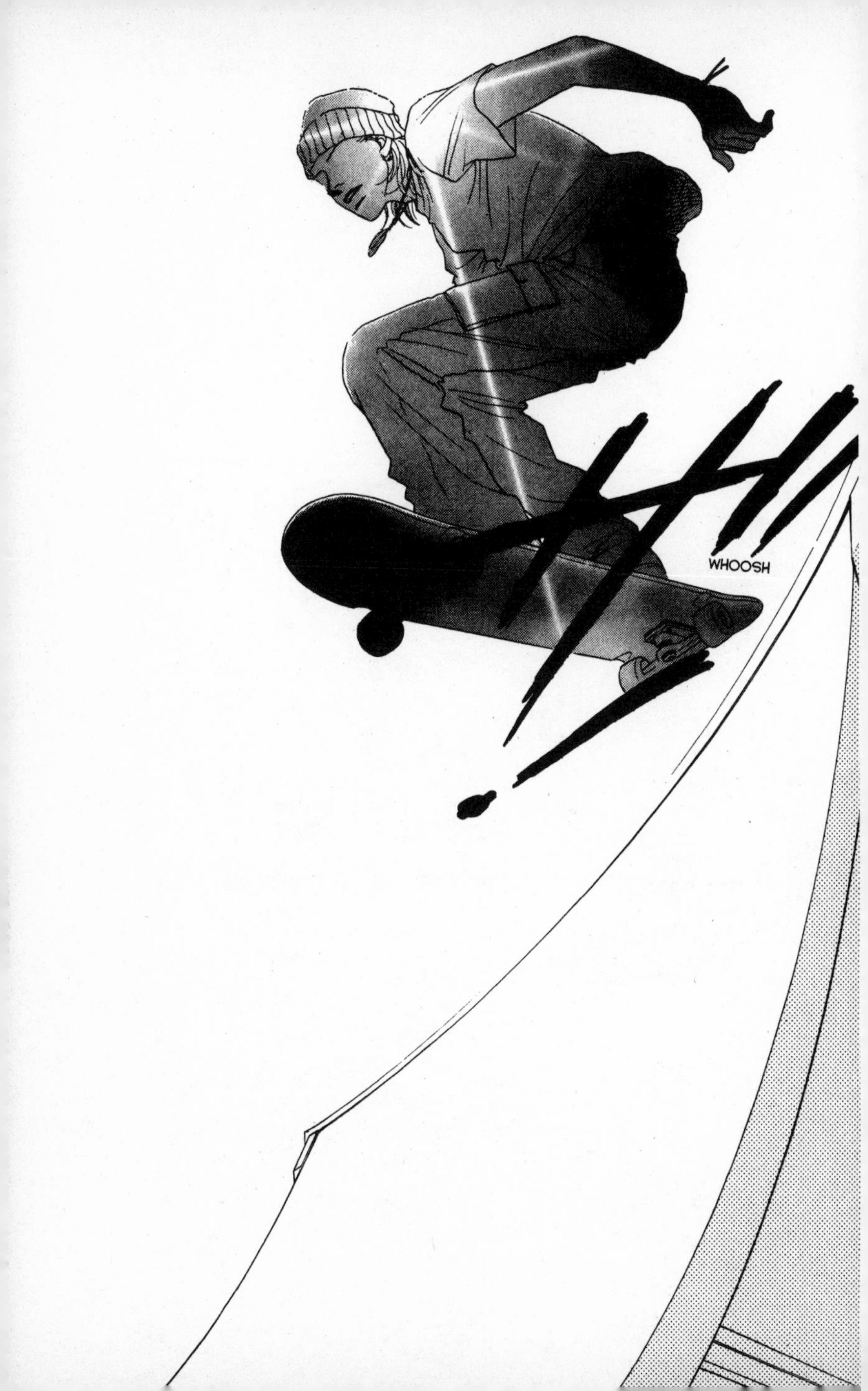
WHOOSH

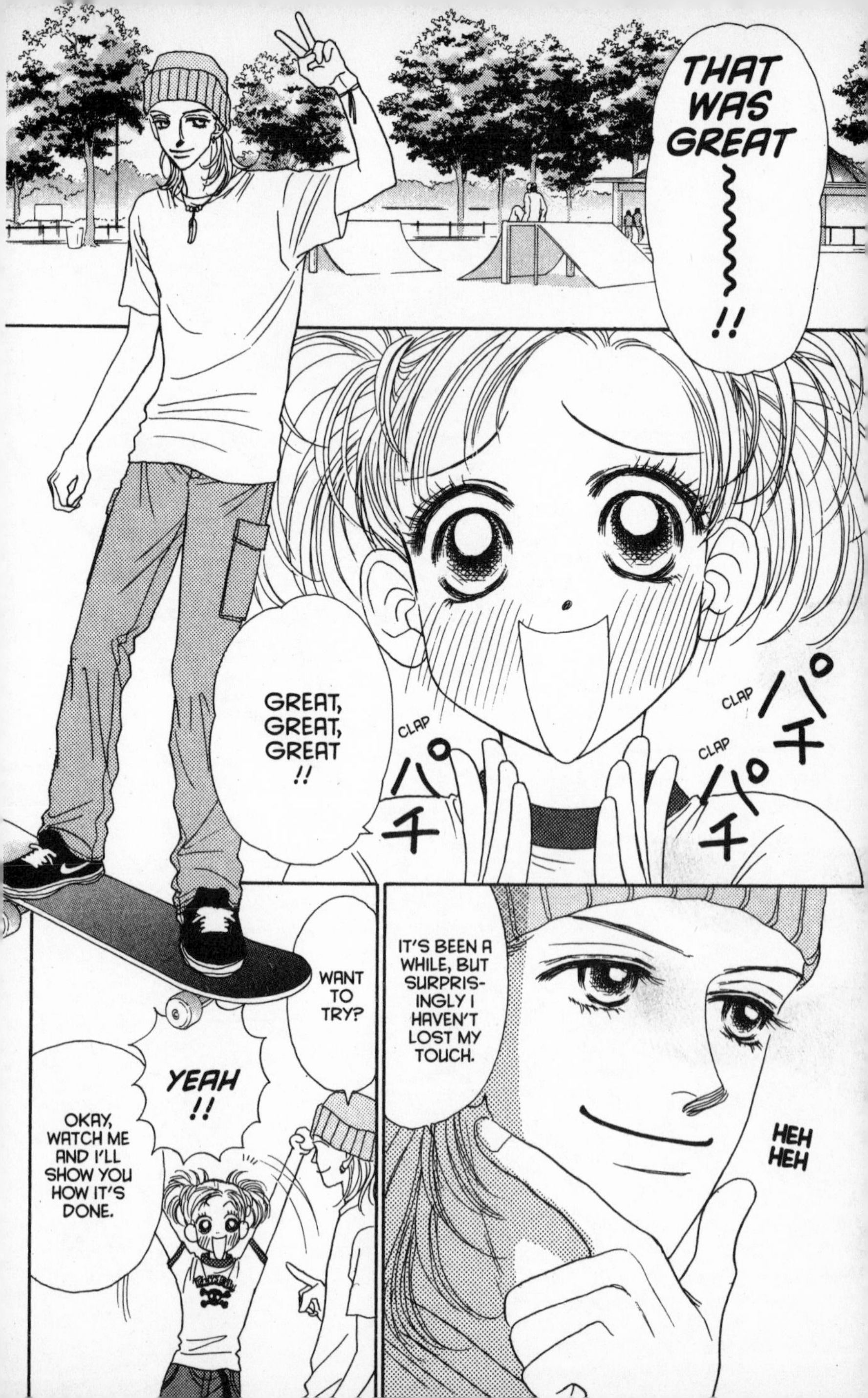
THAT WAS GREAT ~~~!!
CLAP パチ
CLAP パチ
CLAP パチ
GREAT, GREAT, GREAT !!
IT'S BEEN A WHILE, BUT SURPRIS-INGLY I HAVEN'T LOST MY TOUCH.
HEH HEH
WANT TO TRY?
YEAH !!
OKAY, WATCH ME AND I'LL SHOW YOU HOW IT'S DONE.

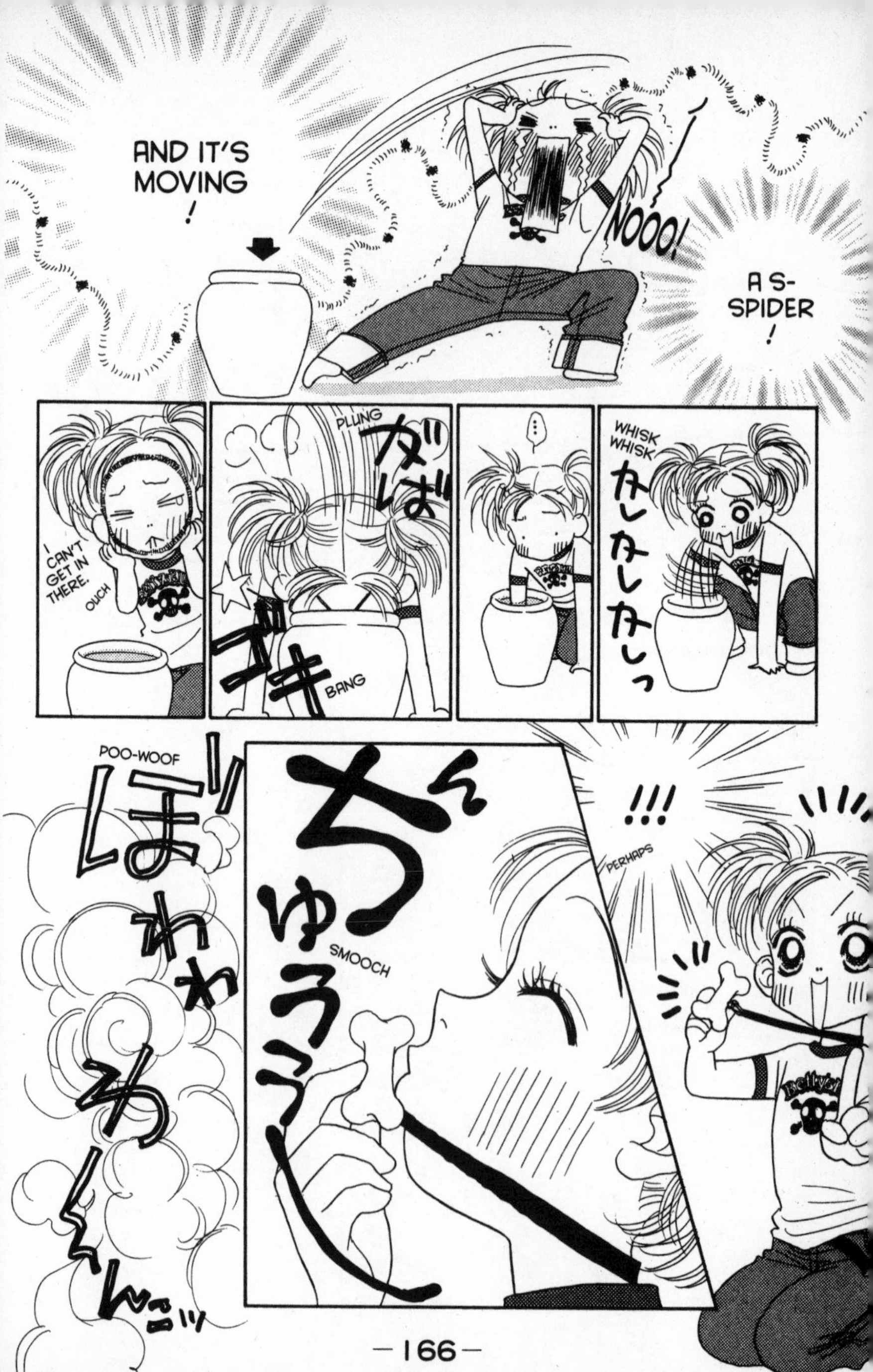
A S-SPIDER!
NOOO!
AND IT'S MOVING!
WHISK WHISK
カレカレカしっ
PLUNG
ガば
ゴキ
BANG
I CAN'T GET IN THERE.
OUCH
!!!
PERHAPS
ちゅううし
SMOOCH
ぽわわわ～ん
POO-WOOF

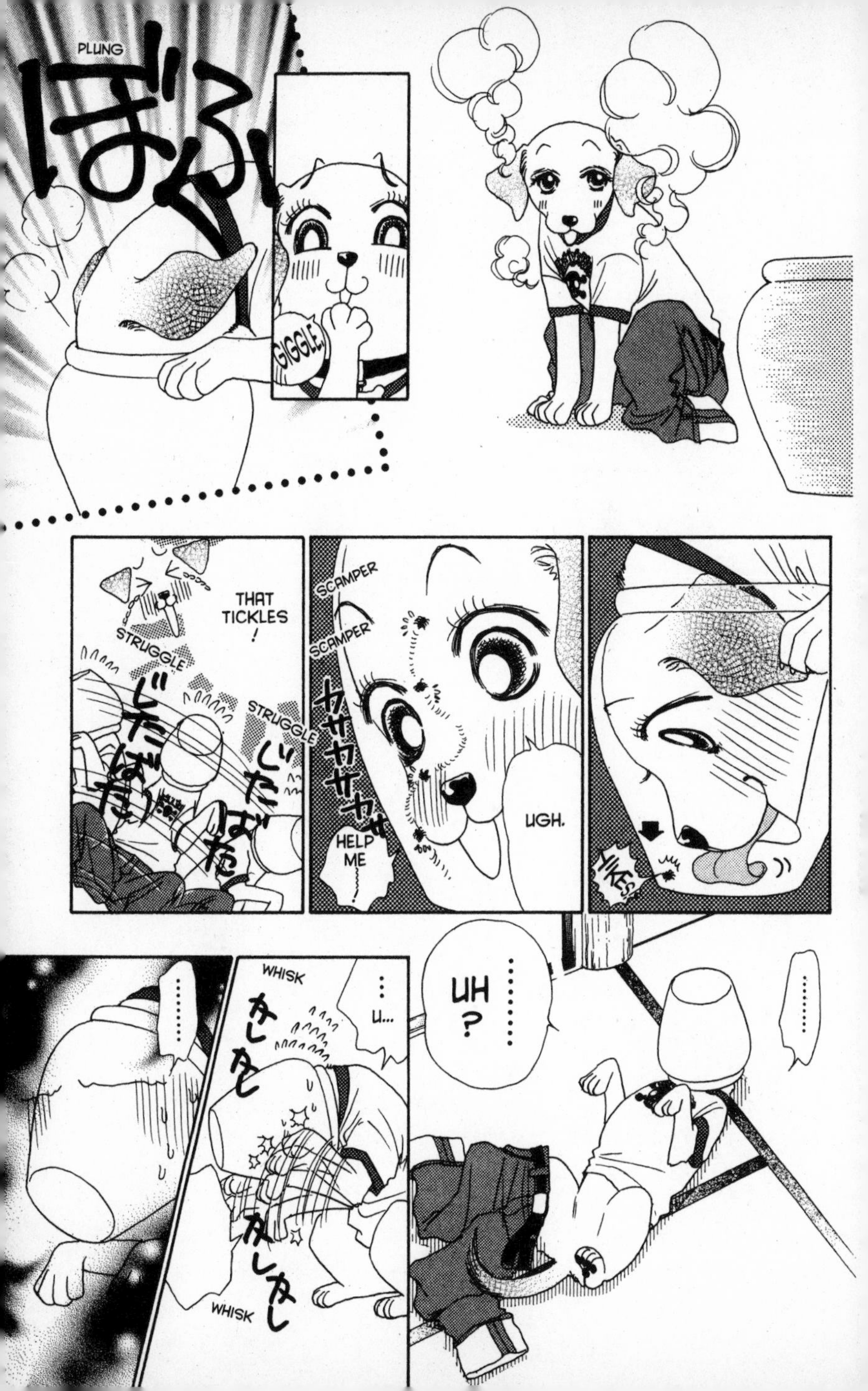
PLUNG
GIGGLE
YIKES!
UGH.
SCAMPER
SCAMPER
HELP ME
THAT TICKLES!
STRUGGLE
STRUGGLE
....
....
UH?
WHISK
... u...
WHISK
....

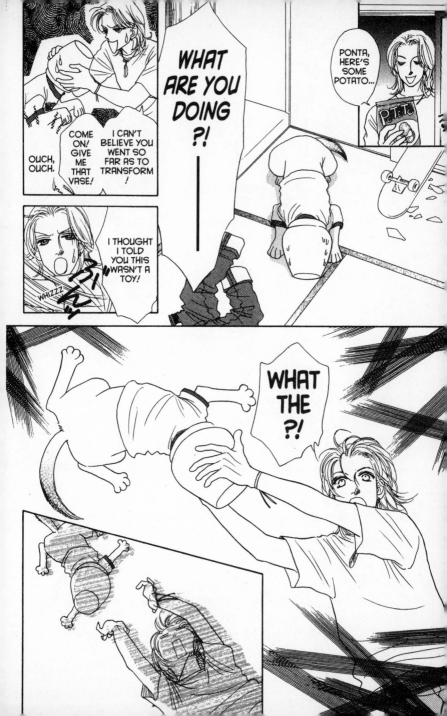

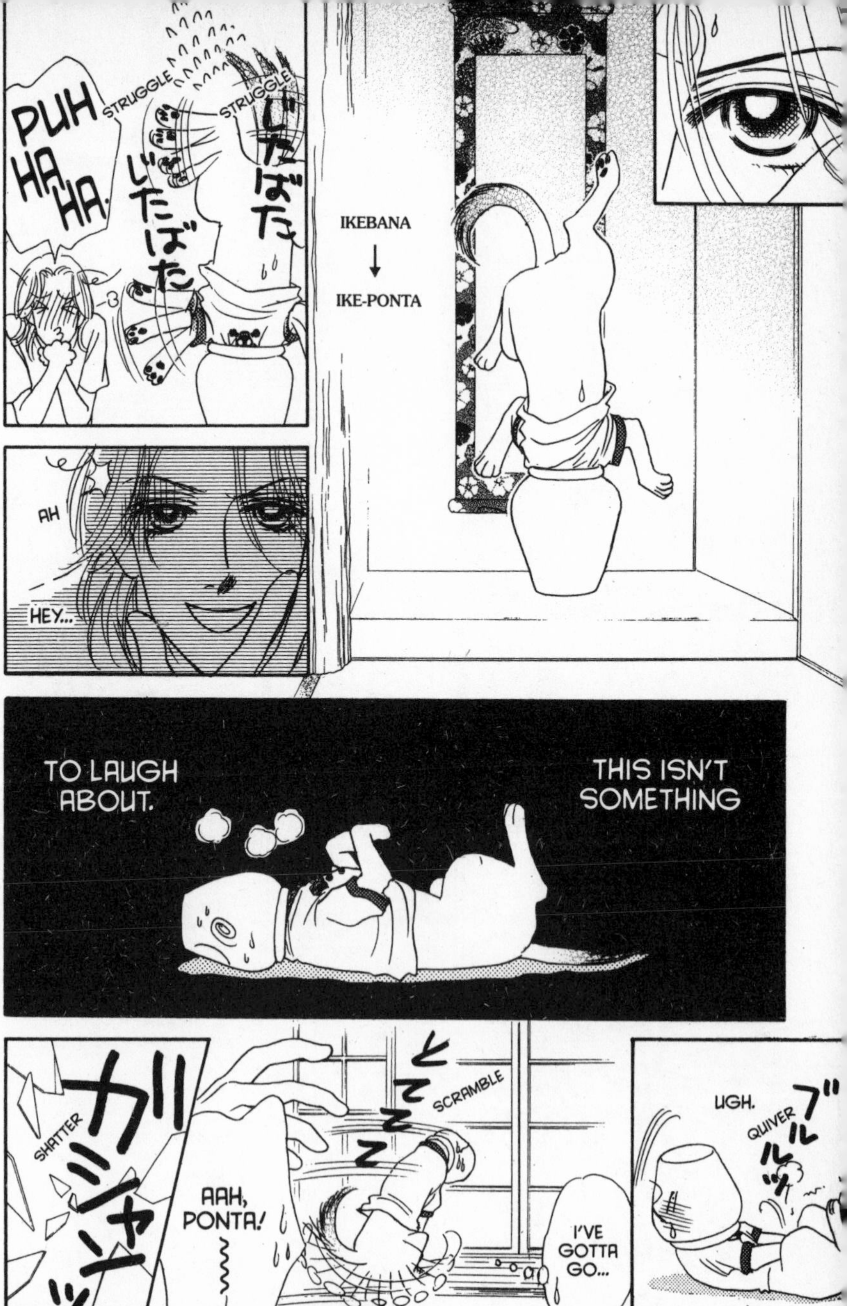
IKEBANA
↓
IKE-PONTA
STRUGGLE
STRUGGLE
じたばた
じたばた
PUH HA HA.
AH
HEY...
THIS ISN'T SOMETHING
TO LAUGH ABOUT.
UGH.
QUIVER
ブルルッ
SCRAMBLE
I'VE GOTTA GO...
AAH, PONTA!
SHATTER
ガシャーンッ

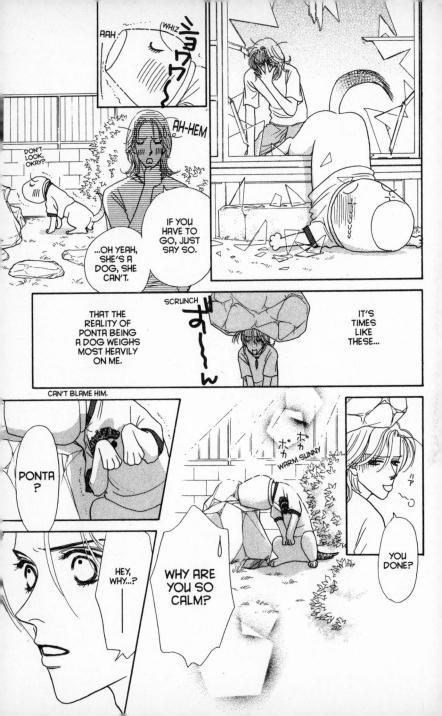

AAH. WHIZ

AH-HEM

DON'T LOOK, OKAY?

IF YOU HAVE TO GO, JUST SAY SO.

...OH YEAH, SHE'S A DOG, SHE CAN'T.

IT'S TIMES LIKE THESE...

SCRUNCH

THAT THE REALITY OF PONTA BEING A DOG WEIGHS MOST HEAVILY ON ME.

CAN'T BLAME HIM.

PONTA?

WARM SUNNY

YOU DONE?

PONTA?

HEY, WHY...?

WHY ARE YOU SO CALM?

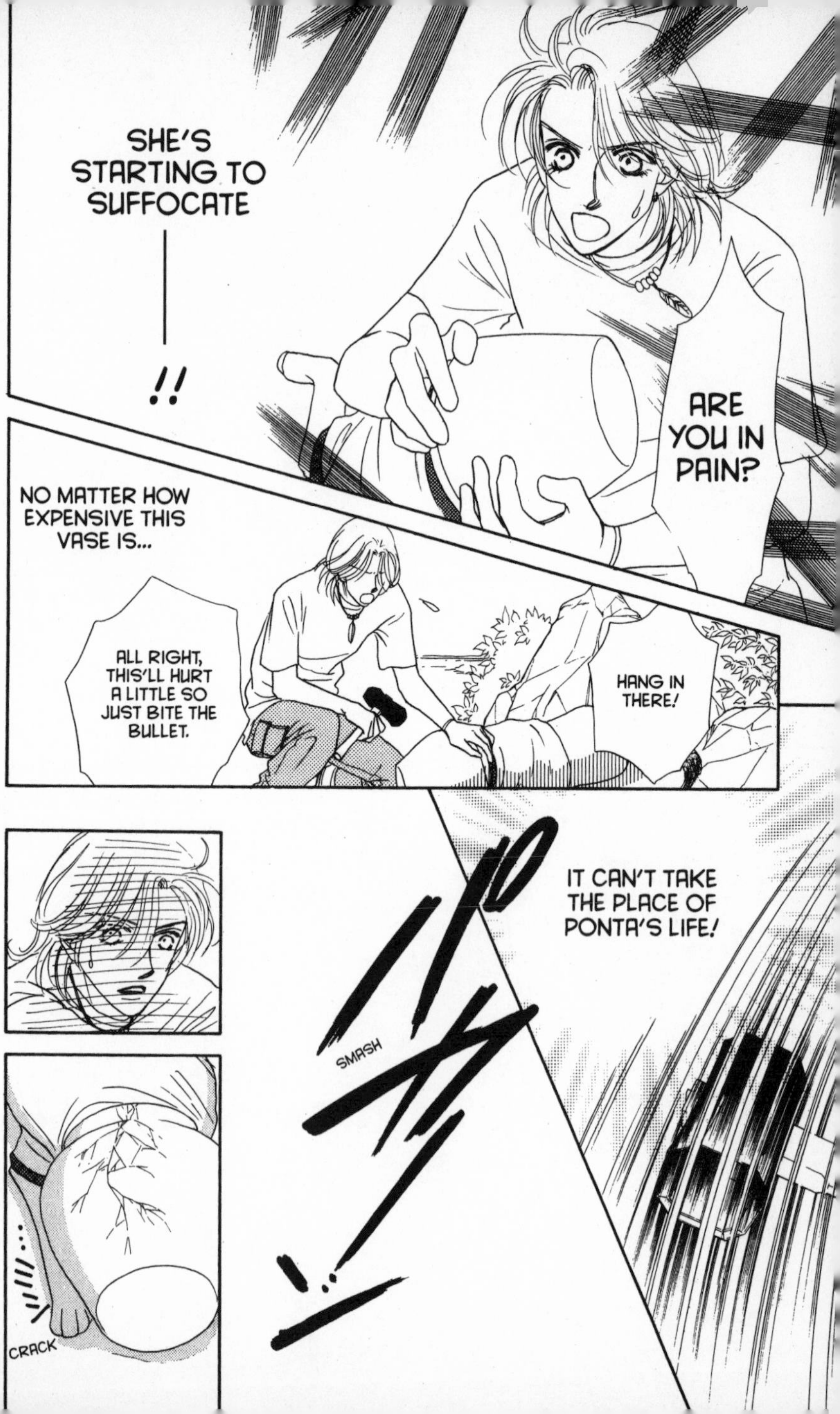
ARE YOU IN PAIN?
SHE'S STARTING TO SUFFOCATE
!!
HANG IN THERE!
NO MATTER HOW EXPENSIVE THIS VASE IS...
ALL RIGHT, THIS'LL HURT A LITTLE SO JUST BITE THE BULLET.
IT CAN'T TAKE THE PLACE OF PONTA'S LIFE!
SMASH
CRACK

HA HA ∞ う は は HA は は HA は は

ANYWAY, EVERY-THING'S ALL RIGHT. EVERY-THING'S ALL RIGHT.

EVERY-THING'S ALL RIGHT.

THAT CAN'T BE SAID FOR EVERYTHING.

BUT...

FOCUS じ

BEFORE YOU ASK WHY, FIRST, FIX YOUR FACE.

EVEN WHEN TRANS-FORMED, HER HEAD'S SHAPED LIKE A VASE.

WHY?!

RATS! IT HAD TO BE DURING SPRING BREAK...

WE CAN'T HAVE FUN FOR A WHILE SO YOU'LL HAVE TO BEAR WITH ME, PONTA,

HELP WANTED

INQUIRE INSIDE.

HEY! IT SAYS, 'HELP WANTED. INQUIRE INSIDE.'

PART TIME JOB?

WHY CAN'T WE HAVE FUN?

OHH, YOU HAVE NO IDEA WHAT I MEAN.

PART TIME JOB.

I HAVE TO PAY FOR THE VASE.

YOU WORK AT THIS SORT OF PLACE AND YOU GET MONEY.

I WANT TO DO IT TOO! I WANT A PART TIME JOB!

AND WITH THAT MONEY...

ANTIQUE SHOP

MIRAI-KUN?

アルバイト パート募集

SWIVEL

SWIVEL

キョロ キョロ

AND HERE TOO.

AND OVER THERE TOO!

WHAT?!

???

WHY?

WHA HA HA HA

THAT'S FUNNY! THAT'S NOT FOR YOU!

THERE'S QUITE A FEW PART TIME JOBS.

SHE'S HAPPY TO READ HER FIRST WORDS.

HELP WANTED

11-7P.M. 850 YEN*/HOUR.

HERE'S AN-OTHER ONE.

OH!

*ABOUT $8.30

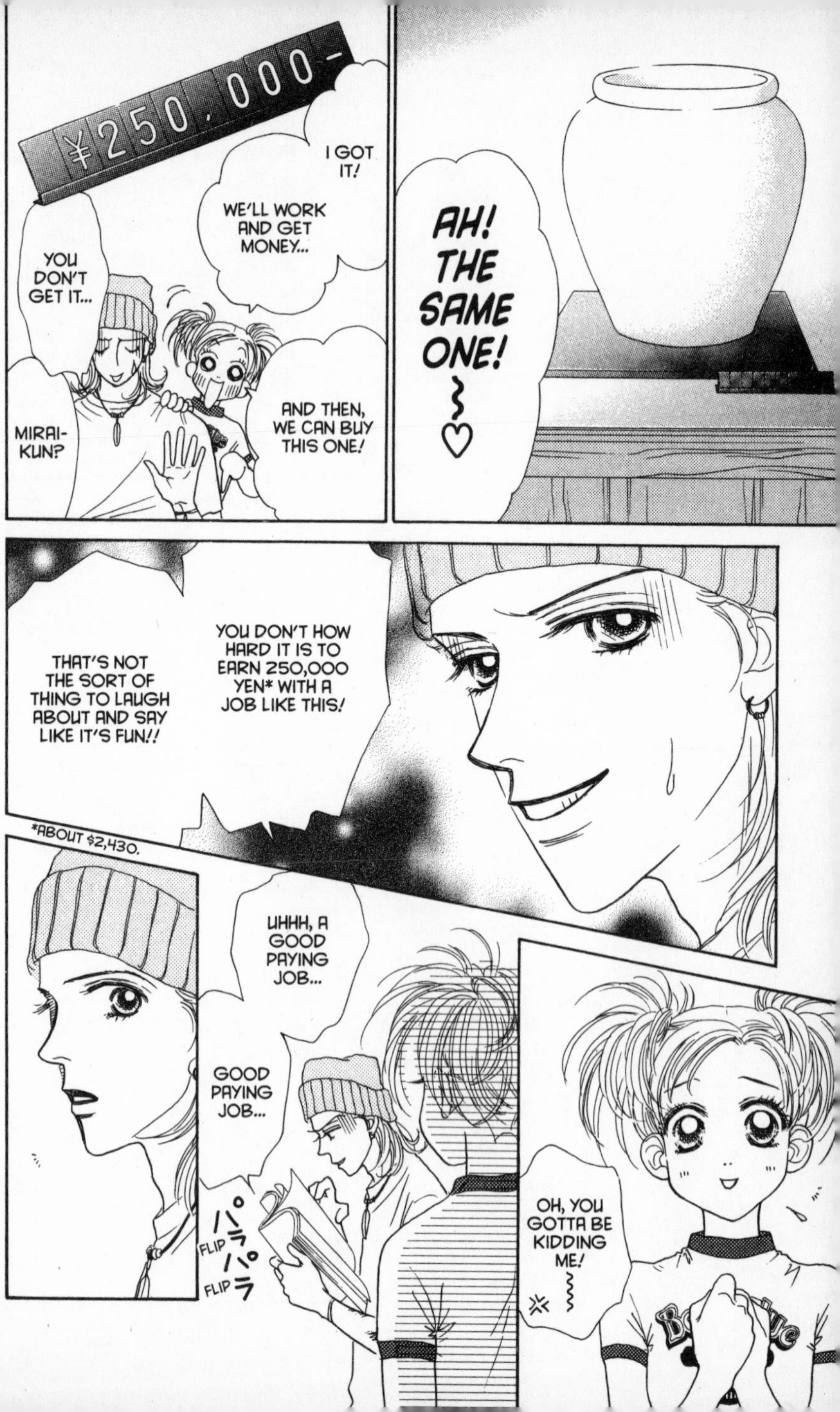
AH! THE SAME ONE!
I GOT IT!
WE'LL WORK AND GET MONEY...
AND THEN, WE CAN BUY THIS ONE!
¥250,000-
YOU DON'T GET IT...
MIRAI-KUN?
YOU DON'T HOW HARD IT IS TO EARN 250,000 YEN* WITH A JOB LIKE THIS!
THAT'S NOT THE SORT OF THING TO LAUGH ABOUT AND SAY LIKE IT'S FUN!!
OH, YOU GOTTA BE KIDDING ME!
UHHH, A GOOD PAYING JOB...
GOOD PAYING JOB...
パラ FLIP
パラ FLIP
*ABOUT $2,430.

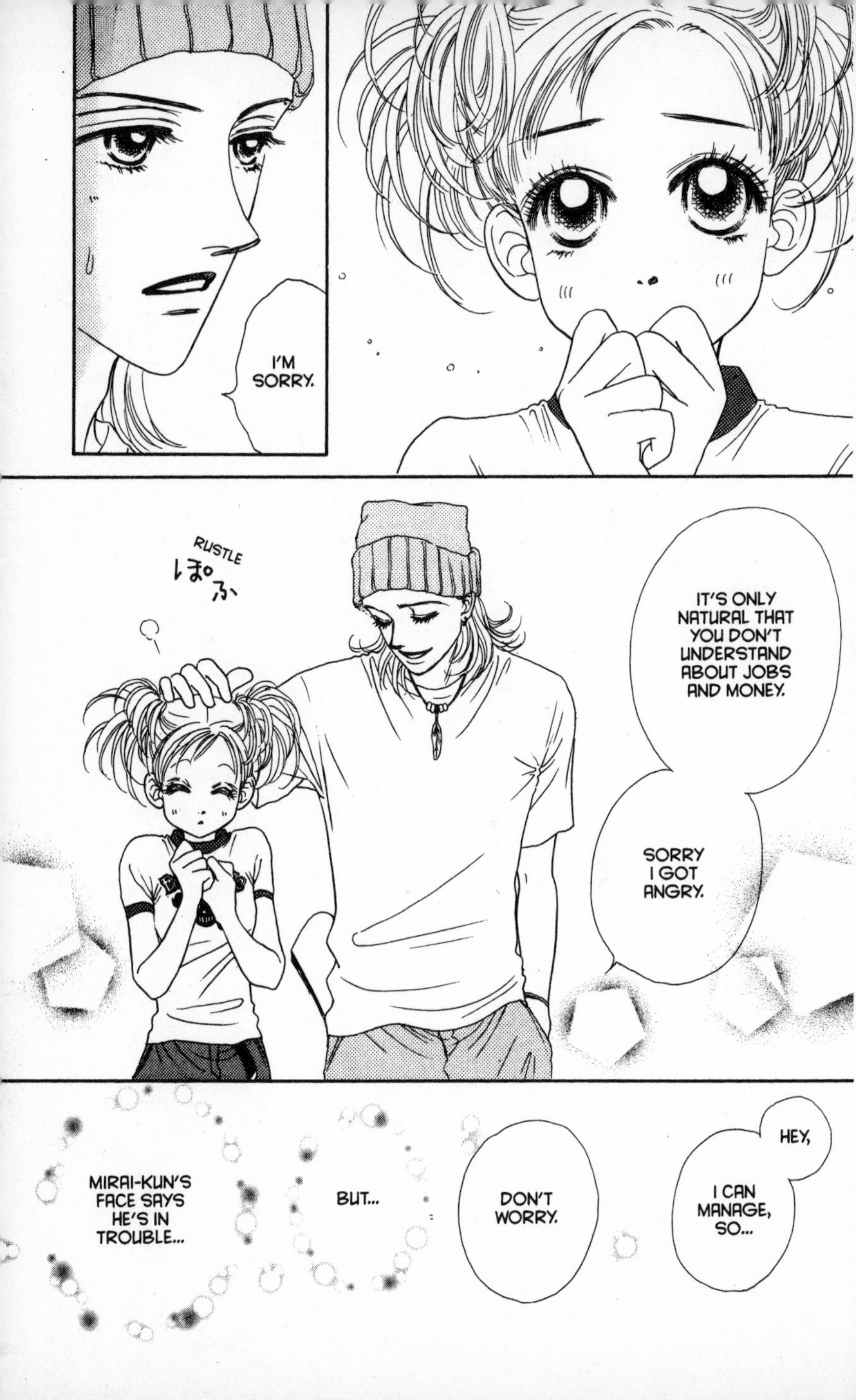

I'M SORRY.
IT'S ONLY NATURAL THAT YOU DON'T UNDERSTAND ABOUT JOBS AND MONEY.
SORRY I GOT ANGRY.
RUSTLE
ぽふ
HEY,
I CAN MANAGE, SO...
DON'T WORRY.
BUT...
MIRAI-KUN'S FACE SAYS HE'S IN TROUBLE...

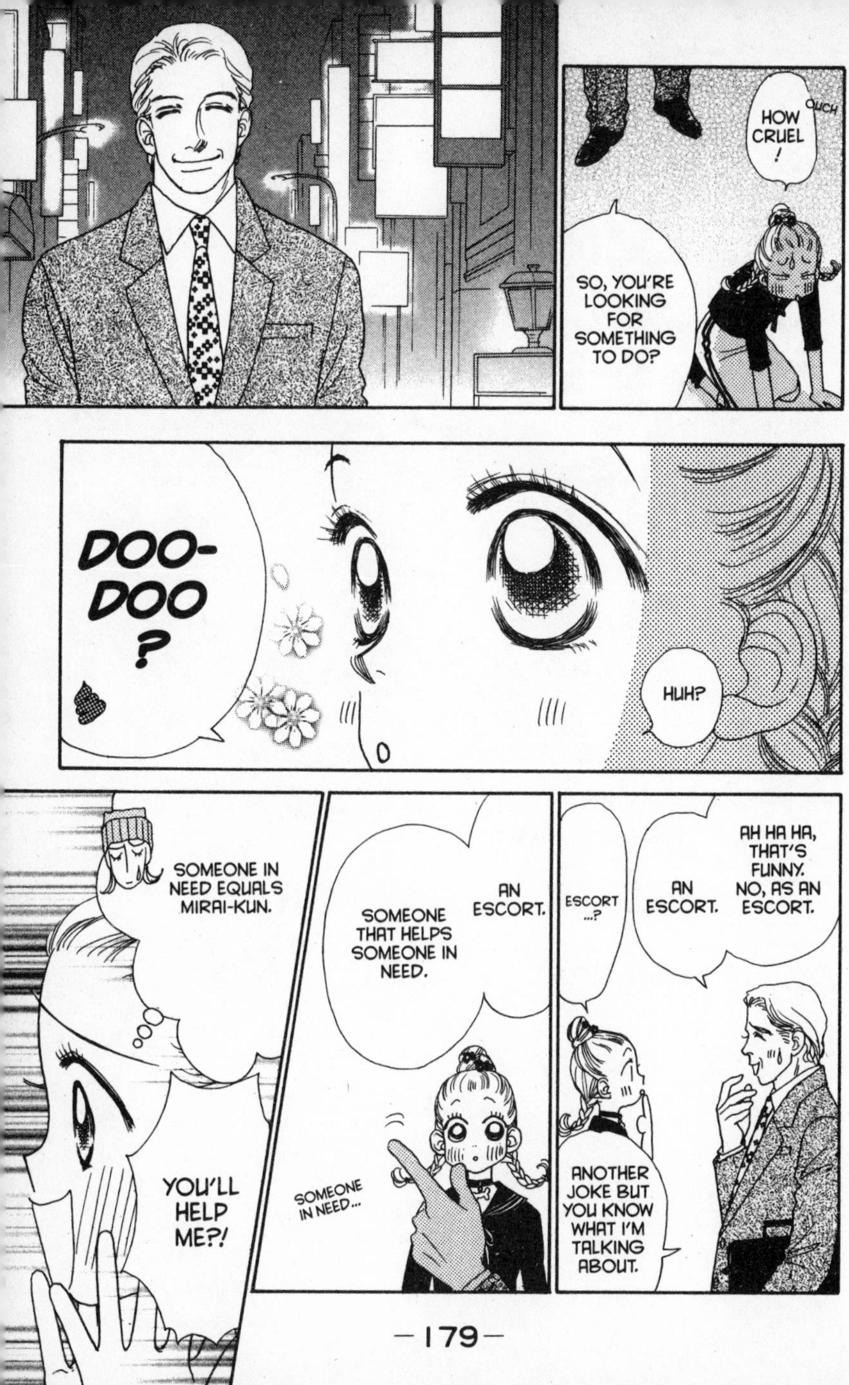
OUCH
HOW CRUEL!
SO, YOU'RE LOOKING FOR SOMETHING TO DO?
HUH?
DOO-DOO?
ESCORT...?
AN ESCORT.
AH HA HA, THAT'S FUNNY. NO, AS AN ESCORT.
ANOTHER JOKE BUT YOU KNOW WHAT I'M TALKING ABOUT.
AN ESCORT.
SOMEONE THAT HELPS SOMEONE IN NEED.
SOMEONE IN NEED...
SOMEONE IN NEED EQUALS MIRAI-KUN.
YOU'LL HELP ME?!

PONTA

?

HEY!

CLASP

WHAT'RE YOU DOING STANDING AROUND SPACING OUT?!

HAH?!

WITH

I'M HERE SWALLOWING MY TEARS, WORKING AND SHE'S OUT HAVING A NIGHT OUT ON THE TOWN.

CRAP!

CLANK

CLANK

GET THE LEAD OUT!

THAT CREEP!

WHEEZE

WHEEZE

WHEEZE

KNEAD

KNEAD

KNEAD

KNEAD

IT'S HARD TO IMAGINE A DOG HAVING A NIGHT ON THE TOWN.

⌐ HE'S HUGE.

THIS IS GREAT FOR JUST EATING TOGETHER.

THIS ESCORT STUFF IS A GOOD JOB!

AH HA HA. YOU'RE JUST EXAGGERATING.

YOU'RE GIVING ME THIS MUCH?!

← SHE SAYS THIS WITHOUT CONSIDERING THE AMOUNT, JUST THE NUMBER OF BILLS (HA HA)

BUT DEPENDING ON WHAT YOU WANT TO DO...

YOU CAN GET MORE MONEY...?

BYE BYE

OKAY THEN, SEE YOU LATER OJI-SAN!

PONTA, YOU GOT A JOB?!

YOU HELPED ME SO MUCH, THANK YOU.

WELL, THAT'S FINE.

I DON'T KNOW... BUT SHE'S A REMARKABLY CHEERFUL GIRL.

SHE SEEMS GAME...

HEH HEH

LA DEE DAH.

I'LL DO A LOT MORE OF THIS PAID ESCORT THING

AND GET A LOT MORE MONEY...

AND I'LL HELP OUT MIRAI-KUN A LOT!
...♡

THAT CREEP'S STILL AT IT.

GRRR

YOU WANNA GO A FEW ROUNDS WITH ME? AH?

ARE YOU STILL...

SLACKING OFF?

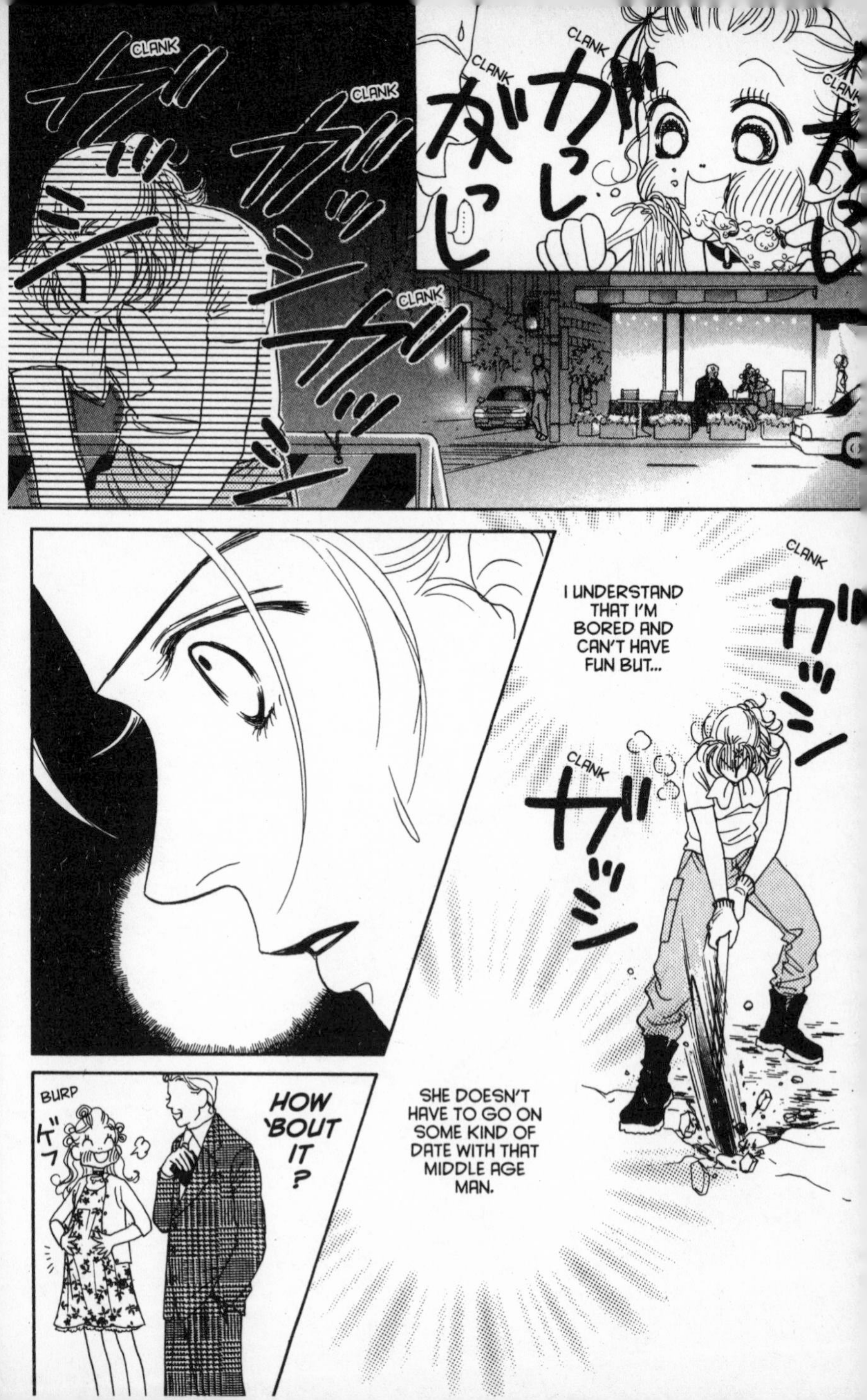
CLANK
CLANK
...
CLANK
CLANK
CLANK
CLANK
CLANK
I UNDERSTAND THAT I'M BORED AND CAN'T HAVE FUN BUT...
CLANK
SHE DOESN'T HAVE TO GO ON SOME KIND OF DATE WITH THAT MIDDLE AGE MAN.
HOW 'BOUT IT?
BURP

*ABOUT 9.44. **ABOUT 9.66.

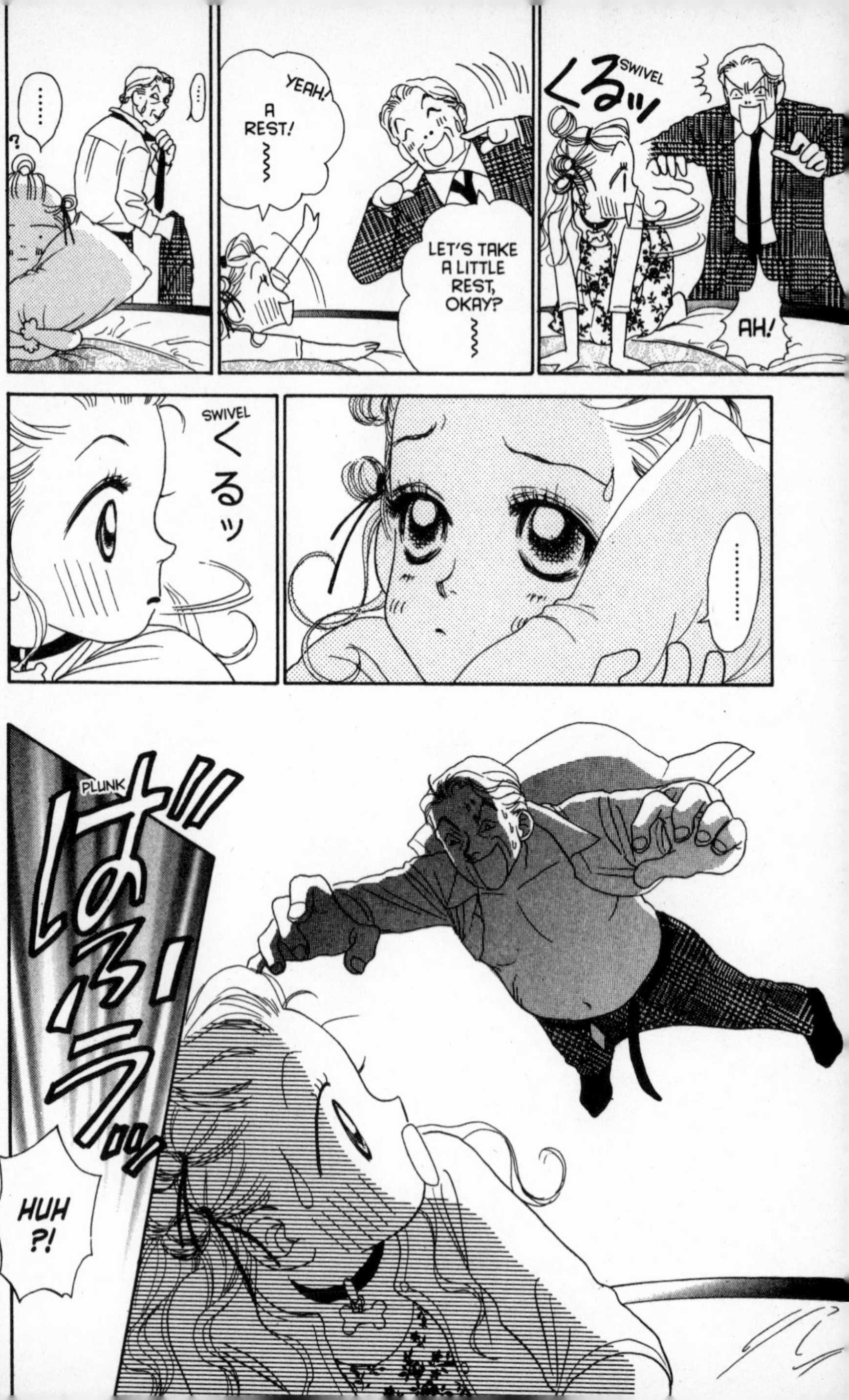

SWIVEL くるッ
AH!
YEAH! A REST!
LET'S TAKE A LITTLE REST, OKAY?
......
?
......
......
SWIVEL くるッ
PLUNK ぼふっ
HUH ?!

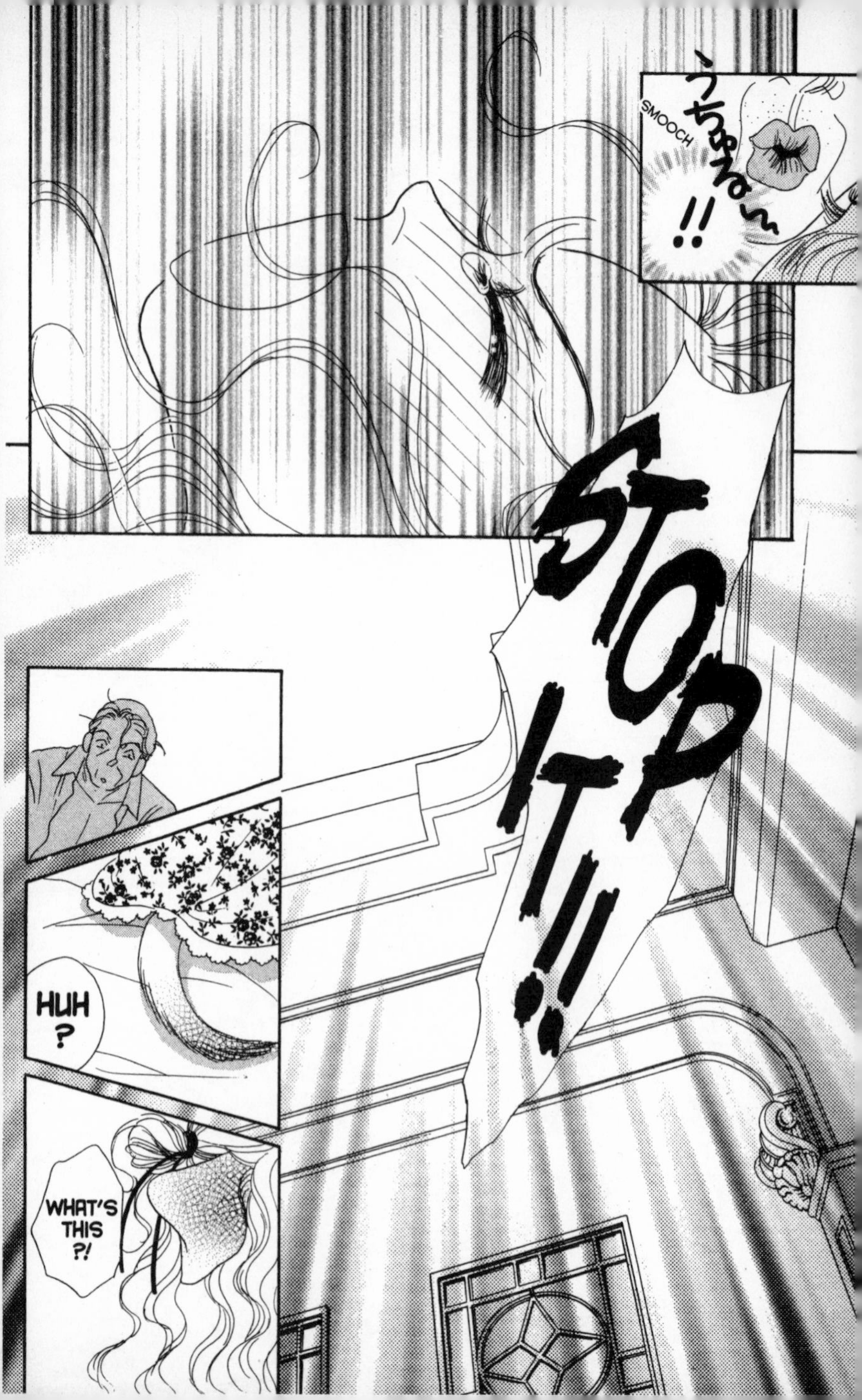

うちゅる〜!!
SMOOCH
STOP IT!!!
HUH?
WHAT'S THIS?!

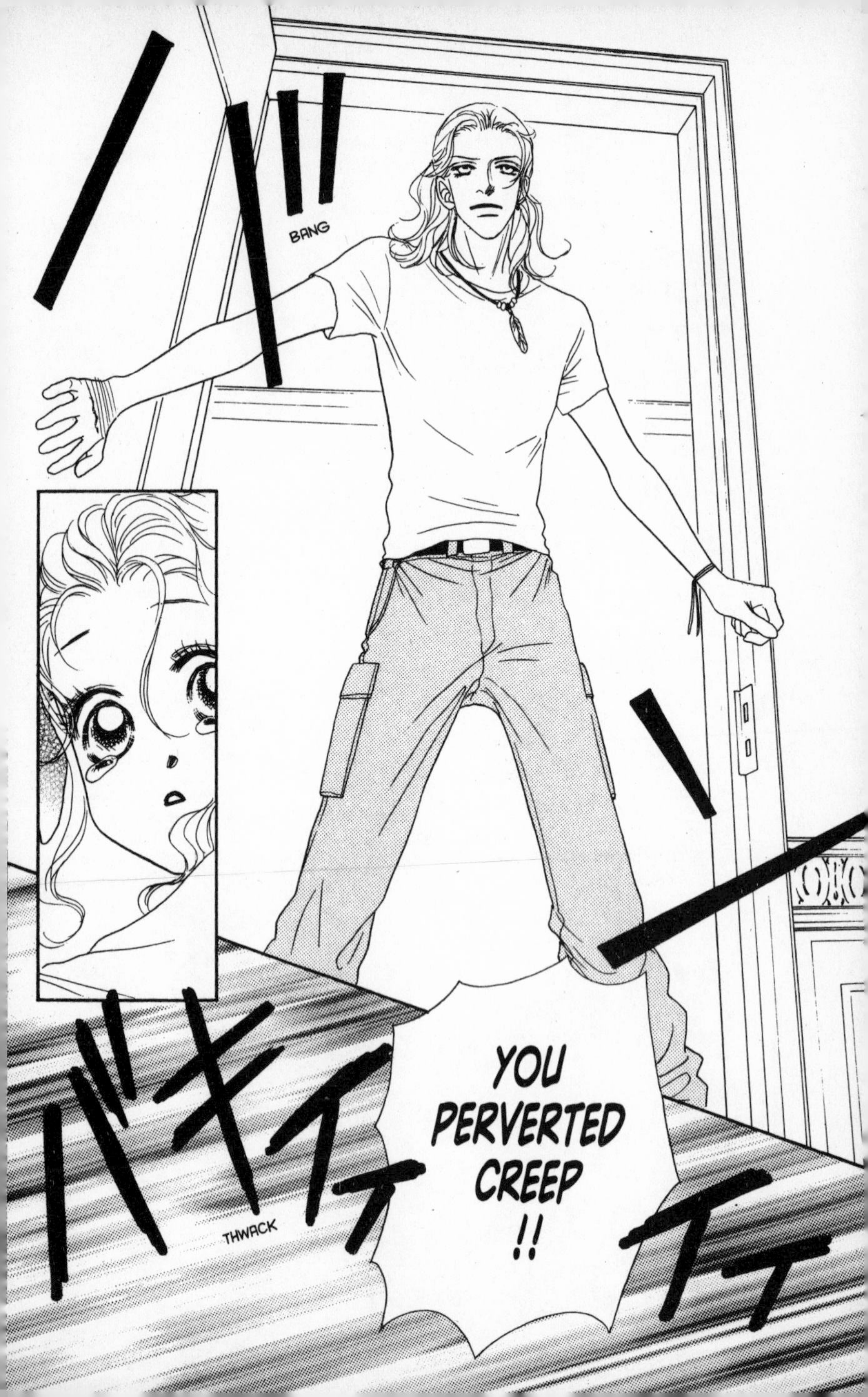
BANG
YOU PERVERTED CREEP !!
THWACK

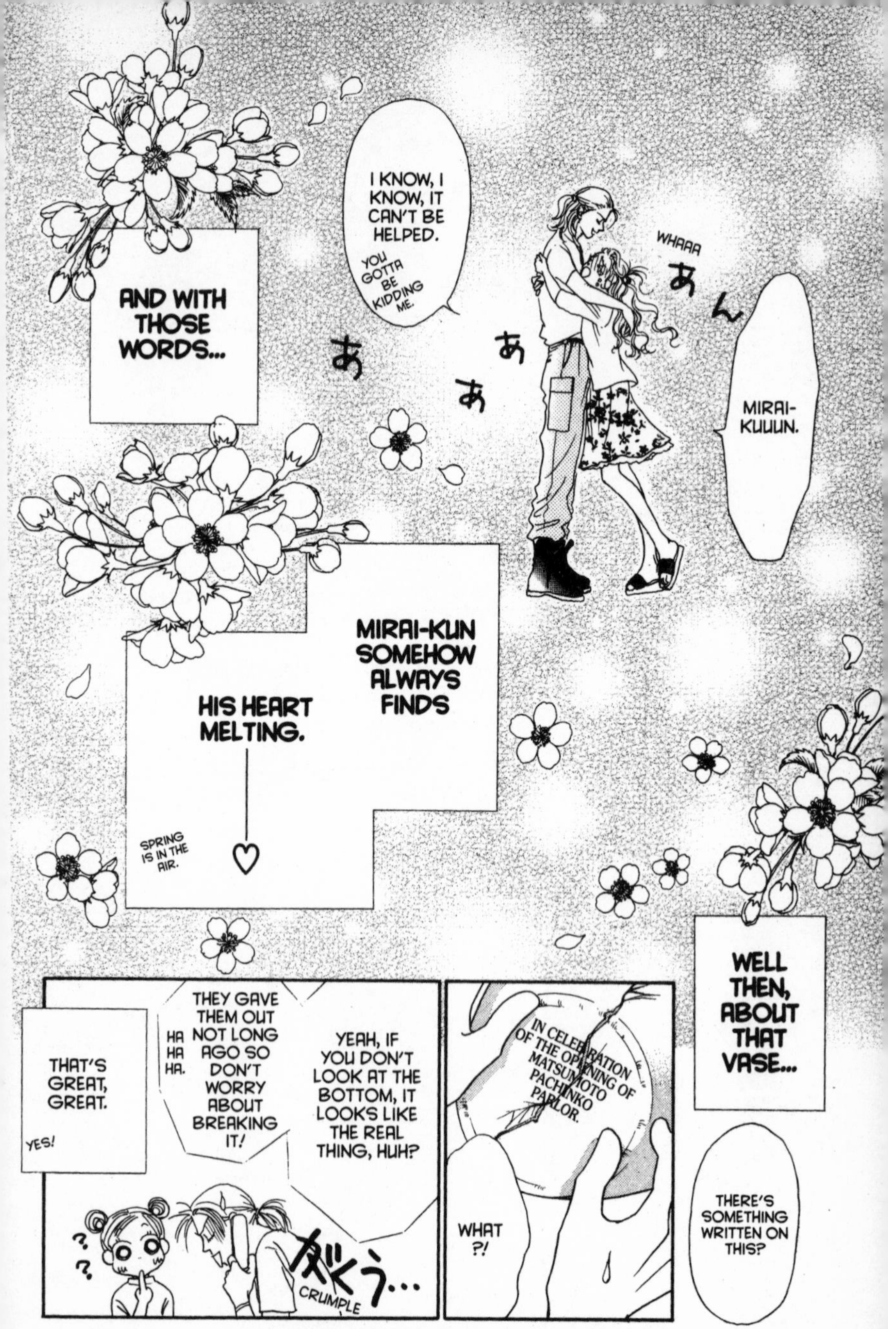
MIRAI-KUUUN.
WHAAA
あん
I KNOW, I KNOW, IT CAN'T BE HELPED.
YOU GOTTA BE KIDDING ME.
あ あ あ
AND WITH THOSE WORDS...
MIRAI-KUN SOMEHOW ALWAYS FINDS
HIS HEART MELTING.
SPRING IS IN THE AIR.
WELL THEN, ABOUT THAT VASE...
THERE'S SOMETHING WRITTEN ON THIS?
IN CELEBRATION OF THE OPENING OF MATSUMOTO PACHINKO PARLOR.
WHAT?!
YEAH, IF YOU DON'T LOOK AT THE BOTTOM, IT LOOKS LIKE THE REAL THING, HUH?
THEY GAVE THEM OUT NOT LONG AGO SO DON'T WORRY ABOUT BREAKING IT!
HA HA HA.
THAT'S GREAT, GREAT.
YES!
CRUMPLE

CONTINUED IN GURU GURU PON-CHAN 3

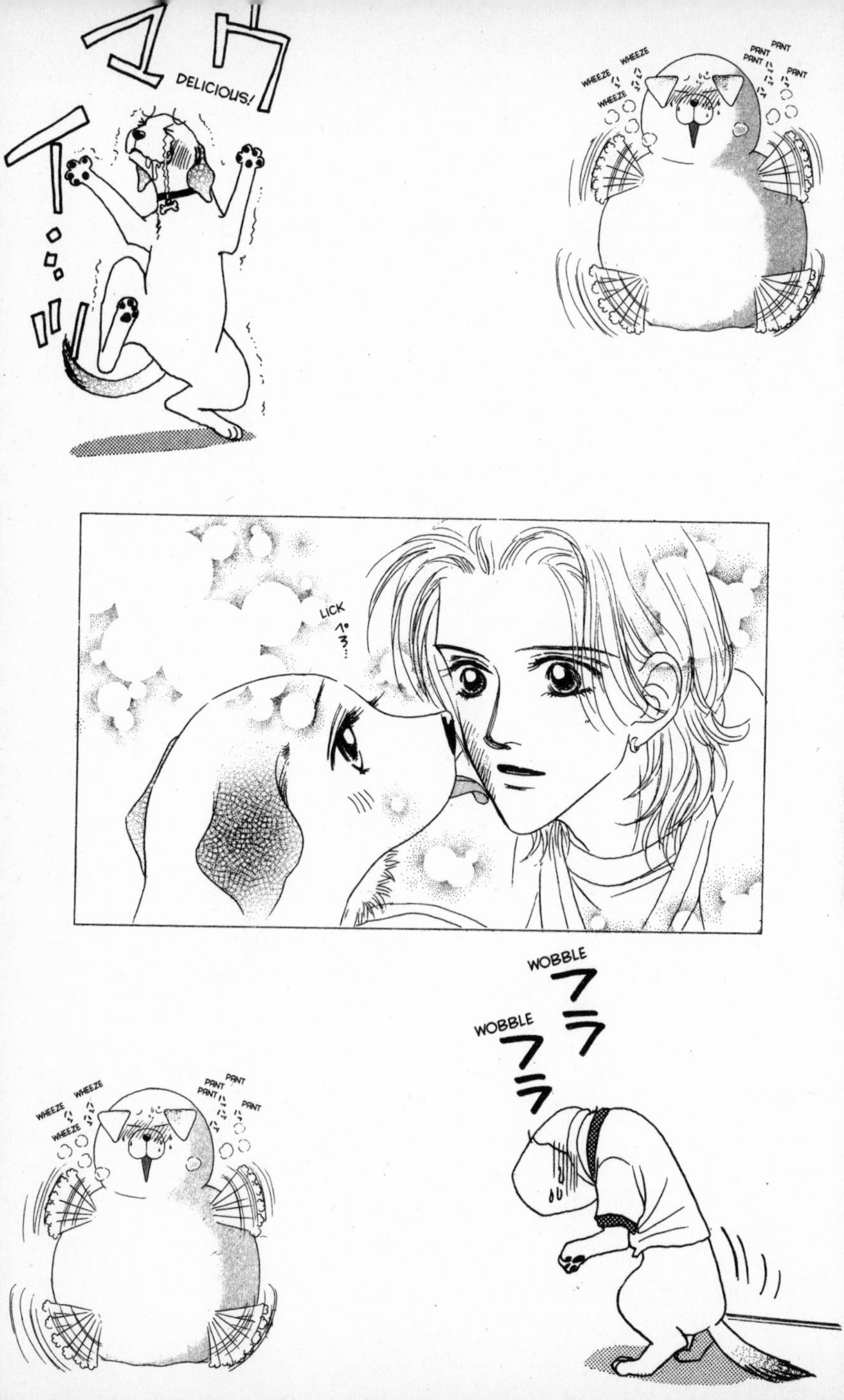

PANT
PANT
PANT
PANT
WHEEZE
WHEEZE
WHEEZE
ウマイ
DELICIOUS!
LICK
ぺろ…
WOBBLE
フラ
WOBBLE
フラ
PANT
PANT
PANT
PANT
WHEEZE
WHEEZE
WHEEZE

About the Creator

Satomi Ikezawa, a prolific manga-ka, finished *Guru Guru Pon-chan* in 2000.

Ikezawa won the 24th Kodansha Manga Prize in 2000 for *Guru Guru Pon-chan*.

She has two Labradors, named Guts and Ponta. Both are male, despite the Ponta of *Guru Guru Pon-chan* being a girl.

Volumes 1, 2 and 3 of *Guru Guru Pon-chan* are available now.

Translation Notes

Japanese is a tricky language for most Westerners, and translation is often more art than science. For your edification and reading pleasure, here are notes on some of the places where we could have gone in a different direction in our translation of the work, or where a Japanese cultural reference is used.

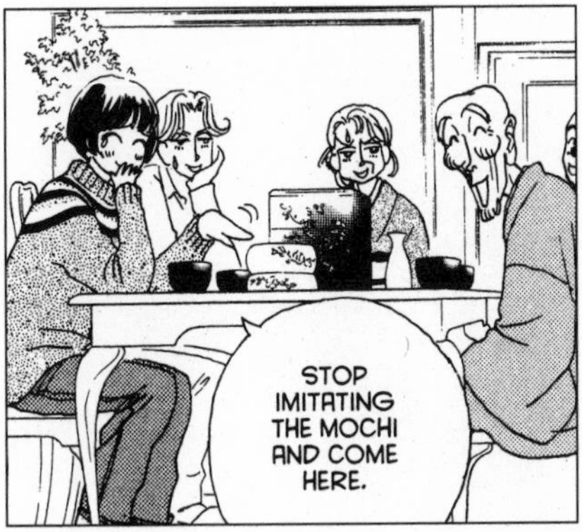
STOP IMITATING THE MOCHI AND COME HERE.

Mochi, page 38

Mochi is a glutinous rice cake that is eaten all year round but is traditionally associated with the New Year holiday. It is baked, grilled, boiled, and eaten by itself or with other dishes.

Osechi Ryori, page 39

Osechi ryori is a special cuisine eaten during the New Year's holiday. *Osechi ryori* is akin to Thanksgiving dinner in that the leftovers are eaten for days afterwards.

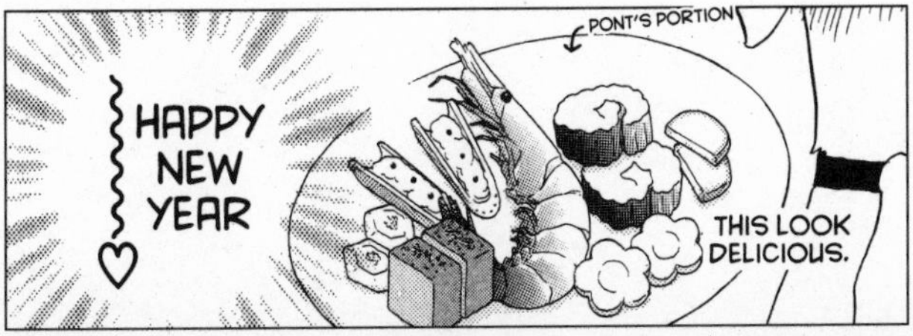
HAPPY NEW YEAR
PONT'S PORTION
THIS LOOK DELICIOUS.

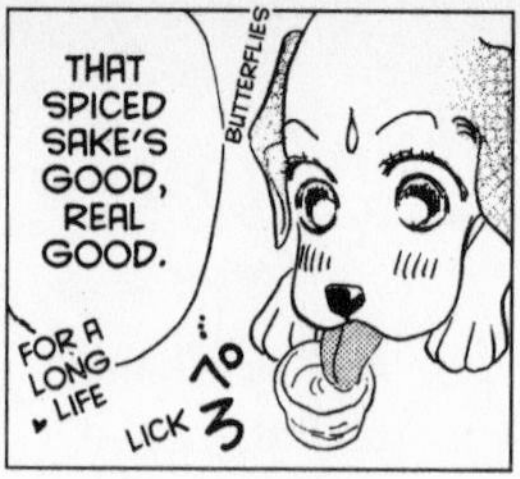
THAT SPICED SAKE'S GOOD, REAL GOOD.
BUTTERFLIES
FOR A LONG LIFE
LICK

O-toso, page 40

O-toso is a spiced sake drunk during the New Year's holiday.

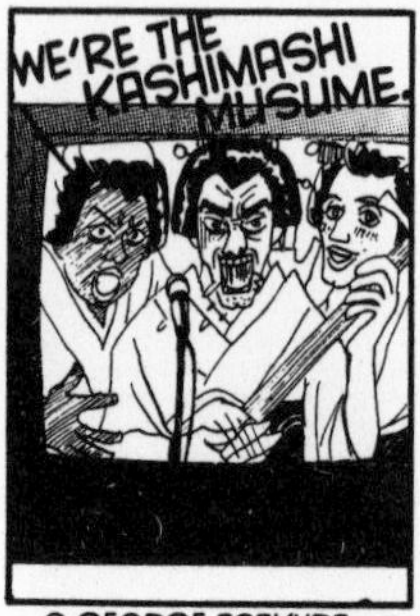
WE'RE THE KASHIMASHI MUSUME.

© GEORGE ASAKURA♥♥♥

George Asakura, page 41

George Asakura is the popular manga artist who created *A Perfect Day for Love Letters*. These are her characters dressed up as the Kashimashi Musume, a trio of sisters who are performers in Japan.

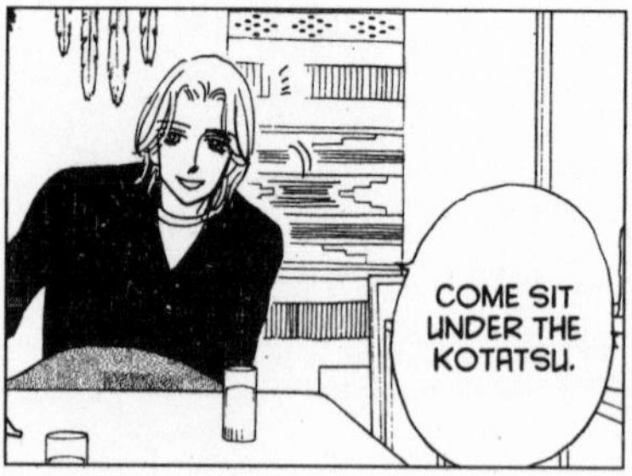
COME SIT UNDER THE KOTATSU.

Kotatsu, page 43

A *kotatsu* is a low table with an attached electric heater and a blanket sandwiched between the table and the tabletop. People enjoy sitting under it during the winter.

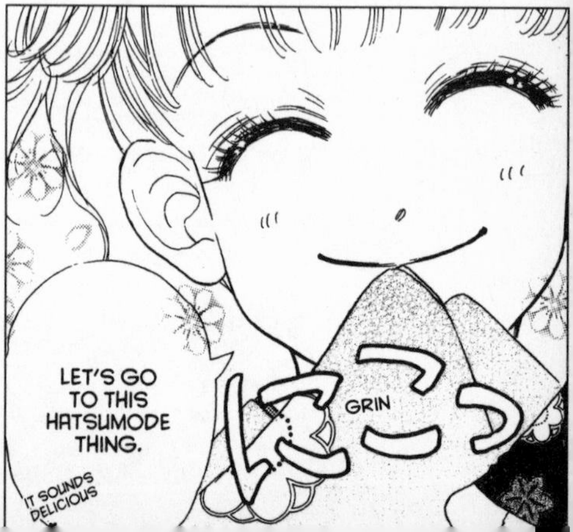
LET'S GO TO THIS HATSUMODE THING.
GRIN
IT SOUNDS DELICIOUS

Hatsumode, page 52

Hatsumode is the Japanese term for the first visit to a shrine or temple in the new year.

Ronin, page 64

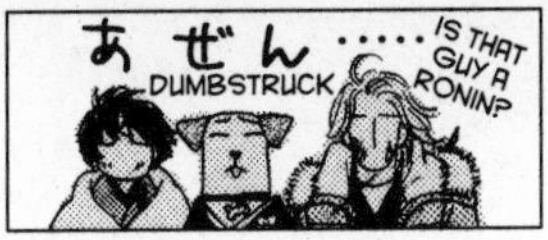
あぜん……
DUMBSTRUCK
IS THAT GUY A RONIN?

Ronin were masterless samurai who took on freelance jobs to pay the bills. Nowadays, *ronin* refers to high school students whose grades aren't good enough to get them into a decent university, so they take a year off to study and take the test again.

The Kinki Kids, page 77

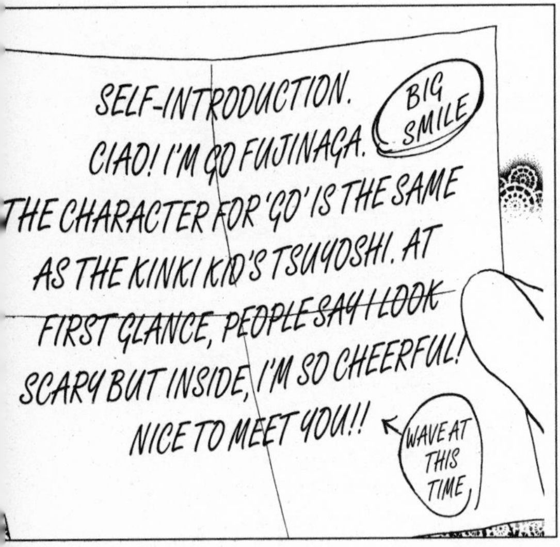
SELF-INTRODUCTION.
CIAO! I'M GO FUJINAGA.
THE CHARACTER FOR 'GO' IS THE SAME
AS THE KINKI KID'S TSUYOSHI. AT
FIRST GLANCE, PEOPLE SAY I LOOK
SCARY BUT INSIDE, I'M SO CHEERFUL!
NICE TO MEET YOU!!
BIG SMILE
WAVE AT THIS TIME

The Kinki Kids are a J-pop duo comprised of Tsuyoshi Domoto and Koichi Domoto (unrelated). Their ubiquitous songs and good looks have made them very popular in Japan, where they appear on several variety shows. Their name refers to the Kinki region of Japan, which encompasses Osaka, Kyoto, and Kobe.

Valentine's Day, page 84

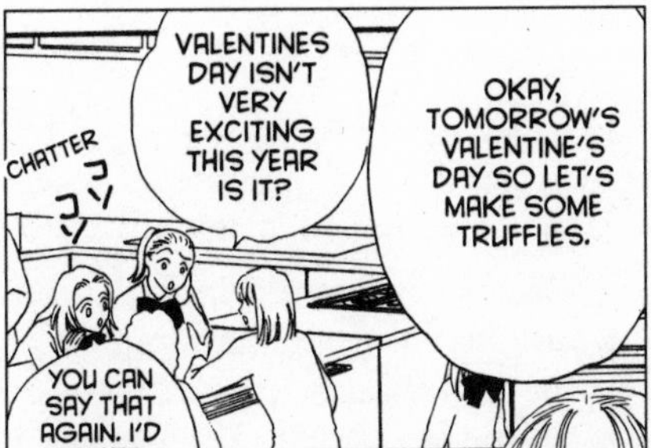
OKAY, TOMORROW'S VALENTINE'S DAY SO LET'S MAKE SOME TRUFFLES.
VALENTINES DAY ISN'T VERY EXCITING THIS YEAR IS IT?
CHATTER
コソコソ
YOU CAN SAY THAT AGAIN. I'D RATHER RECEIVE THAN GIVE.

Valentine's Day in Japan is a little different than it is here. Only women give chocolates or presents to the men they like, including friends and/or relatives. Men have their own day to give women presents/chocolate called White Day, which is one month later on March 13th.

PIN PON PIN PON!
IS CHOCOLATE ?

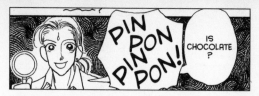

Pin Pon!, page 91

Pin Pon is a phrase the Japanese use to signify you've hit the nail on the head. It comes from the sound used in game shows that signifies a correct answer.

SALE!!
PRIME CUT BEEF

Shabu Shabu, page 94

Shabu Shabu is a famous dish in Japan where thinly sliced meat is dipped in hot broth and eaten.

I WAS PLANNING ON MAKING DASHIMAKI EGGS ANYWAY.
BREAK THEM AND BEAT THEM. YOU SAVED ME A LOT OF WORK.
DASHIMAKI EGGS?

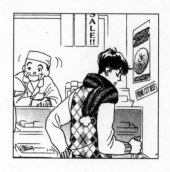

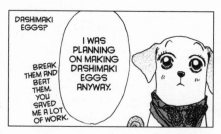

Dashimaki Eggs, page 96

Dashimaki eggs, a thin layer of fried eggs rolled into a sushi roll, are usually found in osechi ryori mentioned earlier.

Under your Nose..., page 124

Notice how the space between Go's nose and lip seems to be stretching? This is a literal example of the Japanese phrase *Hana no shita ga nobiru* or, "the part under your nose is getting longer." It's used to describe someone head over heels in love or lust.

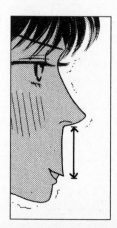

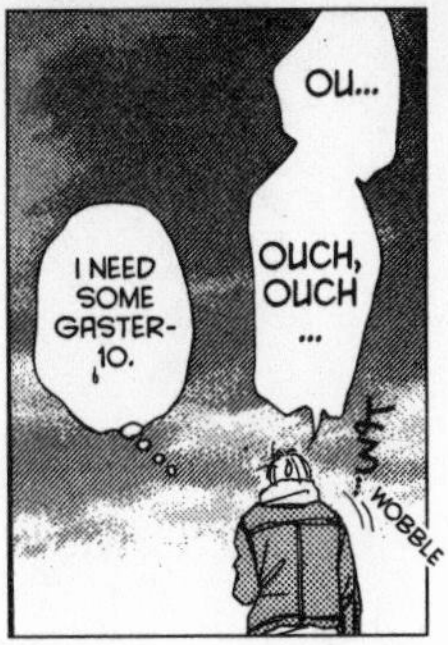
OU...
OUCH, OUCH ...
I NEED SOME GASTER-10.
WOBBLE

Gaster-10, page 136

Gaster-10 is an extremely popular over-the-counter drug that treats heartburn.

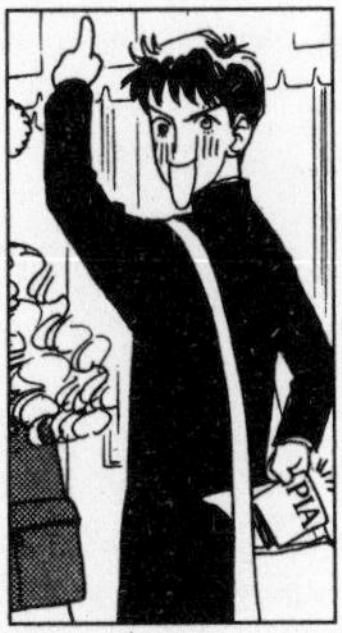
PIA

Pia, page 137

Pia is a guidebook that features information about restaurants, events, festivals, etc. for each region in Japan.

Ikebana, page 170

Ikebana is the traditional Japanese art of flower arrangement. Ike-Ponta would therefore be the traditional Japanese art of dog arrangement...

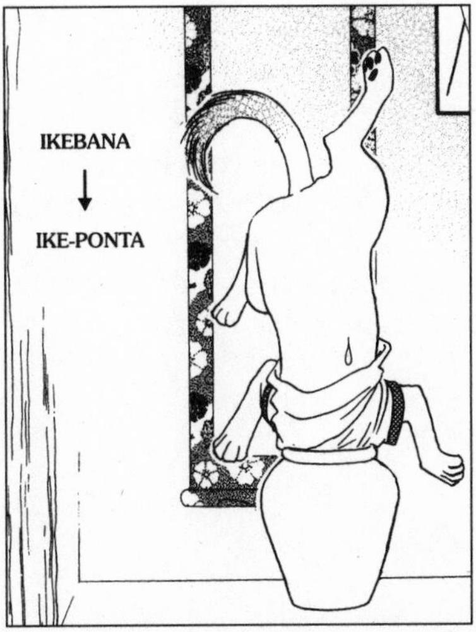
IKEBANA
↓
IKE-PONTA

DOO-DOO?
HUH?

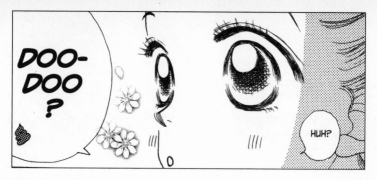

Doo-Doo?, page 179

In the original Japanese, the man uses the term *enkou*, which is an abbreviation for *enjokous*, or teen prostitute. Ponta, with her limited vocabulary, mistakes *enkou* for *unko*, the word for poop. *Enjokousai* refers to teenage prostitution, where a young, usually high school–aged girl "escorts" elderly men in order to get money for expensive items.

Love Hotels, page 186

Kyukei is the word for "rest" or "break," and at a love hotel—hotels in Japan where couples go for an intimate repose—it's akin to renting a room by the hour.

ARE YOU REALLY GOING TO GIVE A LOT MORE MONEY THAN YESTERDAY FOR JUST HAVING A REST WITH YOU?!
INFORMATION
REST 4500 YEN*
LODGING 6800 YEN**
HOTEL

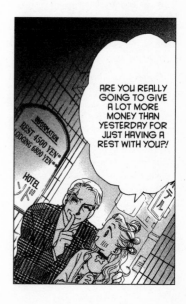

Preview of Volume 3

We're pleased to present you with a preview from Volume 3. This volume is available now and here's a taster of the Japanese original.

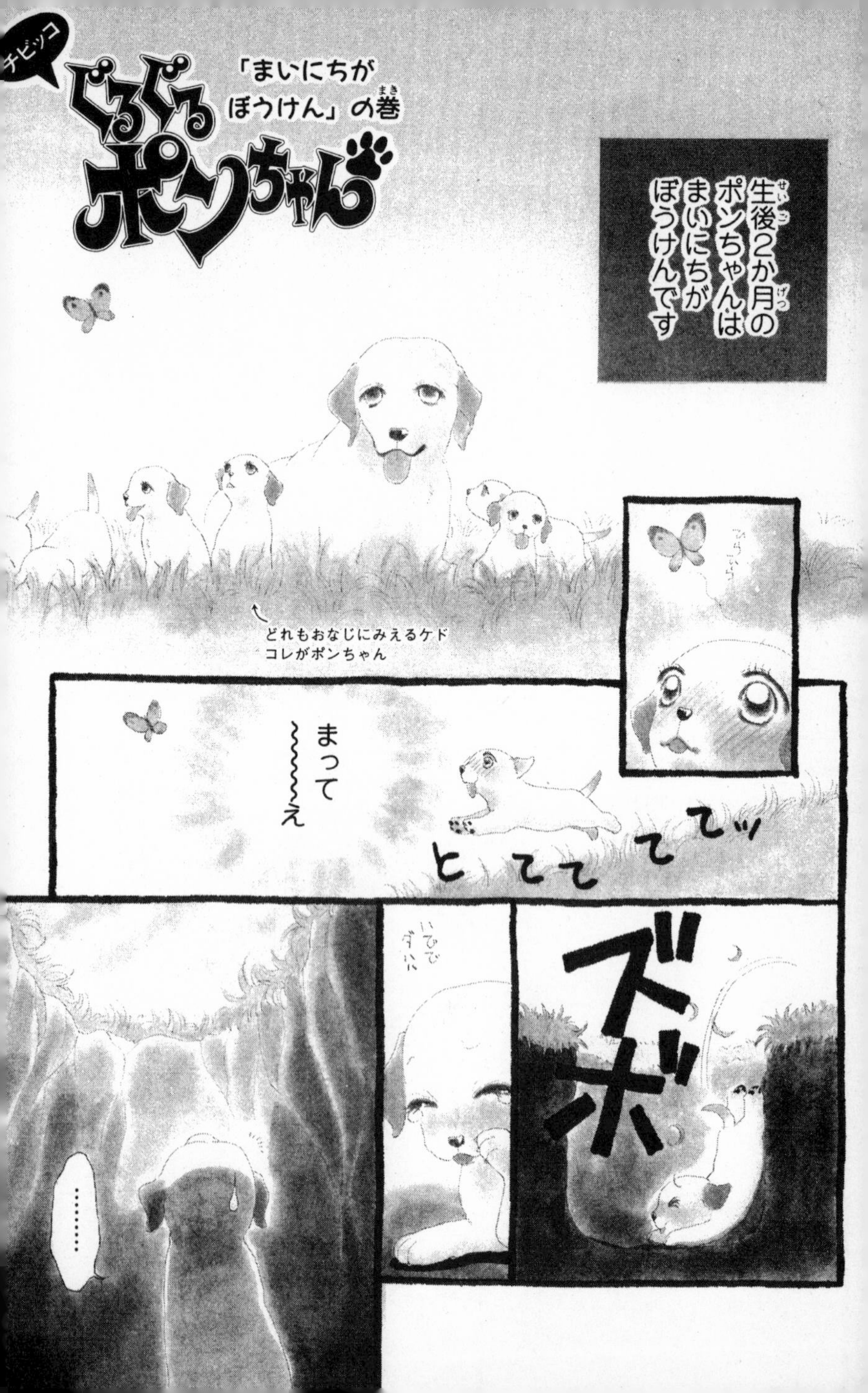
チビッコ
ぐるぐるポンちゃん
「まいにちがぼうけん」の巻
生後2か月のポンちゃんはまいにちがぼうけんです
どれもおなじにみえるケドコレがポンちゃん
まって〜〜〜〜え
とててててッ
ズボッ
……

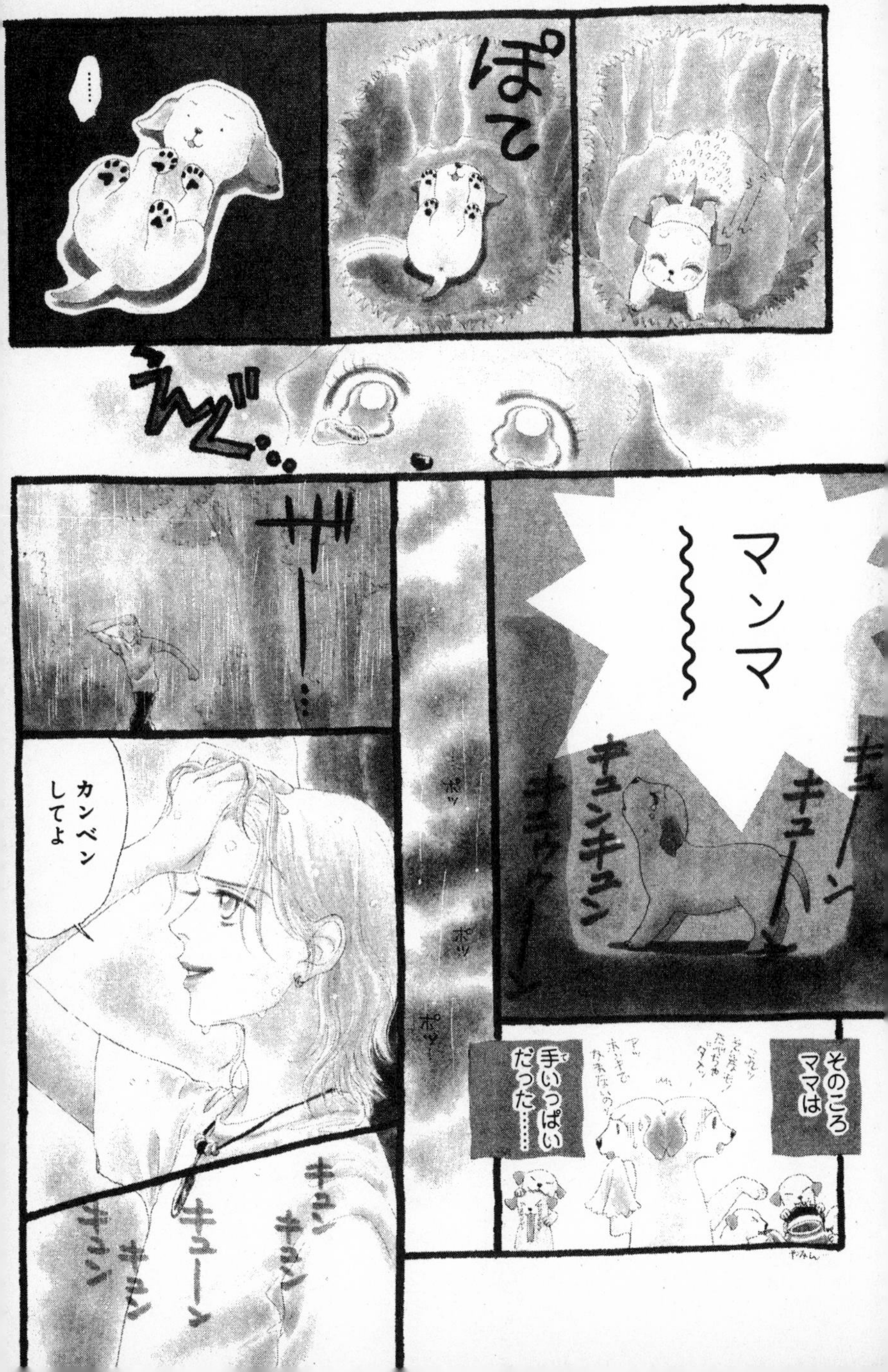
ぽて
……
えんぐ…
マンマ〜〜〜
キューン キューン
キュンキュン キュウ〜ン
そのころママは
手いっぱいだった……
ザー…!!…
ポツ
ポツ
ポツ
カンベンしてよ
キュン キュン キューン キュン キュン

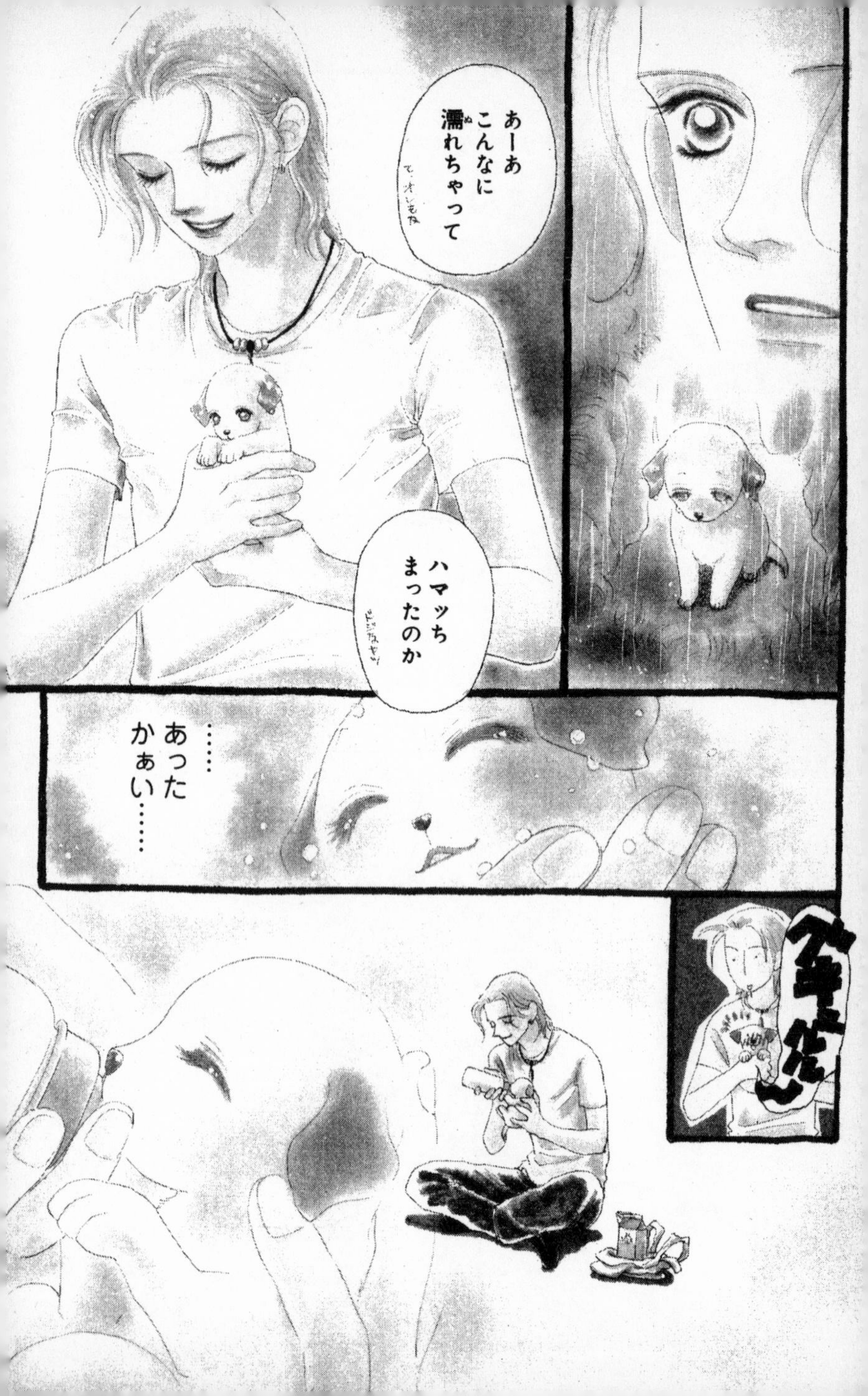
あーあ
こんなに
濡れちゃって
ハマッち
まったのか
……
あったかぁい……

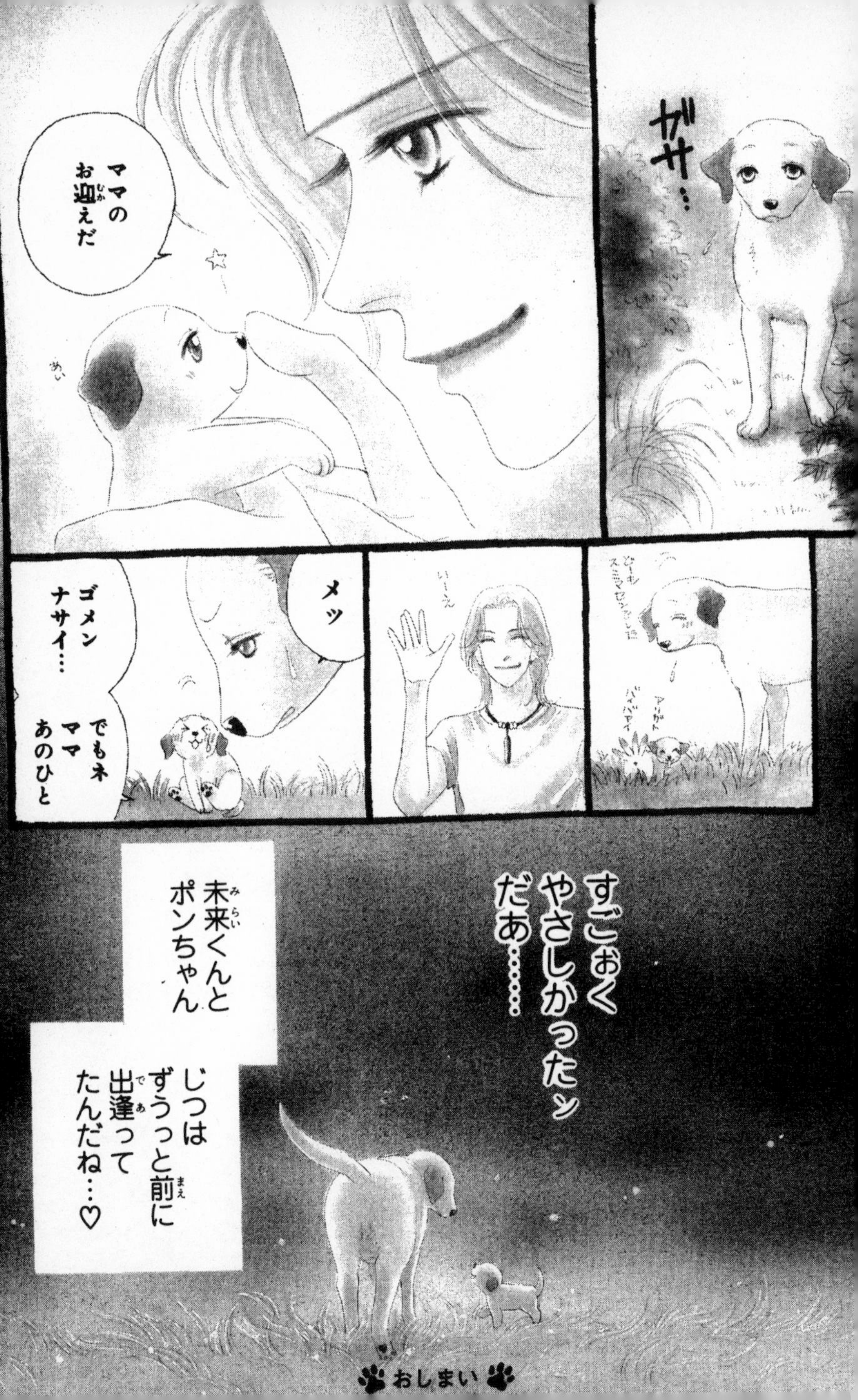
ガサ…
ママの お迎えだ
どーも スミマセンでした
アリガト
バイバイ
いーえ
メッ
ゴメン ナサイ…
でもネ ママ あのひと
すごぉく やさしかったンだあ……
未来くんと ポンちゃん
じつは ずうっと前に 出逢ってたんだね…♡
おしまい

Basilisk

ORIGINAL STORY BY FŪTARO YAMADA
MANGA BY MASAKI SEGAWA

THE BATTLE BEGINS

The Iga clan and the Kouga clan have been sworn enemies for more than four hundred years. Only the Hanzo Hattori truce has kept the two families from all-out war. Now, under the order of Shogun Ieyasu Tokugawa, the truce has been dissolved. Ten ninja from each clan must fight to the death in order to determine who will be the next Tokugawa Shogun. The surviving clan will rule for the next thousand years.

But not all the clan members are in agreement. Oboro of the Iga clan and Gennosuke of the Kouga clan have fallen deeply in love. Now these star-crossed lovers have been pitted against each other. Can their romance conquer a centuries-old rivalry? Or is their love destined to end in death?

Mature: Ages 18 +

Special extras in each volume! Read them all!

BY JIN KOBAYASHI

SUBTLETY IS FOR WIMPS!

She . . . is a second-year high school student with a single all-consuming question: Will the boy she likes ever really notice her?

He . . . is the school's most notorious juvenile delinquent, and he's suddenly come to a shocking realization: He's got a huge crush, and now he must tell her how he feels.

Life-changing obsessions, colossal foul-ups, grand schemes, deep-seated anxieties, and raging hormones—School Rumble portrays high school as it really is: over-the-top comedy!

Ages: 16 +

Coming soon in January 2007!
Special extras in each volume! Read them all!

BY CLAMP

Watanuki Kimihiro is haunted by visions. When he finds himself irresistibly drawn into a shop owned by Yûko, a mysterious witch, he is offered the chance to rid himself of the spirits that plague him. He accepts, but soon realizes that he's just been tricked into working for the shop to pay off the cost of Yûko's services! But this isn't any ordinary kind of shop . . . In this shop, Yûko grants wishes to those in need. But they must have the strength of will not only to truly understand their need, but to give up something incredibly precious in return.

Ages: 13 +

Special extras in each volume! Read them all!

TSUBASA

VOLUME 1
BY CLAMP

SAKURA AND SYAORAN RETURN!

But they're not the people you know. Sakura is the princess of Clow—and possessor of a mysterious, misunderstood power that promises to change the world. Syaoran is her childhood friend and leader of the archaeological dig that took his father's life. They reside in an alternate reality . . . where whatever you least expect can happen—and does. When Sakura ventures to the dig site to declare her love for Syaoran, a puzzling symbol is uncovered—which triggers a remarkable quest. Now Syaoran embarks upon a desperate journey through other worlds—all in the name of saving Sakura.

Ages: 13 +

Includes special extras after the story!

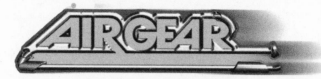

AIRGEAR

BY OH!GREAT

AIRGEAR
1
Oh!great

Itsuki Minami needs no introduction—everybody's heard of the "Babyface" of the Eastside. He's the strongest kid at Higashi Junior High School, easy on the eyes but dangerously tough when he needs to be. Plus, Itsuki lives with the mysterious and sexy Noyamano sisters. Life's never dull, but it becomes downright dangerous when Itsuki leads his school to victory over vindictive Westside punks with gangster connections. Now he stands to lose his school, his friends, and everything he cares about. But in his darkest hour, the Noyamano girls give him an amazing gift, one that just might help him save his school: a pair of Air Trecks. These high-tech skates are more than just supercool. They'll enable Itsuki to execute the wildest, most aggressive moves ever seen—and introduce him to a thrilling and terrifying new world.

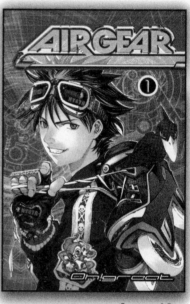

Ages: 16+

Coming in October 2006!
Special extras in each volume! Read them all!

tanoshimi

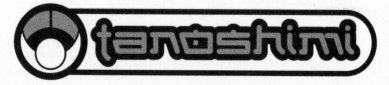

wallpapers
icons
previews
downloads
competitions

tanoshimi

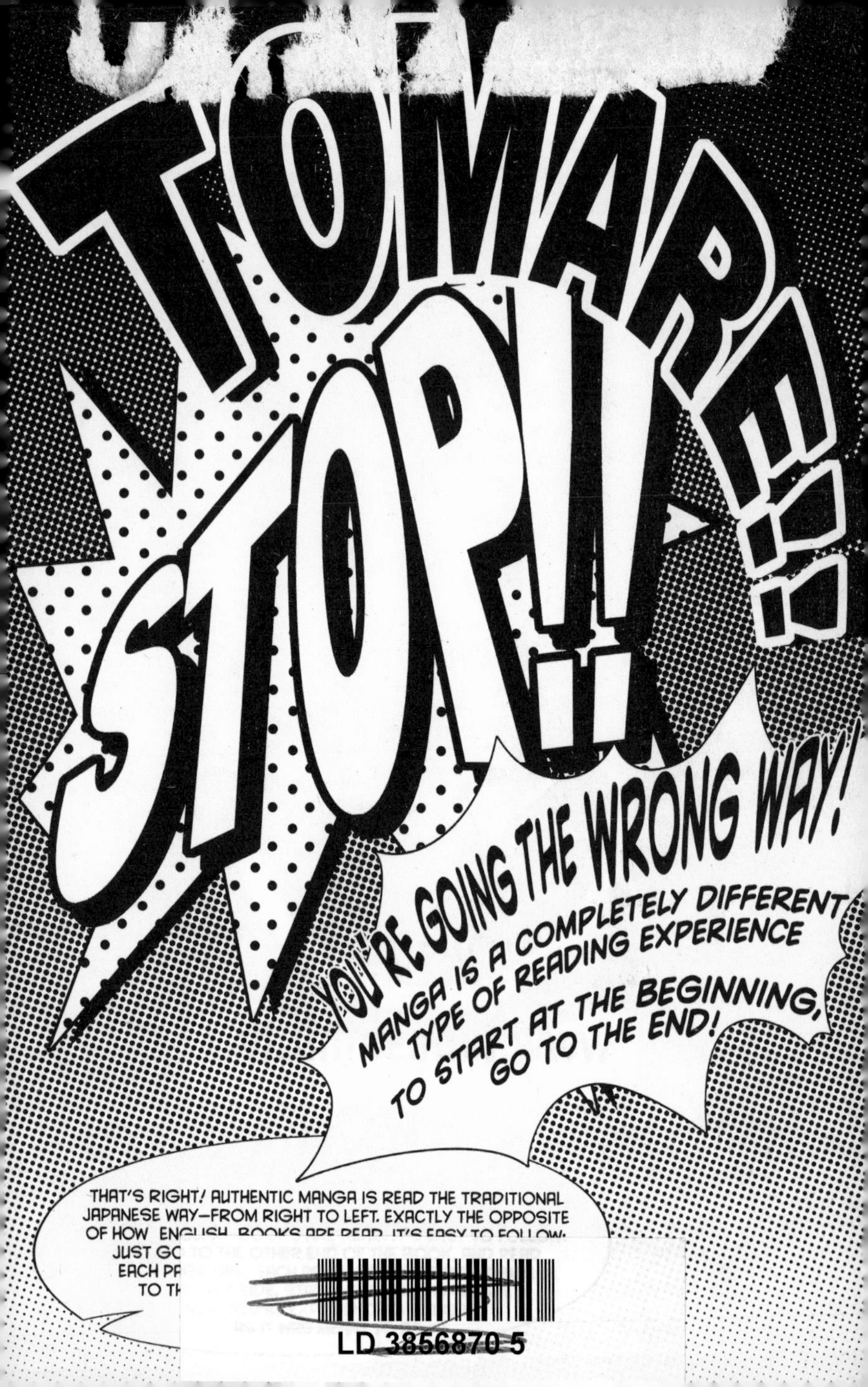
TOMARE!!
STOP!!
YOU'RE GOING THE WRONG WAY!
MANGA IS A COMPLETELY DIFFERENT TYPE OF READING EXPERIENCE
TO START AT THE BEGINNING, GO TO THE END!
THAT'S RIGHT! AUTHENTIC MANGA IS READ THE TRADITIONAL JAPANESE WAY—FROM RIGHT TO LEFT. EXACTLY THE OPPOSITE OF HOW ENGLISH BOOKS ARE READ. IT'S EASY TO FOLLOW: